EXPANDING FREE EXPRESSION IN THE MARKETPLACE

Expanding Free Expression in the Marketplace

BROADCASTING AND THE PUBLIC FORUM

Dom Caristi

QUORUM BOOKS

New York
Westport, Connecticut
London

Library of Congress Cataloging-in-Publication Data

Caristi, Dom.
    Expanding free expression in the marketplace : broadcasting and
the public forum / Dom Caristi.
       p. cm.
    Includes bibliographical references and index.
    ISBN 0-89930-720-5 (alk. paper)
    1. Broadcasting—Law and legislation—United States. 2. Freedom
of speech—United States. I. Title.
    KF2805.C365 1992
    343.7309'94—dc20   91-40950
    [347.303994]

British Library Cataloguing in Publication Data is available.

Library of Congress Catalog Card Number: 91-40950
ISBN: 0-89930-720-5

First published in 1992

Quorum Books, One Madison Avenue, New York, NY 10010
An imprint of Greenwood Publishing Group, Inc.

Printed in the United States of America

The paper used in this book complies with the
Permanent Paper Standard issued by the National
Information Standards Organization (Z39.48–1984).

10 9 8 7 6 5 4 3 2 1

CONTENTS

ACKNOWLEDGMENTS

Writing this book was not easy. It required the assistance of a great number of people. In particular, I must mention Jeffery A. Smith of the University of Iowa, School of Journalism and Mass Communication. While being the work's major critic, he offered continual support and encouragement. He was the first to encourage me to publish this book. While our theories of the First Amendment are not always the same, he has been quite tolerant of my views. He is a meticulous editor and exacting scholar.

A portion of this book appeared earlier in an article I wrote for *Suffolk University Law Review*. I extend my appreciation to editors Warren Kaplan and Colleen Arnot for their suggestions.

I have had the good fortune of being employed by two fine colleges during the writing of this book. The library staffs of both have been essential to my research, especially since neither college has a law college library. At Saint Mary's, I especially thank Br. Paul, Mary, Maryanne, and Rose for all their assistance. At Missouri Southern, Gaye, Bob, Cindy, Terre, Mary Lou, Dick, and both Charlies provided valuable assistance. Bill Crozier of Saint Mary's has been a dear friend, good critic, and computing genius. Thanks to department secretary Sharen Brown for the use of her printer.

Research while teaching requires both time and resources, which are available only with administrative support. My thanks to Br. Paul Grass, John Johnson, and Bill Medland at Saint Mary's. At Missouri Southern,

I have again been fortunate to find administration aid. Department Head Richard Massa and Dean Ray Malzahn have both been very helpful.

I sincerely appreciate the efforts of Eric Valentine of Quorum Books. Timeliness is very important for legal writing, and I appreciate his quick responses in getting this book published.

Of course there is a litany of friends and family who deserve my thanks: far too many to mention here. I only hope all those colleagues who have supported me know how much I appreciate their thoughts.

Finally, and most important, is my family. My immigrant parents had only seven years of formal education between the two of them, yet their three sons all have advanced degrees. I deeply appreciate their support and recognition of the importance of learning. My children, Tony and Nicole, have had to tolerate my frustration. My greatest debt of gratitude goes to my lovely and understanding wife, friend, and companion, Kim. Without her support, none of this would have been possible.

1 INTRODUCTION: THE VALUE OF ADDITIONAL VOICES

More means of communication exist in America than have ever existed before. Public oration and publishing have been supplemented by broadcast media of all kinds, wired networks, and even "in-home" media, such as camcorders and personal copiers. Yet, while it is true that more means of communication exist, many Americans may not have an adequate opportunity to speak freely in the media. Traditional media (e.g., newspapers, radio, and television) require huge investments, making them subject to editorial choices made by their owners. Even home devices, such as video cameras and personal computers, are typically available only to the affluent.

If the United States values free expression, clearly it must also value attempts to increase the opportunities for all to be able to exercise that freedom. This book examines the value of providing increased opportunities for free expression, means by which those opportunities have been expanded, and possible prospects for their continued expansion in years to come.

That the First Amendment's guarantee of freedom of speech is often interpreted differently is evidenced by the hundreds of books and Supreme Court decisions attempting to shed light on its precise meaning. The quantity alone suggests the difficulty associated with trying to provide the one, definitive meaning for free expression in contemporary American society. This chapter examines many of the meanings given for free expression, and the criticisms associated with each approach.

One concept guides this discourse: if free expression is valued, steps should be taken to encourage the greatest opportunity for that expression to take place. Policies that increase free expression outlets ought to be viewed favorably, while those narrowing the choices for speakers should be suspect.

In order to better understand what constitutes free expression, it is essential to determine first why free expression has value: what about it makes it worthy of protection? The meaning of freedom of expression is bound by political and cultural contexts.[1] For example, if free speech is valued because of its contribution to the political process,[2] regulation of speech that does not serve this purpose is necessarily problematic. Conversely, indecent speech that is political in nature should not be restricted if the system is established to protect political expression. It is appropriate to begin by examining the variety of reasons given for protecting free expression.

Thomas Emerson proposes that the essentially four main values protected by the First Amendment are:[3]

1. A means of assuring individual self-fulfillment.
2. A process for advancing knowledge and discovering truth.
3. An essential provision for participation in decision making by all members of society.
4. A method of achieving a more acceptable and therefore stable community.[4]

Individually, each of Emerson's values requires determination of whether a particular form of speech is entitled to constitutional protection based on a content criterion. For example, if discovering truth is the underlying value protected by the First Amendment, then speech that does not attempt to advance truth does not merit such protection. Intentional lies are not to be protected, because the speaker is aware that such expression does not advance the discovery of truth. Further, advertisements encouraging the purchase of a product by means of hyperbole and symbolism may convey no "truth" about the product, nor attempt to advance the cause of truth, while truthful advertising that provides product information, under such a scheme, is worthy of constitutional protection.

Of course, Emerson does not suggest that only one of these values is worthy of protection, but rather that all the values, collectively, imbue the reason expression merits protection.[5] Unfortunately, Emerson also does not provide a hierarchy of values, allowing instead for the constant balancing done by the Supreme Court and others,[6] whenever the rights of free expression come into conflict with other rights, or with other free expression rights.[7] The current legal uncertainty that surrounds defamation law is indicative of the result of balancing free expression against itself. In the interest of promoting the democratic process, defamatory remarks regarding public figures are afforded greater protection than those directed toward private individuals.[8] What constitutes a public or private figure, however, has been the crux of many defamation cases for more than twenty years.[9] In addition, the value of discovering truth has been subordinated in defamation law. If truth is the dominant value, it seems appropriate that once a falsehood is discovered, the law requires a correction. Quite the contrary, the Supreme Court found such a requirement unconstitutional.[10] In the area of defamation law, assessing a monetary damage capable of driving the defamer out of business is constitutional; a statute requiring the publication of a correction is not.[11]

All four of Emerson's values support a correlative value: that of increasing the amount of free expression available. If one accepts the premise that free speech is good, each of Emerson's values supports the notion that more free speech is better. If free expression is protected because it assures self-fulfillment, it follows that as much speech as possible should be protected in order to assure that self-fulfillment can be realized. Likewise, if free speech is valued because it contributes to the democratic process, more speech ought to be protected to allow increased participation in the democracy. While this argument does not assume that all speech must be permitted, it is logical to assert that increased opportunities should increase the likelihood that the stated values will realize greater protection.

Some proponents of increased opportunities for free expression, using diversity as their rationale, argue that increased opportunity for expression results in diversity of viewpoints, which in the end encourages the pursuit of truth and the democratic process. This, however, results in a different, but nonetheless difficult, content criterion for determining whether a particular expression is worthy of protection. While diversity may in fact be the end result of increased opportunities for free expression, it does not necessarily follow.[12] If diversity is the value behind protecting free expression, then repetitious communications do not deserve constitutional protection. This certainly suggests that most advertising is not entitled to First Amendment protection, but such an approach goes further. Political speakers who merely reiterate positions stated previously by themselves or others, no matter how impassioned, do not increase diversity, and as such, deserve no special attention under this scheme.

To assert that increased speech opportunities add to the values inherent in free expression does not ignore the reality that rights still come into conflict. Saying that increased speech opportunities have value does not result in the elimination of rights of privacy, fair trial, or even reputation. Instead, such an assertion establishes a priority for First Amendment theorists: whenever possible, opportunities for increased expression must be expanded. First Amendment theories will be examined from this basic assumption.

FIRST AMENDMENT THEORIES CONNOTING VALUES

The complexity of First Amendment doctrine has made it impossible to establish any single test or rule that is applicable for all situations. The flexibility of general language used in defining free expression rights is testimony to "avoid doctrine that inevitably lags behind reality."[13] Instead of a single rule, it may be appropriate to consider the dimensions that rules must incorporate. In an attempt to develop a comprehensive free speech theory, constitutional scholar Laurence Tribe provided four dimensions that must be included in formulating constitutional legal theory.[14] The second of these is a structural element in which he calls for a free speech theory to provide reference to the value that it embodies.[15]

A number of existing approaches are theories of First Amendment interpretation but ignore the question of the value of free expression. Intent of the framers is one such theory. Some argue that any appropriate interpretation of First Amendment meaning requires an examination of original intent.[16] A plethora of scholarship exists on this subject.[17] The Supreme Court has also used framers' intent as rationale in dicta. "The protection given speech and press was fashioned to assure unfettered interchange of ideas for the bringing about of political and social changes desired by the people."[18] In discussing the search for intent, one author stated that "there is not one instance in which it may be said that the Court has definitively established the intent of the Convention on any important issue."[19] Many of the cited works are in conflict, and add little to this thesis. "If the intent is not clear, then it cannot be the determinative factor in constitutional interpretation of freedom of the press."[20] Perhaps some of the confusion and contradiction results from disagreement over whose writings should be used in determining original intent: philosophers hundreds of years previous, state ratifying conventions, members of Congress, or politicians' statements as much as forty years later.[21]

Another interesting theory that provides no information on free expression values is the question of whether affirmative rights exist under the First Amendment, or if it merely prohibits government intervention.[22] While a valid concern, this, also, begs the question, what is the value of free expression?

Theories supporting the First Amendment abound in a variety of forums. Supreme Court dicta can be analyzed for theoretical assumptions. Scholarly legal journals also provide insight, as do texts on free speech, constitutional law, and political philosophy. Throughout the hundreds of sources, there are surprisingly few approaches that differ significantly from any of Emerson's four values. A review of First Amendment theories shows the strengths and weaknesses of each.[23]

DISCOVERY OF TRUTH/MARKETPLACE OF IDEAS

Often thought of by libertarians as the only value necessary to support free speech, the discovery of truth was used to support free expression long before the Bill of Rights.[24] Although John Milton's argument was primarily designed to support religious rights rather than free expression, the often-quoted passage from *Areopagitica* is still used in legal treatises to support the principle that free speech must be protected as a means of discovering truth.

> And though all the winds of doctrine were let loose to play upon the earth, so Truth be in the field, we do injuriously, by licensing and prohibiting, to misdoubt her strength. Let her and falsehood grapple; who ever knew Truth put to the worse, in a free and open encounter.[25]

This philosophy was adopted by a wide variety of political philosophers, including Jean-Jacques Rousseau,[26] John Locke,[27] and John Stuart Mill.[28] It can also be found in the Supreme Court dicta[29] of such esteemed supporters of free expression as Oliver Wendell Holmes[30] and William Douglas.[31] Within all the texts the message is simple: achievement of truth is difficult, if at all possible. Since no one has preemptive claim on *the* truth, its pursuit requires that all differences of opinion are made available to the public. Those purporting to have something to contribute almost have to be given the opportunity to speak. Any alternative that requires screening speakers to determine whether their speech adds anything to the public's discovery of truth vests too much authority in one body.

The interest in diversity is in fact a sub-value of the search for truth.[32] The purpose of supporting a diversity of speakers is the expectation that the search for truth is enhanced by doing so. The more propositions available to the public, the greater the opportunity to select the best, or rather, the most appropriate.

While the theory has much to recommend it, the search for truth as free expression theory is flawed. First, if a marketplace of ideas is to function effectively, all must have equal access to that marketplace, both to "buy" and "sell" goods. When the goods at issue are ideas, this requires that all participants have the opportunity to both speak and hear a diversity of voices.[33] When one entity (or even a handful of like-thinking individuals) is able to dominate the marketplace, monopolizing opportunities, the marketplace metaphor falls apart. "There is an overwhelming temptation for the ruling minority to use the power of market domination for the self-interested purpose of rationalizing existing unequal arrangements while denying access to ideas that urge reform."[34] This approach has been characterized as the market failure theory.[35]

In addition, this philosophical approach to free expression is problematic because it defines truth as the will of the majority.[36] Nothing is ultimately true unless a majority defines it as such.[37] Conversely, no matter how "correct" a proposition may be, its success rests solely on its ability to be accepted.

Rights of reply and correction statutes find their greatest support in the marketplace approach. Searching for truth requires the presentation of contrasting facts.[38]

It is difficult to define speech that contributes to the search for truth and therefore deserves protecting. Even those who find a marketplace metaphor appealing for the discovery of truth find it troublesome with regard to complex, intangible issues. In 1922 Walter Lippmann stated that "[t]he truth about distant or complex matters is not self-evident, and the machinery for assembling information is technical and expensive."[39] The Supreme Court has stated that "[t]he line between the informing and the entertaining is too elusive for the protection of that basic right. Everyone is familiar with instances of propaganda through fiction. What is one man's amusement teaches another's doctrine."[40]

If the discovery of truth is the value protected by free expression, speech that does not support this purpose need not be protected. Clearly speech intended to confuse or mislead the audience does not deserve protection. In addition, the application of this value is less appropriate in certain areas, such as verifiable truths (as in scientific knowledge).[41] The difficulty in deciding borderline cases should not, however, condemn the approach as unworkable.[42]

SELF-GOVERNANCE

Legal philosopher Alexander Meiklejohn contended that, in a democracy, free expression needs to be protected to facilitate self-governance.[43] The argument was based on quite logical premises. Citizens elect leaders to run the government. In order to make informed judgments regarding who to elect, the citizenry must be informed. Free expression must be protected to ensure an informed electorate, otherwise the concept of representative democracy is pointless.[44] The content of the expression, and its relevance to the discussion of public issues, determines whether the expression is protected speech. "What is essential is not that everyone shall speak, but that everything worth saying shall be said."[45] Of course, the practical problem with this approach is determining when everything worth saying has been said, and by whom the determination is to be made.[46]

Unique to this value of free expression is a right of access to government-held information, often claimed by the media as the "right to know." The rationale is that effective popular sovereignty requires an informed public, and denying access to relevant information is tantamount to denying the right to vote.[47] The irony behind this is that attaching a claim for information to a self-governance right omits much information. Material relevant to collective decision making would be obtainable, yet information relevant only to individual choice, although sometimes life-affecting, would be concealable.[48]

The theory is prevalent in the writings of other scholars including Alexander Bickel[49] and Lillian BeVier.[50]. One scholar offers the constitutional protection of parliamentary privilege as evidence that "protection of speech is needed for the successful operation of the political process and the preservation of self government."[51] Supreme Court justices as politically diverse as William Brennan[52] and Warren Burger[53] have written in support of the self-governance value. Justice Marshall summarized for the Court, "free and open debate is vital to informed decision-making by the electorate."[54] Justice Black stated for the Court, "[w]hatever differences may exist about interpretations of the First Amendment, there is practically universal agreement that a major purpose of that Amendment was to protect the free discussion of governmental affairs."[55]

According to Baker, to protect expression because of its utility to self-governance is to value democratic change.[56] A democratic process of achieving change, sometimes associated with a marketplace of ideas philosophy, is better served by the protection of political speech.[57] He contends that "first amendment theory becomes relevant to the extent that its formal guarantees actually protect participation in" public discussion to change the democratic environment.[58]

One minor modification of the self-governance theory of free expression is the approach that political expression is at the core of the First Amendment, and is therefore more deserving than other expression (which may also be deserving).[59] While this premise may accommodate more expression than a strict Meiklejohnian interpretation, it still operates from the same basic position that political expression is somehow unique.

This is precisely the approach adopted by the Court in *Connick v Myers*.[60] In stringing together quoted fragments from earlier decisions, the Court provided the following calculus:

> speech concerning public affairs is more than self-expression; it is the essence of self-government . . . . Accordingly, the Court has frequently reaffirmed that speech on public issues occupies the highest rung of the hierarchy of [F]irst Amendment values and is entitled to special protection . . . the [F]irst amendment does not protect speech and assembly only to the extent it can be characterized as political.[61]

In another decision, however, the Court suggested differently. "Even though political speech is entitled to the fullest possible measure of constitutional protection, there are a host of other communications that command the same respect."[62]

The self-governance approach to free expression also has difficulties. "To say that speech is valued because it facilitates self government, for example, is simply to push the inquiry a step back: why, after all, is self-government to be valued?"[63] While the self-governance theory of free speech seems consistent with our political heritage,[64] it suffers severe definitional problems. What sorts of speech are political, thus deserving of protection, and what sorts of expression are not entitled to constitutional protection? A democratic socialism perspective "firmly rejects the view that democracy should be limited to the political arena."[65] Meiklejohn himself struggled with the definition. In an earlier writing, he contended that only clearly and directly political expression is entitled to such protection. Later, he recanted, demonstrating that artistic and scientific speech may indirectly affect the political realm.[66] When one starts down the slippery slope of finding expression indirectly relevant to politics, it is difficult to determine what speech is not worthy of protection.[67] Schauer remedies this difficult problem by asserting juries determine whether speech is deserving of protection. Popular sovereignty includes the ability of the majority to decide which expression *not* to protect.[68]

FREE EXPRESSION AS A MEANS OF MAINTAINING SOCIETY

Emerson speaks of the "safety valve" value of free speech. By this he means that allowing members of society the opportunity to express themselves helps to release frustrations. The alternative would be to prohibit expression, which might instead result in individuals and groups taking more drastic action: perhaps rioting and even attempting overthrow of the government. People given the opportunity to vent their frustrations are less likely to have pent up hostilities that eventually become explosive. The analogy is to a pot of boiling water. If steam is released slowly, no problems result and the pot's condition is stable. If, however, the pot is sealed, preventing the gradual escape of pressure, the steam builds until it finally destroys the vessel.

While Emerson sees the safety valve value of free expression as a good thing, Marxists take the process one step further. They argue that not only does free expression allow individuals and groups to vent their frustrations, it also results in their willingness to continue with the situation as it exists.[69] The safety valve thus acts to maintain the status quo, and while it provides for free expression, it offers little in the way of change. Using the metaphor of the boiling water, Marxists point out that allowing steam to escape results in no change for the pressurized water, while allowing the pot to explode from excessive pressure, although violent, puts an end to the water boiling. It is further asserted that demonstrations provide a "warning device" for governments, giving them the opportunity to prepare for and dispel a possible crisis.[70]

Advocates of a clear and present danger approach to protecting speech rights often adopt maintenance of an ordered society as a value of free expression.[71] Only when speech approaches a clear and present danger should it be prohibited. An outgrowth of this approach is the fighting words doctrine, which regulates speakers whose speech is inflammatory and likely to incite a violent response.[72] In fact, Zechariah Chafee, believed to have been the one who persuaded Holmes to adopt the clear and present danger test,[73] also endorsed the safety valve value of expression. While Emerson asserted that free expression helps prevent discontent to the extent of violence, Chafee felt that speech could go so far as to make the nation euphoric. Freedom of speech "creates the happiest kind of country. It is the best way to make men and women love their country."[74]

While this theoretical approach may in fact protect some expression that is caustic, its protection extends only to expression that is spoken by impassioned speakers. Protecting free speech because it acts as an escape valve ignores speech that is purely commercial. Advertising for a product is not necessarily entitled to protection, yet advocacy advertising is at the heart of the safety valve value.

Ironically, for free expression to provide a safety valve that maintains the peaceful society, the expression could not be too effective. An individual speaker attempting to convince a crowd to revolt is "letting off steam" by expressing himself. If the speaker is too effective, however, in convincing the crowd to take violent action, the expression results in the same violent upsurgence it was designed to alleviate. For that reason, the safety valve approach to free expression is difficult to reconcile. Ineffective speakers are given the opportunity to speak, while those who are more effective must have limits imposed on them in the interest of an orderly society. Disregarding the difficulties such an approach presents for equal protection questions, administration of such rules is likely to be arbitrary, capricious, and prone to error on the side of order. Government agents charged with maintaining order (in most cases police departments) are more likely to prevent a potential uprising than wait for the violence to begin.

EDITORIAL AUTONOMY: THE PRESS AS FOURTH BRANCH

The value served by editorial autonomy is not among Emerson's four values for free expression. Vincent Blasi uses the term "checking value" of the First Amendment[75] to connote the value of having a press free from government inhibition to serve as "watchdog" on the government:[76] the unofficial fourth branch in the system of checks and balances. He asserts that free expression needs to be protected in order to provide a check on the abuse of official power at the federal, state, and local levels.

Perhaps the most recognized proponent of the watchdog theory was Justice Potter Stewart. In a speech at Yale Law School,[77] Stewart argued that the free press provision of the First Amendment must be a structural provision of the Constitution, otherwise the phrase would be no more than a "constitutional redundancy."[78] Stewart quoted from a dissent by Justice Brandeis fifty years earlier[79]to support his proposition that "[t]he primary purpose of the constitutional guarantee of a free press was . . . to create a fourth institution outside the government as an additional check on the three official branches."[80] Of course this position is not without its detractors.[81] The principal concern is that affording the press such special status also requires that it act responsibly, and can be held accountable for violating its trust.[82]

The Supreme Court has embraced this theory of free speech in some of its analyses. In the words of Justice Black, "[t]he press was protected so that it could bare the secrets of government and inform the people. Only a free and unrestrained press can effectively expose deception in government."[83]

Protecting editorial autonomy is actually a sub-value of the watchdog value of free expression.[84] Arguments that the government must not intervene in editorial decision making are often incomplete, leaving the audience to discern for itself the appropriate justification. If editorial discretion is protected, that assumes the structural approach advocated by Justice Stewart.

Despite Chief Justice Stewart Burger's rejection of a separate right for the press,[85] he argues the importance of editorial autonomy. In just six short pages of opinion, Burger uses the phrases "journalistic role" (twice), "journalistic independence" (twice), "journalistic 'free agent,' " "journalistic freedom," "journalistic judgment" (twice), "journalistic decisions," "journalistic discretion," and "processes of editorial evaluation."[86] He adopts the position that editorial autonomy is the value that must be protected. "[I]t would be anomalous for us to hold, in the name of free expression, that the day-to-day editorial decisions of broadcast licensees are subject to the kind of restraints urged. . . ."[87] At the other end of the political spectrum from Burger, Justice Douglas also supported editorial autonomy. He wrote that "the old-fashioned First Amendment that we have is the Court's only guideline, and one hard and fast principle which it announces is that government shall keep its hands off the press."[88]

In another decision, the Court "reaffirm[ed] unequivocally the protection afforded to editorial judgment."[89] In *Miami Herald v Tornillo*,[90] the Court writes considerably about the sacrosanct rights of editors.[91] The Court has also asserted that "[w]e know from experience that 'liberty of the press is in peril as soon as the government tries to compel what is to go into a newspaper.' "[92]

FREE EXPRESSION AS SELF-FULFILLMENT

Perhaps most liberal of all theories of free expression is the concept that free expression is worthy of protection because it contributes to individual self-fulfillment.[93] This perspective might be attributable to a number of philosophers including Dewey, Kant, and Spinoza.[94] An essential distinction of self-fulfillment proponents is their advocacy of social reforms or changes in the environment to increase individuals' freedoms, or the number of people who enjoy a particular freedom.[95] "Freedom of expression lies at the very heart of the concept of human rights in that it is both a crucial end in itself and a vital means to the securing of other ends."[96] Adoption of a human or natural rights perspective of free expression eliminates the need to determine the social good. "If speaking freely is a 'natural right,'[97] then the liberty of speaking out ought to be protected by a properly constituted state regardless of whether it is in the public interest to do so."[98] This approach is purely deontological: "speaking is part of what it is to be a person, and restrictions on that expression of personhood by the state are simply wrong."[99]

The legal scholar who most embraces this approach to free expression is Martin Redish.[100] He contends that all distinctions about acceptable speech based on content considerations are inappropriate under a self-realization analysis. "[A] government determination that one type of expression fosters this value better than another is itself a rejection of the self-realization principle, premised on the value of individual choice and intellectual development."[101]

Redish does not propose anarchy. Rather than construct rules that determine acceptable speech, he favors a system of judicial discretion, tempered with an understanding that expression rights occupy a preferred position.[102] While leaving such determinations to the judiciary might make some scholars nervous,[103] Redish believes this structure is necessary to "seek general guidelines of interpretation that simultaneously provide the strong deference to free speech interests that the language and the policies of the [F]irst [A]mendment command while allowing the judiciary the case-by-case flexibility necessary to reconcile those interests with truly compelling and conflicting societal concerns."[104]According to Redish, there is less to fear from judicial application of broad values than from overly-restrictive rules that constrict application of law without regard for the context of the case.

In this way, Redish differs from Ronald Dworkin, who also sees the value of free expression as individual, rather than social good. Dworkin's position is that individual rights are worthy of protection, even if they harm the public good. The "fundamental" right of free speech should be protected, even if the government is persuaded that the majority would be better off restricting speech.[105] Dworkin, however, does not leave it to individual case determination, but rather seeks to establish a "principle of free speech," that protects the "core value" of expression more than theories of free expression. He suggests "a particular rule . . . to protect an individual right."[106] Dworkin asserts that protecting expression as an individual right is more encompassing than protecting expression as a social good. He is concerned that legal scholars might settle on only one theory of First Amendment interpretation, and he prefers that it be one that incorporates more speech, rather than limits the amount.[107]

Other First Amendment scholars have also adopted this approach. Baker, in what he terms the "liberty model," argues that expression is a right of the individual because it has value to the individual rather than some grander societal value. "The liberty theory justifies protection because of the way the protected conduct fosters individual self-realization and self-determination without improperly interfering with the legitimate claims of others."[108] He is quick to point out, however, that this approach is not absolute. Classes of expression that are not part of self-realization, such as advertising, would not necessarily enjoy protection.[109] If the caveat is added that fulfilling speech that harms others can be restricted, much more expression can be proscribed.[110] The difficulty is exacerbated in that Mill's harm principle never elucidates what constitutes harms.[111]

Supreme Court use of self-fulfillment alone as free expression value has been limited. "Most theorists and judges have preferred utilitarianism and have been suspicious of the doctrine that there are natural rights."[112]

In *Cohen v California*, the Court seems to value free expression for its contribution to both self-government and self-fulfillment.[113] In vacating the conviction of a man for wearing a jacket bearing "Fuck the Draft," the Court examined the "constitutional backdrop." It stated that free-expression

is designed and intended to remove governmental restraints from the arena of public discussion, putting the decision as to what views shall be voiced largely into the hands of each of us, in the hope that use of such freedom will ultimately produce a more capable citizenry and more perfect polity and in the belief that no other approach would comport with the premise of individual dignity and choice upon which our political system rests.[114]

While the decision speaks of a "perfect polity" it is couched in "individual dignity and choice." The Court also asserts that "the Constitution leaves matters of taste and style so largely to the individual."[115] This approach is parallel to one taken thirty years earlier by First Amendment scholar Zechariah Chafee, who saw a dual purpose in protecting expression. "There is an individual interest, the need of many men to express their opinions on matters vital to them if life is to be worth living, and a social value in the attainment of truth. . . ."[116] Former Justice William Brennan, a frequent author of opinions valuing free speech for self-fulfillment, cautioned against an approach that values *only* self-fulfilling speech. Self-expression, of value to the individual, is only half of the equation. To Brennan, the social interest in self-government is the other half.[117] This combination of the individual right and the social good is a common thread among many philosophers who claim to believe the value of free expression is self-realization. For example, Robert Neville distinguishes personal and social freedoms.[118] He defines social freedoms as those freedoms we enjoy because of participation in groups, and personal freedoms as those that are neither social nor religious freedoms. While he is cautious to point out that the freedoms overlap, he mistakenly categorizes speech as social opportunity and social pluralism.[119] Similarly, individual rights and social goods are often "combined," or at least, confused. "It is certainly a characteristic of our time that more and more liberties are demanded both as indispensable foundations of the democratic way of living, and in order to protect the individual's well-being."[120]

Robert Picard presents an interesting reversal of this theme. Rather than assert that self-fulfillment serves the greater social good, Picard claims that democratic ideals cannot exist without the commitment to the rights of the individual. "The instruments through which true democracy is made possible are those rights and privileges that protect individual liberty and individuals' ability to seek self-realization."[121] Without a commitment to the value of self-realization, Picard argues, democracy has little value. In promoting the democratic socialist press theory, Picard states that individuals should have participation in all spheres of life that affect them, and that government's role is to assure that means are available for the realization of that participation.[122] High degrees of self-actualization and participation in society are intertwined.[123] Redish supposes not that they are interwoven, but that political participation is but one means by which individuals are self-realized.[124]

Similarly, John Stuart Mill proposed that society needs to foster individuality for society's own benefit. The more individuals develop, the more valuable they become to themselves, thus they become more valuable to others.[125] "Mill's primary contention is that the human race collectively and over the long run benefits from the cultivation of individuality."[126]

Self-fulfillment as free expression value also has its detractors. BeVier states that, while the value itself is appealing, any attempt to attach it to First Amendment analysis is inappropriate.[127] Her position is that if self-fulfillment were given First Amendment status, it would undo much of our social order and undermine our system of majority rule.[128]

Frederick Schauer is critical of the self-fulfillment theory of free speech for a variety of reasons.[129] First, he asserts that claiming a right because something is self-fulfilling requires application of that right to all self-fulfilling behavior.[130] Clearly, this should be of concern, especially when one examines the writings of proponents such as John Dewey, who would have the state protect human interaction with nature.[131] Despite the difficulty, this slippery slope argument is unpersuasive. Constitutional rights to bear arms, to religious freedom, and to fair trial do not prohibit the government from establishing limits to these rights under certain circumstances. Claiming that some rights of self-fulfillment deserve constitutional protection does not imply that all must be protected. Second, Schauer claims that the inability to reconcile self-fulfillment with contemporary First Amendment doctrine should make it unworkable.[132] Rather, this argues for a balancing approach advocated by Redish.[133]

SUMMARY

The First Amendment has been interpreted in a variety of ways by many scholars. Most First Amendment theories provide insights into what makes free expression worth protecting. Some theories can be seen as more narrow, or limiting of free expression, while others can be characterized as expansive.

This analysis began with a proposition that there can be no *one* First Amendment theory. The preceding illustrates that there is much to recommend each of the approaches. Likewise, each approach has its own practical and theoretical problems. Selection of one of these runs the risk of alienating the reader and discounting much sound analysis. I, however, assert that self-fulfillment as free expression value seems to merit the greatest weight. In an attempt to provide the greatest expression opportunities to the most individuals, the value of self-fulfillment is the most inclusive of the values cited. As Tribe so eloquently stated, "[t]o posit that expression is an element of the human may be controversial, but this at least moves discussion to the limits of language more directly than is otherwise possible with instrumental claims."[134]

Chapter 2 examines the legal history of access through actions taken by the courts, Congress, and the Federal Communications Commission either to limit or expand the opportunities that exist for individuals to speak freely. Precedents are compared to determine whether there exists an implicit public policy regarding individual access to forums for free expression. What are the venues that the government has sought to make available for free expression, and what means can be used to distinguish them from other forums? Legal history is also analyzed for affirmative action by the state to provide the means for accessing the forums of communication.

NOTES

1. J. COHEN & T. GLEASON, SOCIAL RESEARCH IN COMMUNICATION AND LAW 54 (1990).

2. "[P]ublic discussion is a political duty . . . this should be a fundamental principle of the American government." Whitney v California, 274 U.S. 357, 375 (1926) (Brandeis, J., concurring).

3. T. EMERSON, THE SYSTEM OF FREEDOM OF EXPRESSION 6–8 (1970).

4. Emerson's list is not exhaustive. For example, omitted is editorial autonomy *see infra* notes 75–92 and accompanying text. Karst claims Emerson's first three values are part of the larger equality principle that values the equal opportunity of expression for all. Karst, *Equality as a Central Principle in the First Amendment*, 43 U. CHI. L. REV. 20 (1975). John Rawls adopts the position that equality is the leading value. D. TUCKER, LAW, LIBERALISM AND FREE SPEECH 39–42 (1985). He asserts provision of basic liberties must be equal. Rawls, *The Basic Liberties and Their Priorities* in THE TANNER LECTURES ON HUMAN VALUES III (S. McMurrin ed. 1982). Additionally, a philosophy-of-language approach to expression values free speech in order for language to have meaning. "It implies that there is no 'speech' except free speech, because speech is dialogue to learn the meaning of words." Chevigny, *Philosophy of Language and Free Expression*, 55 N.Y.U.L. REV. 157, 177 (1980).

5. One scholar suggests it is imprudent to evaluate general principles to fashion one, general theory of free expression. H. KALVEN, A WORTHY TRADITION 3 (1988).

6. Without a scheme for weighting one value above others, Emerson's list is subject to ad hoc balancing. Hodge, *Democracy and Free Speech: A Normative Theory of Society and Government,* in THE FIRST AMENDMENT RECONSIDERED 149 (B. Chamberlain & C. Brown eds. 1982).

7. For an excellent review of the conflict between the free expression values of self-governance and self-fulfillment, *see* Bollinger, *The Press and the Public Interest: An Essay on the Relationship Between Social Behavior and the Language of First Amendment Theory,* 82 MICH. L. REV. 1447, 1447–1449 (1984).

8. "[D]ebate on public issues should be uninhibited, robust and wide-open, and . . . may well include vehement, caustic, and sometimes unpleasantly sharp attacks on government officials." New York Times v. Sullivan, 376 U.S. 254, 270 (1964). "[P]rivate individuals are not only more vulnerable to injury than public officials and public figures; they are also more deserving of recovery." Gertz v Welch, 418 U.S. 323 (1974).

9. *See, e.g.,* Rosenblatt v Baer, 383 U.S. 75 (1966); Curtis Publishing Co. v Butts, 388 U.S. 130 (1967); Monitor Patriot Co. v Roy, 401 U.S. 265 (1971).

10. The Supreme Court rejected any requirement that access be legally required, even in the form of paid advertising. "[E]diting is what editors are for. . . . Calculated risks are taken in order to preserve high values." CBS v DNC, 412 U.S. 94, 124–125 (1973). *See also* Miami Herald Publishing v Tornillo, 418 U.S. 241 (1975). Chief Justice Burger suggests that editorial autonomy is the principle worthy of constitutional protection. Alas, by alluding to the "high values" that editorial autonomy preserves without any elucidation, no logical analysis can be applied. The proposition begs the question, Why is determination of what advertising to accept, not even an editorial decision for most media, worthy of constitutional protection?

11. Miami Herald v Tornillo, 418 U.S. 241 (1974). Justice Brennan's concurrence tried to except retraction statutes from the ban on government compulsion of publication, but the majority did not adopt his position. *Id.,* at 258–259.

12. An increase in electronic channels has not been accompanied by an increase in diversity. Hyde, *FCC Action Repealing the Fairness Doctrine: A Revolution in Broadcast Regulation,* 38 SYRACUSE L. REV. 1175, 1188 (1987). *Accord* R. PICARD, THE PRESS AND THE DECLINE OF DEMOCRACY 77 (1985) ("The mere existence of media plurality does not ensure diversity.")

13. Schauer, *The Role of the People in First Amendment Theory,* 74 CAL L. REV. 761, 784 (1986).

14. Tribe, *Toward A Metatheory of Free Speech,* 10 S.W.U.L. REV. 237, 239 (1978).

15. *Id.* The other three dimensions were premises, methods, and boundaries.

16. R. BERGER, GOVERNMENT BY JUDICIARY 363–372 (1977).

17. *See, e.g.*, I. BRANT, THE BILL OF RIGHTS (1965); Blasi, *The Checking Value in First Amendment Theory*, 3 AM. BAR. FOUND. RES. J. 521 (1977); Bogen, *The Origins of Freedom of Speech and Press*, 42 MD. L. REV. 429 (1983); L. LEVY, EMERGENCE OF A FREE PRESS (1985); J. SMITH, PRINTERS AND PRESS FREEDOM (1988); Anderson, *The Origins of the Press Clause*, 30 UCLA L. REV. 455 (1983).

18. Roth v U.S., 354 U.S. 476, 484 (1957).

19. P. BOBBITT, CONSTITUTIONAL FATE 11 (1982).

20. COHEN & GLEASON, *supra* note 1, at 60. *See also* Brest, *The Misconceived Quest for the Original Understanding*, 60 B.U.L. REV. 204 (1980); Abrams, Book Review, N.Y. TIMES BOOK REV. 30 (Nov. 1, 1987) ("perils of reliance on inevitably contradictory historical data as the primary basis for interpreting the Constitution.")

21. *See* Wright, *A Rationale from J. S. Mill for the Free Speech Clause*, 1985 SUP. CT. REV. 149, 150; Joyce, Book Review, 75 J. AM. HIST. 924 (Dec. 1988) ("It is unclear where the energizing sources of historical change are located.")

22. *See* Emerson, *The Affirmative Side of the First Amendment*, 15 GEORGIA L. REV. 795 (1981); Note, *Access to Cable Television: A Critique of the Affirmative Duty Theory of the First Amendment*, 70 CAL. L. REV. 1393 (1982); Taylor, *What's Wrong With Negative Liberty*, in THE IDEA OF FREEDOM 177 (A. Ryan ed. 1979); Nemming, *Negative and Positive Press Freedom*, IPI REPORT (Sept. 1969) 8.

23. It is pointless to search for the *one* correct theory of free expression. One text suggests "few serious students would suggest that we have developed a satisfactory theoretical framework for discussing freedom of expression." COHEN & GLEASON, *supra* note 1, at 56.

24. In fact, discovery of truth has been argued since at least the sixteenth century. *See* J. SMITH, *supra* note 17, at 32. As the arguments of Peter Wentworth and others have been largely ignored until Milton, discourse prior to 1644 is superfluous.

25. *Areopagitica* in 2 COMPLETE PROSE WORKS OF JOHN MILTON 504 (D. Wolfe ed. 1975).

26. *See* J. ROUSSEAU, THE SOCIAL CONTRACT 128 (G. Cole trans. 1950).

27. "For truth certainly would do well enough if she were once left to shift for herself." J. LOCKE, *A Letter Concerning Toleration* (1689) in THE SECOND TREATISE OF GOVERNMENT 153 (J. Gough ed. 1966).

28. "If the opinion is right, they are deprived of the opportunity of exchanging error for truth: if wrong, they lose, what is almost as great a benefit, the clearer perception and livelier impression of truth, produced by its collision with error." J. MILL, ON LIBERTY 18 (1859, 1975).

29. According to one researcher, thirteen different justices authored opinions using the metaphor of a marketplace of ideas for free expression. Sweeney, *The Marketplace of Ideas: An Economic Analogy for Freedom of Speech*, p. 10 (paper presented at Association for Education in Journalism and Mass Communication Convention, Aug. 1984).

30. "But when men have realized that time has upset many fighting faiths, they may come to believe even more than they believe the very foundations of their own conduct that the ultimate good desired is better reached by free trade in ideas—that the best test of truth is the power of the thought to get itself accepted in the competition of the market, and that truth is the only ground upon which their wishes can be safely carried out." Abrams v U.S., 250 U.S. 616, 630 (1919) (Holmes, J., dissenting).

31. "When ideas compete in the marketplace for acceptance, full and free discussion exposes the false and they gain few adherents." Dennis v U.S., 341 U.S. 494, 584 (1951) (Douglas, J., dissenting).

32. Robert Picard claims instead that diversity "serves the ends of democratic participation" and thus would be a sub-value of self-governance. R. PICARD, *supra* note 12, at 43. Conceivably it serves both end values.

33. More than fifty years ago, constitutional scholar Zechariah Chafee foresaw this paradox. He asserted that for the marketplace to function properly, it would require government intervention. Z. CHAFEE, 2 GOVERNMENT AND MASS CCOMMUNICATIONS 471 (1947).

34. Reich, *Affirmative Action for Ideas*, 38 CASE W. RES. L. REV. 632, 636 (1988).

35. Baker, *Scope of the First Amendment Freedom of Speech*, 25 UCLA L. REV. 964, 981–990 (1978).

36. Schauer calls this a "consensus theory of truth." F. SCHAUER, FREE SPEECH: A PHILOSOPHICAL INQUIRY 20 (1982).

37. "A theory of majority rule for truth distorts out of all recognition our use of words like 'truth,' 'good,' 'sound,' or 'wise.' " *Id.*, at 22.

38. D. TUCKER, *supra* note 4, at 53–56.

39. W. LIPPMANN, PUBLIC OPINION 202 (1922).

40. Winters v N.Y., 333 U.S. 507, 510 (1948).

41. F. SCHAUER, *supra* note 36, at 32.

42. Wright, *supra* note 21, at 169.

43. "The principle of the freedom of speech springs from the necessities of self-government." A. MEIKLEJOHN, FREE SPEECH AND ITS RELATION TO SELF GOVERNMENT 66 (1948).

44. J. ALTSCHULL, AGENTS OF POWER 182 (1984) ("the democratic assumption . . . holds that democracy is nurtured and furthered when an informed citizenry makes wise judgments in choosing those who will represent them in government.")

45. A. MEIKLEJOHN, *supra* note 43, at 25.

46. Karst, *supra* note 4, at 40.

47. F. SCHAUER, *supra* note 36, at 37–40, *See also* Berman, *The Right to Know: Public Access to Electronic Information* in 2 NEW DIRECTIONS IN TELECOMMUNICATIONS POLICY 39 (P. Newberg ed. 1989); Reid, *An Affirmative First Amendment Access Right,* COM. & L. 39 (June 1988) (free expression intended to assure discussion of public affairs).

48. Redish, *The Value of Free Speech,* 130 U. PA. L. REV. 591, 607 (1982).

49. "The social interest that the First Amendment vindicates is . . . the interest in the successful operation of the political process." A. BICKEL, THE MORALITY OF CONSENT 62 (1976).

50. BeVier, *The First Amendment and Political Speech: An Inquiry Into the Substance and Limits of Principle,* 30 STANFORD L. REV. 299 (1978). BeVier argues that the only logical construction of the First Amendment is restricted to political speech, and that while other rules protecting additional expression may be legitimate, to claim they are constitutionally protected is a disservice to the framers' intent, the Constitution as a whole, and the government structure. *Id.,* at 302, 305.

51. Bogen, *supra* note 17, at 435.

52. New York Times v Sullivan, 376 U.S. 254, 270 (1964) (national commitment to uninhibited debate on public issues).

53. CBS v DNC, 412 U.S. 94, 122 (1973) (citing Meiklejohn).

54. Pickering v Board of Education, 391 U.S. 563, 571–572 (1968).

55. Mills v Alabama, 384 U.S. 214, 218 (1966).

56. Baker, *The Process of Change and the Liberty Theory of the First Amendment,* 55 S. CAL L. REV. 293, 330 (1981).

57. *Id.,* at 331.

58. *Id.,* at 327.

59. One author suggests that speech that impacts the electoral process is a *basic* right, while other speech may only be an *important* right. Hodge, *supra* note 6, at 157. For criticism of a core approach, see L. BOLLINGER, THE TOLERANT SOCIETY 43–75 (1986).

An interesting parallel exists in the first amendment area of freedom of religion. *See* Note, *The "Core"-"Periphery" Dichotomy in the First Amendment Free Exercise Clause Doctrine: Goldman v Weinberger, Bowen v Roy, and O'Lone v Estate of Shabazz,* 72 CORNELL L. REV. 827 (1987) (dichotomy allowing courts to avoid factual inquiry inappropriate).

60. 461 U.S. 138 (1983).

61. *Id.,* at 145, 147, citing Garrison v Louisiana, 379 U.S. 64, 74–75 (1964); NAACP v Claiborne Hardware Co., 458 U.S. 886, 913 (1982); Carey v Brown, 447 U.S. 455, 467 (1980); Mine Workers v Illinois Bar Assn., 389 U.S. 217, 223 (1967); Thomas v Collins, 323 U.S. 516, 531 (1945).

62. City Council v Taxpayers for Vincent, 104 S. Ct. 2118, 2135 (1984).

63. Tribe, *supra* note 14, at 241.

64. "I believe that history confirms Dr. Meiklejohn but goes beyond his position. The basic right to freedom of expression was not meant to be

confined to the political realm." Emerson, *Colonial Intentions and Current Realities of the First Amendment*, 125 U. PA. L. REV. 737, 742 (1977).

65. R. PICARD, *supra* note 12, at 30.

66. Specifically, those subjects Meiklejohn identifies as tangential to the political realm were: education, philosophy, science, literature, the arts, and "public issues." Meiklejohn, *Is the First Amendment an Absolute*? 1961 SUP. CT. REV. 245.

67. "[T]o justify music and sculpture as only more remote contributions to intelligent political choice, is to deprive the theory's premises of binding force and thereby render its structure essentially boundless." Tribe, *supra* note 14, at 242.

68. Schauer, *supra* note 13, at 780. According to Schauer, this is precisely what has been done with obscenity and libel judgments. *Accord* Scanlon, *A Theory of Freedom of Expression*, 1 PHIL. & PUB. AFF. 204, 223 (1972) ("[T]he value to be placed on having certain kinds of expression flourish is something which should be subject to popular will in the society in question.")

69. *See* A. GRAMSCI, SELECTIONS FROM THE PRISON NOTEBOOKS (Q. Hoare & G. Nowell-Smith eds. 1977).

70. D. TUCKER, *supra* note 4, at 137.

71. "Those who won our independence . . . knew that order cannot be secured merely through fear of punishment for its infraction; that it is hazardous to discourage thought, hope and imagination; that fear breeds repression; that repression breeds hate; that hate menaces stable government; that the path of safety lies in the opportunity to discuss freely supposed grievances and proposed remedies; and that the fitting remedy for evil councils is good ones." Whitney v California, 274 U.S. 357, 375–377 (1926) (Brandeis, J., concurring).

72. "[F]ighting words—those which by their very utterance inflict injury or tend to incite an immediate breach of the peace . . . are of such slight social value as a step to truth that any benefit that may be derived from them is clearly outweighed by the social interest in order and morality." Chaplinski v New Hampshire, 315 U.S. 568, 572 (1941). *See also* Cantwell v Connecticut, 310 U.S. 296, 310 (1939).

73. Ragan, *Justice Oliver Wendell Holmes Jr., Zechariah Chafee Jr., and the Clear and Present Danger Test for Free Speech*, 58 J. AM. HIST. 23 (1971).

74. Z. CHAFEE, FREE SPEECH IN THE UNITED STATES 564 (1941).

75. Blasi, *supra* note 17. Redish claims the checking function is merely a sub-value of the self-realization approach. Redish, *supra* note 48, at 616.

76. "The press is often likened to a watchdog guarding against the abuse of government power." Abrams, *The Press Is Different: Reflections on Justice Stewart and the Autonomous Press*, 7 HOFSTRA L. REV. 563, 591 (1970).

77. Stewart, *Or of the Press*, 26 HASTINGS L. J. 631 (1975).

78. *Id.*, at 633. If no other phrase in the constitution contained redundancy, Stewart's argument might have greater weight. Does one explain "[t]he

Senate shall choose their other Officers, and also a President pro tem-
pore . . . " by claiming the president pro tem is not an officer of the Senate?
U.S. CONST. art. I, sec. 3. What is one to make of phrases such as "liable and
subject to Indictment," *Id.* and "Treason, Felony and Breach of the Peace,"
U.S. CONST. art. I sec. 6 (is treason not a felony)?

79. Myers v U.S. 272 U.S. 52, 293 (1926).

80. Stewart, *supra* note 77, at 634.

81. *See, e.g.* Lewis, *A Preferred Position for Journalists?* 7 HOFSTRA L.
REV. 595 (1979); First National Bank of Boston v Bellotti, 435 U.S. 765
(1978) (Burger, C. J., concurring) (corporations have free speech rights).

82. Bollinger, *supra* note 7, at 1451, 1455.

83. New York Times v U.S., 403 U.S. 713, 717 (1971) (voiding injunc-
tion on publication of the Pentagon Papers).

84. "If . . . the press's central function is to serve as a counterforce to
public and private centers of power within society, protection of independent
editorial judgment is essential." Bezanson, *The New Free Press Guarantee*, 63
VA. L. REV. 731, 767 (1977). Although Bezanson expands the press role to
include watching private as well as public malfeasance, the rationale remains
the same. This is consistent with a democratic socialist press theory. "[A]n
individual's liberty must be protected not only from state encroachment but
from the encroachment of other individuals and of the economic and other
institutions of society." R. PICARD, *supra* note 12, at 30.

85. "[T]he history of the clause does not suggest that the authors contem-
plated a 'special' or 'institutional' privilege." First National Bank v Bellotti,
435 U.S. 765, 798 (1978).

86. CBS v DNC, 412 U.S. 94, 116–121 (1973).

87. *Id.*, at 120.

88. *Id.*, at 160–161.

89. Pittsburgh Press Co. v Human Relations Comm'n., 413 U.S. 376,
391 (1973) (prohibition of "male" and "female" help wanted listings not
unconstitutional).

90. 418 U.S. 241 (1974).

91. *Id.*, at 254–258.

92. Bigelow v Virginia, 421 U.S. 809, 829 (1975).

93. Redish prefers the term "self-realization" to self-fulfillment. It is his
contention that the former is more encompassing, including all the other values
proposed by Emerson. Redish, *supra* note 48, at 593–594.

94. The list of philosophers who affirm the freedom of self-realization
includes Hobbes, Voltaire, Edwards, Hume, Priestly, Burke, Freud, and
Malinowski. For a list, *see* M. ADLER, THE IDEA OF FREEDOM, Vol. 1,
171–201 (1961).

95. *Id.*, Vol. II, at 8.

96. L. MACFARLANE, THE THEORY AND PRACTICE OF HUMAN RIGHTS
73 (1985).

97. Anthony Smith sees natural rights as "a fresh, internationally acceptable liberal view of public interest." Smith, *The Public Interest and Telecommunications* in 1 NEW DIRECTIONS IN TELECOMMUNICATIONS POLICY 334, 357 (P. Newberg ed. 1989). Communication as human right has been promoted by UNESCO. *See* D. FISHER, THE RIGHT TO COMMUNICATE: A STATUS REPORT (1982).

98. Schauer, *supra* note 13, at 771 (citation omitted).

99. *Id.*, at 772.

100. *See* M. REDISH, FREEDOM OF EXPRESSION: A CRITICAL ANALYSIS (1984).

101. *Id.*, at 5.

102. *Accord* R. LADENSON, A. PHILOSOPHY OF FREE EXPRESSION AND ITS CONSTITUTIONAL APPLICATIONS 144–148 (1983) (judicial review appropriate means of protecting fundamental rights).

103. "The essential meaning of the First Amendment is that, already, in the making and maintaining of the Constitution, the procedure of 'balancing' has been undertaken and completed. . . . And that principle denies . . . to any other branch of government, authority, case by case, to abridge the political freedom of the people." Meiklejohn, *The First Amendment and Evils that Congress Has a Right to Prevent,* 26 IND. L. J. 478, 485 (1951); Bork, *Neutral Principles and Some First Amendment Problems,* 47 IND. L. J. 1 (1971) (First Amendment protects only political speech, and courts should not creatively interpret it).

104. *Id.*, at 4, 197–200, 255–257.

105. R. DWORKIN, TAKING RIGHTS SERIOUSLY 191 (1978).

106. R. DWORKIN, A MATTER OF PRINCIPLE 375 (1985).

107. *Id.*, at 388.

108. Baker, *supra* note 35, at 966.

109. *Id.*, at 996. Redish, however, disagrees with this analysis. Most advertising, he asserts, contributes to decision making and is thus self-actualizing. Redish, *supra* note 48, at 630. This, however, would be overinclusive, suffering the same definitional problems as claiming that art is political speech.

110. Schauer, *supra* note 13, at 772. Excluded are "defamatory statements, acerbic book reviews, critical evaluations of restaurants and newly opened plays, public racial epithets or revelations (true or false) about a political candidate's past."

111. D. TUCKER, *supra* note 4, at 13.

112. *Id.*, at 33.

113. 403 U.S. 15 (1971).

114. *Id.*, at 24.

115. *Id.*, at 25.

116. Z. CHAFEE, *supra* note 74, at 33.

117. Brennan, *Press and the Court: Is the Strain Necessary?* EDITOR & PUBLISHER (Oct. 27, 1979), at 10.

118. R. NEVILLE, THE COSMOLOGY OF FREEDOM 6–7 (1974).

119. *Id.*, at 222–223, 242–245.

120. Shmueli, *The Right to Self-Realization and Its Predicaments*, in THE PHILOSOPHY OF HUMAN RIGHTS 159 (A. Rosenbaum ed. 1980).

121. R. PICARD *supra* note 12, at 11.

122. *Id.*, at 27. The approach is similar to that of Karst, *supra* note 4.

123. *Id.*, at 37.

124. Redish, *supra* note 48, at 601.

125. R. LADENSON, *supra* note 102, at 37.

126. *Id.*, at 38.

127. BeVier, *supra* note 50, at 318.

128. *Id.*, at 320. *See also* Bollinger, *supra* note 7, at 1455. "The problem with the public interest (i.e., self fulfillment perspective) is that it seems to place control over speech freedom in the hands of the public itself."

129. F. SCHAUER, *supra* note 36, at 47–58.

130. Schauer, *supra* note 13, at 772.

131. R. ROTH, JOHN DEWEY AND SELF REALIZATION 4–9 (1962).

132. *Id.*, at 773.

133. Redish, *supra* note 102–104 and accompanying text.

134. Tribe, *supra* note 14, at 241.

2   LEGAL HISTORY OF ACCESS

The question of access to an appropriate forum for expression is not necessarily a new one, but it has taken a variety of forms over the past century. In the first case heard by the Supreme Court, access to appropriate forums was not seen as correlative to the right of free expression. In fact, the decision in *Davis v Massachusetts*[1] established the position that free speech on public property could be prohibited unless approved by the mayor. The Court reasoned that the Constitution "does not have the effect of creating a particular and personal right in the citizen to use public property in defiance of the constitution and laws of the State."[2]

On the other hand, the first case heard by the Supreme Court regarding access to the broadcast media occurred more than seventy years later, with quite a different result. In a unanimous decision, the Court upheld the personal attack clause of the Fairness Doctrine, determining that individuals did have a right of access to the broadcast media under certain, well-defined circumstances.[3]

This chapter examines the history of claims of access to a variety of forums for the purpose of expression. While cases differ significantly based on the particular forum, a number of similarities make all claims for access to facilitate expression consistent.

COMPARING RED LION AND TORNILLO

In 1964, radio station WGCB in Red Lion, Pennsylvania, aired a syndicated religious program called "Christian Crusade." The program that aired on November 25 of that year contained a venomous attack of Fred J. Cook, author of the book *Goldwater: Extremist on the Right*. The Reverend Billy James Hargis, host of the syndicated program and initiator of the two-minute attack, believed Cook's book to be at least partly responsible for Goldwater's failed presidential bid.[4]

Cook reacted by writing letters to the more than two hundred stations that regularly carried the Hargis broadcast informing them that the law requires the stations to provide him with time to respond free of charge.[5] WGCB was one of several stations willing to provide Cook reply time, however, at his expense.[6] Convinced the Fairness Doctrine required more than what WGCB was willing to offer, Cook took his case to the Federal Communications Commission (FCC).

Eleven months after the Hargis broadcast, the commission determined that Cook was entitled to free reply time. After an unusual sequence of events including appeals, proposed rule makings, and revised rules,[7] the case reached the Supreme Court. The Court's decision upheld the commission's rules regarding the Fairness Doctrine and the personal attack clause.

Miami Herald v Tornillo also involved a case that decided the constitutionality of a right of access under specific circumstances.[8] Patrick Tornillo, a candidate for state legislature in Florida, had demanded the right to respond to an editorial in the *Miami Herald*. The state of Florida had at the time a right-of-reply statute for candidates. When the *Herald* denied his request, Tornillo took his claim to court, leading to its eventual disposition by the Supreme Court.

As with *Red Lion*, the Supreme Court was unanimous in its decision. There, however, the similarity ends. In *Tornillo*, the Court supported the medium's right to decide for itself what content should fill the available space. The Court found Florida's right-of-reply statute to be a violation of the First Amendment. When the case was argued before the Court, Tornillo used the precedent from *Red Lion* as a central premise. The Supreme Court, however, never mentioned *Red Lion*, either to distinguish the cases or to limit the previous decision. Legal literature abounds with attempts to reconcile the two cases.[9]

Three possible approaches to their reconciliation distinguish them on the basis of differences in the (a) media, (b) speakers, or (c) content. The most obvious way to distinguish between *Red Lion* and *Tornillo* is to point out that one involved broadcasting while the other involved a print medium. (The reconciliation of differing treatment for print and broadcast media is discussed in Chapter 3.) Another possible reconciliation of the cases is the ability of a candidate to receive media attention compared to the relative inability of a "common" book author to do so. This claim contends that those who can achieve media attention without government intervention should do so: access regulations should be used only in those cases where access would not be achieved without government assistance. Finally, while both were personal attacks, one dealt with a book review while the other dealt with the suitability of a candidate for public office. A Meiklejohnian approach that distinguishes between political speech "at the core" of the First Amendment and commercial speech, entitled to limited if any protection, has no difficulty making such a distinction.

An additional possibility is presented by Craig Smith, who speculates that a difference exists in the Supreme Court's confidence in the audience. "In the *Miami Herald* case, the Supreme Court considered a newspaper reader sophisticated and intelligent enough to form his or her own opinion. In *Red Lion*, however, the radio listener was treated as one who must be protected by a governmental agency that assures fairness."[10] While this distinction may appear at first simplistic, it may in fact be the most accurate characterization for the Court's apparent inconsistency. The Supreme Court appears concerned with the broadcast audience's ability to fend for itself.

This might be seen as analogous to the Supreme Court's distinction in the *Cohen* and *Pacifica* cases. In two communications involving indecent language, the Court reached two different conclusions. Asserting that one seeing an indecency in a public place might avert one's eyes does not distinguish a case where the same epithet is broadcast and one may avert one's ears (or merely change the channel). The Supreme Court's perspective in *Pacifica* was much more paternalistic.

In the enormous volume of literature that compares *Red Lion* and *Tornillo*, rationalizations for the differing conclusions usually follow one of two arguments. Either the cases are distinguished due to the scarcity[11] of frequencies available, or the argument that licensing of broadcast stations allows the government to impose public service requirements on broadcasters.[12] Sometimes the line between the two is obscured and the arguments are combined although they should be seen as separate issues.

Two other possible distinctions, although not as prevalent in the literature, are presented here for consideration. Henry Geller and others contend that perhaps the only rational distinction to draw in the two cases is a historical one.[13] Historically, newspapers have not been subject to regulation, whereas broadcasting developed amidst mounds of it. In the historical scheme, broadcasters are used to it. This approach is similar to that argued by Bollinger, who proposes that legislative access requirements are appropriate, so long as they remain restricted to one medium.[14] In his words, "By permitting different treatment of the two institutions, the Court can facilitate realization of the benefits of two distinct constitutional values, both of which ought to be fostered: access in a highly concentrated press and minimal governmental intervention."[15]

Finally, it is possible that the Supreme Court completely ignored the *Red Lion* decision in its *Tornillo* ruling[16] simply because it felt uncomfortable with the earlier holding. The only justice not participating in *Red Lion*, Justice Douglas, wrote of his disagreement with the decision four years after *Red Lion*, the year before *Tornillo* was decided.[17]

Despite the varying rationales, the comparison of the two cases represents the overriding premise that access-related regulation is at times appropriate for broadcast media, but not for print.[18] While existing cases call into question some of the premises from the *Red Lion* decision,[19] the Supreme Court has never overruled the case, nor has the FCC challenged the appropriateness of the personal attack clause.

Perhaps the best way to determine the Court's view of a distinction would be to consider cases since *Tornillo* that refer to both *Red Lion* and *Tornillo*. In Shepardizing decisions since 1974, *Red Lion* is cited by the Court dozens of times, but there are only fourteen cases where both *Red Lion* and *Tornillo* are mentioned.[20] In three of these decisions, the two cases are not cited within the same opinion,[21] and are thus not as valuable in distinguishing the cases.

The most recent Supreme Court decision citing both *Red Lion* and *Tornillo* is *Los Angeles v Preferred Communications*.[22] Unfortunately, the case provides little analysis. The previous cases are cited to explain that the lower court believed cable conditions were analogous to newspapers rather than broadcast media, and thus cable should be subject to a *Tornillo* rather than a *Red Lion* analysis. In remanding the case, the Court elects not to decide on that aspect.

Earlier that same term, the Court heard *Pacific Gas & Electric v Public Utilities Commission*.[23] In that decision, the Supreme Court found a California Public Utilities Commission rule requiring access to utility company mailings unconstitutional. Justice Powell's plurality opinion found the utility envelopes similar to newspapers in *Tornillo*. According to Powell, two First Amendment violations were involved: forcing the utility (or paper) to disseminate views with which it did not agree was a penalty for speaking out, and the organization's editorial discretion was violated.[24] In a footnote, Powell explains that *Red Lion* involved a "scarce, publicly owned resource," and that the U.S. mail was available to all.[25] The inference, then, is that Powell would distinguish *Tornillo* from *Red Lion* based on the claim that broadcasting is both scarce and publicly owned.

Prior to *Preferred*, the most recent case[26] to cite both *Red Lion* and *Tornillo* in the majority opinion is *FCC v League of Women Voters*.[27] This case has been repeatedly cited as "opening the door" to the reexamination of not only the Fairness Doctrine, but of the entire premise of differential regulatory standards for print and broadcast,[28] a view based largely on two footnotes contained in the majority opinion. The first, support for the public interest standard in broadcast licensing, claims that scarcity is the prevailing rationale for broadcast regulation.[29] In the note, the Court points out that the scarcity rationale has been questioned in light of the new communications environment. While the Court elects not to change *its* position on scarcity, it suggests the possibility that Congress or the FCC might send a signal that such a change is warranted.[30] The second footnote states the Court's willingness to reconsider the *Red Lion* decision if it were shown that the Fairness Doctrine impeded, rather than furthered, First Amendment goals.[31]

It appears from the majority opinion in *League of Women Voters* that spectrum scarcity is the dominant reason for the distinction between *Red Lion* and *Tornillo*. The Court also speaks of the spectrum as a public resource,[32] but it does so in passing, without supporting evidence or citation. Using this case as determinative, one would have to assert that *Red Lion* is distinguishable from *Tornillo* based on spectrum scarcity.

In *CBS v FCC*,[33] the Court upheld the reasonable access requirements on broadcasters by candidates for federal office.[34] The Court accepts *Red Lion* as precedent that the rights of the audience supersede those of the broadcaster by asserting a public resource argument.[35] The Court continues by using *Tornillo* as evidence that a limited right of access may exist, but that there is no *general* right.[36] The distinguishing characteristic is the use of the airwaves, which are owned by the people.

In the analysis of cases from more than a decade, the Supreme Court seems to use both the scarcity rationale and the airwaves as public resource approach to distinguish *Red Lion* and *Tornillo*. While the Court also provides evidence that scarcity may no longer be appropriate, no Supreme Court decision has yet drawn that conclusion.

ACCESS TO PUBLIC FORUMS

According to a search of Supreme Court decisions, the term "public forum" has been used in Court decisions only since 1961.[37] To suggest, however, that analysis of public forums and what rights of access may ensue has been considered for only thirty years is naive. In order to understand the applicable cases, it is appropriate to discuss what constitutes the public forum.

A public forum can be defined as a venue where the government determines the character of the expressive activity that is allowed to occur.[38] Thus, a governmental determination that a certain forum will be open to free expression makes it a public forum. The situation is not so easily resolved, however, as the following historical analysis of more than fifty Supreme Court decisions demonstrates.

The first case to consider whether a public place had to be opened to the public for speech purposes was *Davis v Massachusetts*.[39] The City of Boston had enacted a law requiring city approval for a variety of activities on Boston Common, including making any public address.[40] Davis, a preacher, was convicted of violating the ordinance. In a three-page opinion, Justice White wrote for a unanimous Court in stating that the Fourteenth Amendment "does not have the effect of creating a particular and personal right in the citizen to use public property in defiance of the constitution and laws of the state."[41] The Court adopted the premise that Boston was a property owner, and just like individual property owners, did not have to make its areas available for use unless it wanted to.

It was forty years before the Supreme Court again considered the question of whether the government could regulate speech on property owned by the state. In *Lovell v City of Griffin*,[42] the Court was again presented with the question of whether a city could constitutionally require the securing of a permit prior to expression. Once again, the Court was unanimous in its decision, however the response was surprisingly different. Chief Justice Hughes stated that the ordinance was invalid. "Whatever the motive which induced its adoption, its character is such that it strikes at the very foundation of freedom of the press by subjecting it to license and censorship."[43] While the case dealt with pamphleteering rather than public speaking, the issue was the same as in *Davis*: ordinances requiring government permission before permitting expression using the public forum. Nowhere in *Lovell* does the Court cite or refer to *Davis*.

The following year, the Supreme Court was again confronted with the constitutionality of a local ordinance regulating the distribution of printed matter, as well as public parades and assemblies. In *Hague v CIO*,[44] the Court reiterated its position in *Lovell* that free expression requires the protection of means of distribution as well as protection of publication. In this case, the Court chose to specifically refer to both *Davis* and *Lovell*. The petitioners argued that the precedent from *Davis* gave Jersey City the authority to enforce such an ordinance, similar to that permitted in Boston. The plurality disagreed, however, choosing to distinguish the Boston ordinance as one dealing generally with city regulation of parks. "In the instant case the ordinance deals only with the exercise of the right of assembly for the purpose of communicating views entertained by speakers, and is not a general measure to promote the public convenience in the use of the streets or parks."[45] Once *Davis* was distinguished, the Court was free to cite *Lovell* as the appropriate precedent.

The plurality chose to protect speech in public places, which it said were historically used for speech purposes.

Wherever the title of streets and parks may rest, they have immemorially been held in trust for the use of the public and, time out of mind, have been used for purposes of assembly, communicating thoughts between citizens, and discussing public questions. Such use of the streets and public places has, from ancient times, been a part of the privileges, immunities, rights, and liberties of citizens.[46]

Its argument was for protection of speech in venues where speech had historically occurred.

In its very next term, the Court expounded on its public forum position in *Schneider v State*.[47] Four different communities varying in size and geography[48] enacted ordinances restricting the distribution of printed materials. The Supreme Court held that, while some regulation of public streets was appropriate,[49] the constitution greatly limited a state's ability to restrict use of public streets.

The Court used *Lovell* and *Hague* to support its finding that all four ordinances were unconstitutional. Justice Powell, author of the *Hague* plurality, wrote for the *Schneider* majority. The opinion continued the theme that streets are appropriate for expression for historical reasons. Further, it states that "the streets are natural and proper places for the dissemination of information and opinion; and one is not to have the exercise of his liberty of expression in appropriate places abridged on the plea that it may be exercised in some other place."[50] Thus public forums were determined appropriate for speech regardless of whether other forums were provided. While the court pointed out that streets were "natural and proper" places for speech, it failed to explain the characteristics that made them such, or what other sorts of locations were also natural and proper.

Cantwell v Connecticut[51] also dealt with a permit requirement. The Supreme Court overturned Cantwell's conviction for violating an ordinance that required solicitors to register with the secretary of the public welfare council. The secretary was then authorized to "determine whether such cause is a religious one or is a bona fide object of charity and philanthropy and conforms to reasonable standards of efficiency and integrity."[52] While the Court was willing to accept ordinances attempting to protect citizens from clear and present dangers, such was not the case here. The unanimous decision, written by Justice Roberts, found the ordinance "sweeping in a great variety of conduct under a general and indefinite characterization, and leaving to the executive and judicial branches too wide a discretion in its application."[53] The ordinance failed because it went overboard.

One year later, the Supreme Court demonstrated its willingness to find licensing requirements constitutional, provided the ordinances were narrowly constructed and administrative discretion was minimal. The unanimous decision in *Cox v New Hampshire* recognized the historical argument for public forums presented in *Hague*, but added another: there was also a common law argument for police power.

> As regulation of the use of the streets for parades and processions is a traditional exercise of control by local government, the question in a particular case is whether that control is exerted so as not to deny or unwarrantedly abridge the right of assembly and the opportunities for the communication of thought and the discussion of public questions immemorially associated with resort to public places.[54]

Thus, while the Court accepted the premises established in *Lovell* and *Hague*, it distinguished *Cox* by proclaiming that the permit requirement was narrowly constructed.

New Hampshire appeared again before the Supreme Court in 1942 to defend a law limiting speech in a public place. The law proscribed language that was "offensive, derisive and annoying" to others.[55] A unanimous Court upheld the statute, using as justification the "fighting words" doctrine crafted by Zechariah Chafee.[56] The doctrine asserts that words that are so vile that their mere utterance causes injury or incites a breach of peace are undeserving of protection.[57] For the appellant to call a city marshal a "damned Fascist" and a "damned racketeer" was determined by New Hampshire to be such fighting words, and the Supreme Court judged the statute, and its application, constitutional.

The Supreme Court continued to support the right of individuals to distribute pamphlets on public streets. In *Jamison v Texas,*[58] a Jehovah's Witness had been charged with violating a Dallas ordinance prohibiting the distribution of handbills on city streets. The city cited *Davis* as authority for ordinances prohibiting the use of streets for communication. Citing instead *Hague* and *Schneider*, the Court rejected the contention. "One who is rightfully on a street which the state has left open to the public carries with him there as elsewhere the constitutional right to express his views in an orderly fashion."[59]

Less than two months later, the Supreme Court issued its ruling in *Martin v City of Struthers*.[60] In the interest of residents not wishing to be disturbed, the city enacted an ordinance prohibiting door-to-door solicitation. Writing for a narrow majority, Justice Black held that the ordinance not only protected those who wished to be left alone, but also limited reception by those who might want information. In other words, the ordinance went beyond what limits it could legally impose.

Interestingly, Black's opinion stated a desire to protect speech not in the interest of the speaker, but in the interest of the receiver.

> Freedom to distribute information to every citizen *wherever he desires to receive it* is so clearly vital to the preservation of a free society that, putting aside reasonable police and health regulations of time and manner of distribution, it must be fully preserved. The dangers of distribution can so easily be controlled by traditional legal methods, *leaving to each householder the full right to decide* whether he will receive strangers as visitors, that stringent prohibition can serve no purpose. . . .[61]

Marsh v Alabama was the first case where the Court considered the application of public forum principles to strictly private property.[62] Marsh was a Jehovah's Witness who attempted to distribute religious literature in Chickasaw, a suburb of Mobile, Alabama. What made Chickasaw different from Struthers, Dallas, and the other communities in previous cases was that Chickasaw was a "company-owned" town. The entire community, including streets and sidewalks, was privately owned. Justice Black's decision for the Court was that Marsh's First Amendment rights had been violated, even though the speech restriction took place on private property. He reasoned that "[t]he more an owner, for his advantage, opens up his property for use by the public in general, the more do his rights become circumscribed by the statutory and constitutional rights of those who use it."[63] Black thus established the threshold by which future cases were analyzed. Public forum cases dealing with private property were resolved by determining to what extent property had been "opened up" and to what extent the "public in general" was invited to use it.

In 1948 the Supreme Court was confronted with an ordinance attempting to prohibit the use of sound amplifying equipment without permission of the chief of police. The majority in *Saia v New York* held that the ordinance was not narrowly drawn, and thus was unconstitutional.[64] Justice Douglas wrote that the possibility that loudspeakers would be abused was not adequate to allow such regulation. "The hours and place of public discussion can be controlled. But to allow the police to bar the use of loud-speakers because their use can be abused is like barring radio receivers because they too make a noise."[65] Thus the Court followed the precedent that reasonable regulation of the public forum was permissible, but completely prohibiting speech, or restrictions going beyond those necessary, would be strictly scrutinized.

The following year, the Supreme Court heard another case, this time from New Jersey, dealing with amplified sound in the public forum. In *Kovacs v Cooper*, the Court found a Trenton ordinance prohibiting sound trucks constitutional as applied.[66] The plurality rejected the argument from *Saia* that the ordinance was too vague. The terms "loud and raucous" in the ordinance have well-accepted definitions, according to Justice Reed. "While these are abstract words, they have through daily use acquired a context that conveys to any interested person a sufficiently accurate concept of what is forbidden."[67]

The dissenters, led by Justice Black, expressed concern about the Court's apparent repudiation of *Saia*. Further, it was feared that the result of *Kovacs* would be to favor certain means of communication over others, thus resulting in preferential treatment for those who owned certain communication media.

The basic premise of the First Amendment is that all present instruments of communication, as well as others that inventive genius may bring into being, shall be free from governmental censorship or prohibition. Laws which hamper the free use of some instruments of communication thereby favor competing channels. Thus, unless constitutionally prohibited, laws like this Trenton ordinance can give an overpowering influence to views of owners of legally favored instruments of communication.[68]

The same term, the Supreme Court heard a case from Illinois concerning an individual's speech that was determined by the lower court to be a breach of peace. In *Terminiello v Chicago*,[69] the majority avoided the constitutional question of whether the fighting words doctrine enunciated in *Chaplinski* was consistent with First Amendment interpretations. Instead, the opinion, written by Justice Douglas, centered on the interpretation of a "breach of peace" as defined by the trial court. As interpreted, the statute banned speech that "stirs the public to anger, invites dispute, brings about a condition of unrest, or creates a disturbance."[70] The Court ruled that including such speech was unconstitutional. "A function of free speech under our system of government is to invite dispute."[71] In a lengthy dissent, Justice Jackson chastised the majority for ignoring the dicta from unanimous decisions in *Chaplinski* and *Cantwell*.[72]

On one day in 1951, the Supreme Court announced three decisions concerning the right of individuals to use the public forum. The first two cases involved individuals using parks for religious expression: one in Harve de Grace, Maryland,[73] the other in New York City.[74] Both opinions, written by Justice Vinson, were critical of ordinances that vested too much discretion in city officials. The Court reiterated its position that permit requirements could be consistent with the First Amendment, but that in cases at the bar, there were "no appropriate standards"[75] and the refusal to grant permits was "completely arbitrary and discriminatory."[76]

The third case dealt not with a permit requirement, but with the arrest of a speaker who had refused to stop speaking when police officers believed violence was imminent.[77] The Supreme Court opinion, again authored by Justice Vinson, upheld the conviction, asserting that it was an arrest based not on the speech's content but rather on a breach of peace and incitement to riot. "It is one thing to say that the police cannot be used as an instrument for the suppression of unpopular views, and another to say that, when as here the speaker passes the bounds of argument or persuasion and undertakes incitement to riot, they are powerless to prevent a breach of the peace."[78] Dissents, written by Justices Black and Douglas, both questioned why police arrested the speaker to prevent a violent confrontation, rather than arresting the individual in the crowd who had done the threatening.[79]

Later that same term, the Supreme Court upheld an ordinance in Alexandria, Louisiana, prohibiting door-to-door solicitation without the prior approval of owners or occupants.[80] In the First Amendment analysis of the case,[81] Justice Reed's majority opinion stressed the right of the community to determine whether such sales techniques deserved protection. "The Constitutionality of Alexandria's ordinance turn[s] upon a balancing of the conveniences between some householders' desire for privacy and the publisher's right to distribute publications in the precise way that those soliciting for him think bring the best results."[82] The Supreme Court allowed the city to determine that the balance in this particular situation should favor privacy rights. The dissent of Justices Black and Douglas would not have permitted such a balancing, opting instead for a preferred position for free speech.[83]

In the first case to deal with a public transit system as a forum for communication, the Supreme Court held that a city-operated streetcar could play radio programs over a loudspeaker without interfering with the rights of passengers.[84] Justice Burton's opinion for the majority held that the First Amendment right of the passengers to converse with each other was not disturbed by the sound system, and that the system was not being used as a means of propaganda.[85] Justice Douglas's dissent focused on the captive audience. The fact that passengers were forced to listen to messages was for him the deciding factor. "The right to be let alone is indeed the beginning of all freedom."[86] For Douglas, transit passengers should not be subjected to any radio programs, including those that are strictly entertainment, for fear that they may be subjected to political programming in the future. Citizens at home subjected to the very same messages have the option of turning the dial, or turning off the radio, while transit passengers have no such option.

In *Fowler v Rhode Island*, a unanimous Court found a Pawtucket ordinance unconstitutional as applied.[87] A Jehovah's Witness had been found guilty of violating an ordinance prohibiting religious addresses in any public park. The state argued that *Davis* provided the legal precedent, while the appellant claimed that *Davis* had been so limited by subsequent cases that it was no longer valid law. The Supreme Court avoided the question by deciding that the ordinance had been applied to Fowler's speech while other religious speech was exempted. Catholic and Protestant speech had been permitted because it had been included as part of a larger religious service, while the Jehovah's Witness speech was impermissible because of the difference in the way the service was conducted. That, Justice Douglas wrote, "is merely an indirect way of preferring one religion over another."[88]

The first Supreme Court case to actually use the phrase "public forum" was *International Association of Machinists v Street*.[89] The case validated a section of the Railway Labor Act requiring all employees to pay union dues. Justice Brennan's majority opinion argued that employees who objected to having their money spent for particular political causes could restrict their dues to other purposes, thus invalidating any claim that employees were being forced to fund causes they may not support.

The use of the phrase "public forum" appears near the conclusion of Justice Black's dissent. Arguing against a government requirement for participation in a union, he stated that "[u]nions composed of a voluntary membership, like all other voluntary groups, should be free in this country to fight in the public forum to advance their own causes, to promote their choice of candidates and parties and to work for the doctrines or the laws they favor."[90] Nowhere is there an explication of exactly what it is that constitutes the public forum of which Black speaks.

In 1961, 187 black students were arrested for breach of peace after refusing to disperse from the grounds of the South Carolina State House.[91] The Supreme Court held that the students' speech had been peaceful and that their arrest was a violation of the First Amendment. Justice Stewart's majority opinion differentiated the case from *Feiner* and *Chaplinski* on the facts: fighting words and speech that was inciting could still be punished, but the record was void of any such evidence. Quoting *Terminiello*, Stewart wrote "freedom of speech . . . is . . . protected against censorship or punishment, unless shown likely to produce a clear and present danger of a serious substantive evil that rises far above public inconvenience, annoyance, or unrest."[92] No such clear and present danger was seen to exist.[93]

The Supreme Court narrowly decided to overturn the breach of peace conviction of five blacks who protested discriminatory library practices by refusing to leave a segregated regional library.[94] The plurality held that the protesters were within their First Amendment rights: their "silent and reproachful presence, in a place where the protestant has every right to be" was clearly protected.[95] As for the claim that breaches of peace were not constitutionally suspect, Fortas wrote "no claim can be made that use of the library by others was disturbed by the demonstration."[96]

Later that year, Justice Black, who authored the dissent in *Brown*, wrote for the court in *Adderly v Florida*.[97] The Court upheld the conviction of 107 students for trespassing when they refused to leave the grounds of a county jail, where they were protesting. Black reasoned that "[t]he State, no less than a private owner of property, has power to preserve the property under its control for the use to which it is lawfully dedicated."[98] The dissent, led by Justice Douglas, accepted the argument that not all publicly owned property was appropriate for public expression. The dissent cautioned, however, the extension of this premise to exclude the expression in this case.

> There may be some public places which are so clearly committed to other purposes that their use for the airing of grievances is anomalous. There may be some instances in which assemblies and petitions for redress of grievances are not consistent with other necessary purposes of public property. A noisy meeting may be out of keeping with the serenity of the statehouse or the quiet of the courthouse. No one, for example, would suggest that the Senate gallery is the proper place for a vociferous protest rally. And in other cases it may be necessary to adjust the right to petition for redress of grievances to the other interests inhering in the uses to which public property is normally put. But this is quite different from saying that all public places are off limits to people with grievances. And it is further yet from saying that the "custodian" of the public property in his discretion can decide when public places shall be used for the communication of ideas, especially the constitutional right to assemble and petition the government for a redress of grievances.[99]

Two decades after *Marsh*, the Supreme Court was confronted with whether the concept of the public forum should be expanded to include another private property: this time, a shopping mall.[100] The case involved the union's rights to picket a privately owned shopping center. The Court applied the thinking of *Marsh*, finding the shopping center the functional equivalent of the streets of a company-owned town.[101] Thus the company-owned town and the shopping mall were, at least temporarily, treated as public forums for First Amendment purposes.

The Court was then asked to resolve whether public schools were appropriate forums for free expression, to which it responded with a conditional "yes." In *Tinker v Des Moines School District*, the majority held that the wearing of black armbands to protest American involvement in Vietnam did not interrupt the school procedure, thus making the prohibition an unwarranted infringement of First Amendment rights.[102] After stating that First Amendment rights were available to students and teachers, Justice Fortas asserted that "[f]reedom of expression would not truly exist if the right could be exercised only in an area that a benevolent government has provided as a safe haven for crackpots."[103] The majority further held that the school officials were attempting to punish the specific speech in question inasmuch as the school had singled out this particular symbolic speech as deserving of attention.

In a scathing dissent, Justice Black criticized the majority for deciding how the school day should be spent. Further, he reiterated his position, consistent with the ruling in *Cox*, that not all public venues are appropriate for expression. "It is a myth to say that any person has a constitutional right to say what he pleases, where he pleases, and when he pleases."[104]

The Court disposed of *Gregory v Chicago* with little problem.[105] In fact, the unanimous decision written by Chief Justice Warren begins, "[t]his is a simple case."[106] Peaceful demonstrators, who were arrested for disorderly conduct, had had their First Amendment rights violated. The demonstration had been peaceful and conducted on public streets.

In another unanimous decision, the Supreme Court established that the homeowner could limit the type of mail he received.[107] The Court upheld a section of the U.S. Code allowing individuals to block "sexually pandering" mail. Chief Justice Burger wrote that "the right of every person 'to be let alone' must be placed in the scales with the right of others to communicate,"[108] enunciating principles established previously in *Martin*. Of all venues to be let alone, one's own home seemed the most appropriate. The Court adhered to the adage "a man's home is his castle."[109]

The following term, the Court considered whether language that was offensive to many would be permissible in the public forum.[110] Paul Cohen was arrested for offensive conduct for wearing a jacket bearing the words "fuck the draft." The Supreme Court narrowly decided that the arrest was unconstitutional. The Court was unwilling to expand the "captive audience" analysis from *Rowan* to include public displays. Justice Harlan stated that those offended "could effectively avoid further bombardment of their sensibilities simply by averting their eyes."[111] It appeared that one could easier avoid offensive mail, which could remain unopened, than offensive words on clothing visible in public. Two distinctions, not enunciated by the Court or the dissent, explain the differing treatment for Rowan and Cohen. Cohen's speech was clearly a political statement, which is at the heart of the First Amendment. Rowan, on the other hand, was merely selling goods. Second, and more relevant to a public forum analysis, was that the Los Angeles County Courthouse was a traditional public forum, a place where free speech had been historically appropriate, while a mailbox had never been established as such.

In *Lloyd Corp. v Tanner* the Court was again faced with whether private property constituted a public forum for free speech purposes.[112] For the third time, the phrase "public forum" appeared in a Supreme Court dissent.[113] The majority held that a privately owned shopping center could prohibit individuals from distributing handbills. The opinion stated that the *Logan Valley* precedent needed redefinition. "The Court noted that the scope of its holding was limited, and expressly reserved judgment on the type of issue presented in this case."[114] The opinion, written by Justice Powell, distinguished *Lloyd* from *Logan Valley* by considering the nature of the communication. The Court held that free speech did not have to be protected in *Lloyd* because the communication did not have any relationship to the business being conducted at the shopping center (the leaflets dealt with antiwar issues).[115]

Police Department of the City of Chicago v Mosley was the first time the phrase "public forum" was used in the opinion of the Court.[116] In a unanimous decision, the Court voided an ordinance restricting certain picketing near school grounds because the ordinance violated equal protection rights. Justice Marshall wrote, "Selective exclusions from a public forum may not be based on content alone, and may not be justified by reference to content alone."[117] Peaceful labor picketing had been exempted in the Chicago ordinance.

The same day, the Court announced its unanimous decision in *Grayned v City of Rockford*.[118] Rockford had an antipicketing ordinance similar to Chicago's, which the Court quickly invalidated for equal protection reasons. However, the Court upheld an antinoise ordinance that was used to arrest a student protesting outside the school. Using *Tinker* as its touchstone, the Court determined the ordinance and its enforcement were appropriate means of maintaining order in the school. "[E]xpressive activity may be prohibited if it 'materially disrupts classwork or involves substantial disorder or invasion of the rights of others.' "[119]

The dissent in *CBS v DNC* was prepared to establish the broadcast spectrum as a public forum, but the majority did not address the issue.[120] Instead, their analysis involved the FCC's authority to regulate as it believed appropriate, within the parameters established by Congress. The Court held that the Communications Act did not mandate a right of access for editorial advertising. Justice Stewart's concurrence argued that extending the public forum to include broadcasting, as the dissenters proposed, would make broadcasters common carriers, which was explicitly prohibited in the Communications Act.[121]

In 1974, the Supreme Court determined that car cards are not a public forum deserving of First Amendment protection.[122] Harry Lehman challenged a Shaker Heights policy prohibiting political advertising on its transit system. Blackmun's plurality opinion stressed the historical approach in its analysis. "[B]efore you could say whether a certain thing could be done in a certain place you would have to know the history of that particular place."[123] The plurality, and Justice Douglas's concurrence, did not see the car cards as similar to a park or streets.[124] The dissenters, led by Justice Brennan, argued that once the city had elected to open a forum by soliciting advertising, it was precluded from discriminating among users for content reasons.[125]

In 1975 the Court determined that a municipal auditorium and a city-leased theater were "public forums designed for and dedicated to expressive activities."[126] The decision, written by Justice Blackmun, held that Chattanooga's denial of the use of its facilities for the musical "Hair" was an unconstitutional prior restraint. The same year, the Court also invalidated a Jacksonville, Florida, ordinance that made the exhibition of nudity in drive-in movies a public nuisance.[127] The law was facially invalid because of its content-specific language, as well as its overbreadth. While not assessing whether privately owned drive-ins constituted a public forum, the Court reviewed the ordinance's desire to protect passers-by who may see the nudity. In a footnote, the Court states its principle that there is less need to protect people on public streets from offensive expression in part because they are not a captive audience.[128]

In 1976 the Supreme Court returned to the question of whether privately owned shopping centers constitute a public forum. Striking employees picketed a store in a privately owned shopping center.[129] The National Labor Relations Board issued a cease-and-desist order, which the pickets claimed violated their First Amendment rights. Admitting confusing and sometimes conflicting precedent,[130] the Court ruled that the shopping center could not possibly be the functional equivalent of a municipality, for if it were, the Court could never allow discriminatory regulation based on the content of the speech, as had been done in *Lloyd*.[131] The prohibition was affirmed, in effect, because the center was not a public forum for the appellants to claim a First Amendment right.

Later that same month, the Supreme Court stated that a military base is not a public forum.[132] Regulations restricting political speeches and handbilling, even in areas of the base where the public had access, were not unconstitutional. The Court specifically stated that it would be a mistake to think "that whenever members of the public are permitted freely to visit a place owned or operated by the government, then that place becomes a 'public forum' for purposes of the First Amendment. Such a principle of constitutional law has never existed, and does not exist now."[133] Justice Stewart applied the common law approach, stating that military installations were not traditional forms for free expression.[134]

Two concurrences in 1976 saw other venues as public forums. Justice Stevens believed that content-specific regulations in zoning ordinances in Detroit were unconstitutional.[135] The ordinance limited adult motion picture theaters, ignoring others, which Stevens saw as an inappropriate content restriction. Quoting his own plurality decision in *Mosley*, he stated "selective exclusions from a public forum may not be based on content alone."[136] Justice Brennan's concurrence in *Madison School District v Wisconsin Employees Relation Commission* established Board of Education meetings as public forums.[137] He advanced the argument that the state had created a public forum by requiring that meetings be open to public view and participation. Therefore, Brennan held that prohibiting participation by employees, other than union representatives, was a First Amendment violation.[138]

In 1976 the Supreme Court overwhelmingly held a New Jersey ordinance requiring door-to-door solicitors to provide written notice to the police department void for vagueness.[139] The ordinance lacked any information as to what was required as part of the registration, nor was it specific as to who had to comply.

The Supreme Court emphatically stated that prisons are not public forums in *Jones v North Carolina Prisoners Union*.[140] As such, the prison administration was free to determine what groups would be afforded the opportunity to conduct meetings within the prison.

In 1980, the Supreme Court invalidated yet another door-to-door solicitation ordinance.[141] This time, the Court ruled the regulation was overbroad in that there were less restrictive means than the ordinance at issue.

That same year, the Supreme Court was confronted for the fourth time with whether a private shopping center was required to provide opportunities for free speech. Pruneyard Shopping Center in California had asked individuals soliciting signatures on a petition to leave.[142] The situation was somewhat different from earlier shopping mall cases in that the appellants claimed a state constitutional right of free expression. The Supreme Court held that California was permitted to extend free expression rights beyond those provided by the federal constitution, including the determination that public places such as shopping centers must provide for free speech. The Court argued that such a determination by the state did not constitute a Fifth Amendment "taking." Thus, the Supreme Court reasoned that shopping centers could be public forums, provided states made the determination that they were to be treated as such.

The Supreme Court invalidated a Chicago law prohibiting the picketing of private residences for equal protection reasons.[143] The ordinance exempted from the prohibition peaceful labor picketing. The Court followed the precedent from *Mosley* in invalidating the ordinance for distinguishing between peaceful picketing for different purposes.

In a departure from "traditional" venues for free expression, the Court considered whether a prohibition on inserts into monthly utility bills was constitutional.[144] Because the law prohibited only certain inserts, it was not content neutral, thus not acceptable as a time, place, and manner restriction.[145] Nor would the Court accept the argument that the bill recipients were a captive audience, as disposal of the inserts was simple.[146] The Supreme Court held the prohibition unconstitutional. The Court did not declare public utility envelopes were public forums, but it did limit the state's authority to restrict speech in that nonpublic arena.

Dicta in *Hefron v International Society for Krishna Consciousness* adds state fairs to the list of public forums.[147] While the Court let stand Minnesota restrictions on solicitations at the fair, it did so because it saw them as acceptable time, place, and manner restrictions.[148]

The same year, the Supreme Court determined that mailboxes are not public forums, expanding on the theme established ten years earlier in *Rowan*. The Court let stand a postal regulation prohibiting use of a mailbox for any printed matter other than mail delivered by the U.S. Post Office.[149] It noted that mailboxes are not "traditional" public forums, and the regulation did not distinguish based on content.[150] In significant dicta, the Court reiterated its support of public forum doctrine that had become bedrock law in the previous two decades:

> While the analytical line between a regulation of the "time, place, and manner" in which First Amendment rights may be exercised in a traditional public forum, and the question of whether a particular piece of personal or real property owned or controlled by the government is in fact a "public forum" may blur at the edges, we think the line is nonetheless a workable one.[151]

However, the Court claimed that college campuses might be public forums, but that if they are, the colleges are still entitled to different treatment. In *Widmar v Vincent*, the Court invalidated a university's policy prohibiting the use of its facilities by religious groups.[152] While using traditional analysis to void the rule (it was not content neutral) the majority noted that schools did not always have to apply public forum analysis. "A university differs in significant respects from public forums such as streets or parks or even municipal theaters."[153]

If mailboxes are not public forums, and campuses are different public forums, the Court next was asked to decide whether schoolteachers' mailboxes were public forums. A narrow majority stated they were not.[154] The Court divided public property into traditional public forums (such as streets and parks), public property that has been given "revocable" public forum status[155] (such as campuses in *Widmar*), and public property that is neither traditionally nor designated as a public forum (such as mailboxes and military bases). The majority held the schools' mailboxes fit the third description.[156]

The Supreme Court overwhelmingly ruled that its own premises do not constitute a public forum.[157] Justice White's majority opinion stated that the property was not a traditional public forum provided for public expression.[158]

Further, a "meet and confer" session of a public employer is not a public forum.[159] Justice O'Connor could not have been more explicit in stating for the majority that "[a] 'meet and confer' session is obviously not a public forum."[160] There was no long tradition nor designation of the sessions as such.

In 1984, the Supreme Court determined that utility poles do not constitute a public forum.[161] A Los Angeles ordinance prohibiting the posting of signs on public property was held constitutional. The Court rejected the argument that the poles constituted a public forum, opting instead for the position that utility poles are not traditionally open to expression. "The mere fact that government property can be used as a vehicle for communication does not mean that the Constitution requires such uses to be permitted."[162]

The Supreme Court avoided the question of whether national parks in the nation's capital are public forums.[163] While upholding a prohibition on camping on the mall and in Lafayette Park, the Court stated the regulation was an acceptable time, place, and manner restriction assuming, arguendo, that the camping were symbolic speech. Justice Marshall's dissent, however, stated that even if the rule were facially valid, it may not pass constitutional muster in the instant case in that it may vest "standardless discretion in officials empowered to dispense permits for the use of public forums."[164]

Finally, in a narrow 4–3 decision, the Supreme Court ruled that a forum is not necessarily defined by the tangible government property, but could be defined in terms of the access sought by the speaker. A group of nonprofit organizations seeking access to a government-sponsored fund drive among government employees was denied. In *Cornelius v NAACP Legal Defense Fund*[165] the majority held that it was not the entire federal workplace that was the forum at issue, but instead the Combined Federal Campaign (CFC), an annual appeal to employees for contributions.[166] The CFC itself, not the entire workplace, was the forum to which the National Association for the Advancement of Colored People (NAACP) sought access. Using the three-classification system created in *Perry*, the Court ruled the CFC was a nonpublic forum.[167] Once pigeonholed, the Court needed only to show that the regulation was reasonable and the rules viewpoint neutral, which it promptly did. "Reasonable" did not require "most reasonable or the only reasonable limitation."[168] The Court added that in nonpublic forums such as this one, the regulation need not even be narrowly tailored.[169]

The litany of cases above demonstrates the difficulty of applying public forum analysis. Especially difficult seems to be the application of forum analysis to some yet-untried forum, which appears to be the case more and more frequently.

CABLE ACCESS

Unlike the history of the public forum, the history of access to cable has been punctuated by definitive decisions of the FCC and Congress as to its interpretation. Supreme Court decisions alone do not provide an adequate analysis, although there are also several cases illuminating the status of cable access.[170]

Prior to 1965, the FCC claimed it did not have the authority to regulate cable.[171] But in that year the Commission asserted its authority, primarily not in its duty to regulate wired communication, but instead in the interest of television.[172] The Supreme Court upheld such regulation and rationale in stating the FCC's regulation of cable as "reasonably ancillary."[173]

Given the support by the Court, the FCC enacted increased regulation in 1969, requiring systems with 3,500 or more subscribers to originate some local programming.[174] When enacted, only 10 percent of cable systems had enough subscribers to be affected by the regulation.[175] These rules were given the Supreme Court's blessing three years later in a constitutional challenge.[176] Local origination rules were characterized by the Court as appropriate means to promote the commission objective of diversity.[177] This was consistent with the FCC's rule prohibiting cross ownership for cable, premised on the promotion of diversity.[178]

With diversity seen as a rational objective for regulating cable, the commission promulgated cable access rules for the first time in 1972.[179] "[I]t is therefore appropriate that the fundamental goals of a national communications structure be furthered by cable—the opening of new outlets for local expression, the promotion of diversity in television programming, the advancement of educational and instructional television, and increased informational services of local governments."[180] The rules required larger cable systems to provide four separate access channels: one each for public access, educational access, governmental access, and leased access. The channels could be combined if there was no demand. It further ordered that users be provided time on a first-come basis, and that no fees could be assessed (except for leased access) for live programs less than five minutes long.[181]

The rules were in effect for seven years, until another constitutional challenge by Midwest Video, this time successful.[182] The Court ruled the FCC had overstepped its jurisdiction in imposing common carrier rules on a medium that was not a common carrier.[183] More important, in an analysis reminiscent of *Tornillo*, the Court claimed that access requirements were "the negation of editorial discretion otherwise enjoyed by cable operators."[184] Thus, while many cable systems that had access channels continued their operation, they were no longer a requirement.

This was the status until passage of the Cable Communications Act by Congress in 1984. While the act explicitly states cable is not a common carrier,[185] it states that local communities "may establish requirements,"[186] as part of their franchising requirements, and impose restrictions as a condition of the award of the franchise. Frequently, one of those conditions is the provision of access channels.[187] While public, educational, and government access channels *may* be required by local communities, the act requires the provision of leased access channels on larger systems.[188] Rather than define system size by number of subscribers, as the commission had done in its rules, Congress used channel capacity (more than thirty-six channels) to determine which systems would be affected by the regulation.

No Supreme Court decision yet exists that settles the constitutionality of the new rules. Although given the opportunity, the Court did not reach the question in *Preferred*.[189] Several authors have posited their own theories.

Hollinrake proposes that the four-part test devised in *O'Brien* is appropriate for determining the acceptability of access requirements for cable.[190] He cites a lower federal court's decision as evidence that the test can be appropriately applied.[191]

Claims that access channels actually impose a form of media tax on cable systems would justify their elimination.[192] Further, if editorial discretion is the free expression value being protected, cable access requirements seem inappropriate. However, other free expression values, such as the discovery of truth, self-fulfillment, and safety valve values, appear to be enhanced by such a requirement. It remains to be seen which value is stated by the Court in its next assessment of the rules, certain to come before long.

GOVERNMENT ENFORCED ACCESS

Beyond the areas discussed above, there have been a variety of instances where a government-enforced right of access has been asserted. This section examines the variety of conditions and venues under which such have been asserted.

Personal Attack Rule

First among these rights of access is the right of an individual who is personally attacked during a broadcast.[193] Despite revocation of the Fairness Doctrine, the personal attack rule is still very much in effect.[194] The rule provides:

> When, during the presentation of views on a controversial issue of public importance, an attack is made on the honesty, character, integrity or like personal qualities of an identified person or group, the licensee shall, within a reasonable time . . . an offer of a reasonable opportunity to respond over the licensee's facilities.[195]

While the Fairness Doctrine was at issue in *Red Lion*, it was actually only the personal attack rule that Fred Cook invoked when he sought free reply time from WGCB.

If personal attack rules exist as a punitive measure, they appear to be in direct conflict with First Amendment rights. If, however, they exist to correct possible wrong impressions held by the public, they seem most appropriate for those least likely to have access without government assistance. Political and business figures, having a greater ability to defend themselves, do not need a personal attack rule to defend them.[196]

Reasonable Access for Federal Candidates

A statutory right exists for access to broadcast media by qualified candidates for federal office.[197] The rule, it is asserted, is based on the scarcity approach to broadcast regulation.[198] This right to reasonable access was found constitutional by the Supreme Court in *CBS v FCC*.[199] The Carter-Mondale Presidential Committee had requested a thirty-minute block of prime time to promote their reelection campaign.[200] All three commercial television networks declined to sell the requested time to the committee.[201] The election committee decided to file suit, claiming they had been denied reasonable access. In a 6–3 decision, the Supreme Court agreed with the candidates.

The decision's interpretation of the reasonable access requirement is interesting. The networks attempted to characterize the requirement in terms of the overall presentation of candidates, but the Court saw it differently. "Sec 312(a)(7) assures a right of reasonable access to *individual* candidates for federal elective office."[202]

Because of the relatively limited legislative history surrounding the reasonable access rule,[203] an ad hoc basis for determining reasonable access,[204] and the lack of legal opinions, what constitutes reasonable is obviously subjective.[205] Worthy of note in the Carter-Mondale decision is the fact that the FCC decided along strict party lines: the four Democratic commissioners thought access had not been reasonable, while the three Republicans voted that it had been.[206] Candidates are likely to believe access is inadequate, while broadcasters are likely to think they have been generous.[207] Much the same situation currently exists with regard to candidate access. A proposal for free political airtime presented in the Senate was opposed by the National Association of Broadcasters.[208] One commentator recommends the continuance of the reasonable access requirement until cable penetration reaches 65 percent. At that time, he asserts, cable access requirements will be adequate to provide for the same goals sought by Section 312.[209]

Advertising

In all the years of access cases, there has been only one Supreme Court decision referring to a right of access for advertising.[210] The right was very narrowly defined in terms of antitrust violations.[211] A newspaper attempted to drive a radio station out of business by refusing to accept ads from anyone who advertised on that station. The Court determined that the paper's refusal was a violation of the Sherman Antitrust Act.[212]

In light of the case and subsequent limiting decisions,[213] it is difficult to apply the ruling in *Lorain* to any tenets beyond the facts in the case.[214]

The Supreme Court could not have made it clearer that no special right of access for advertising exists in the broadcast media, despite the public interest requirement. In *CBS v DNC*,[215] the Court held that stations were not required to sell advertising time to organizations wishing to make political statements. In examining the legislative history of the Communications Act, the Court emphasized that Congress had been given the opportunity to select from several regulatory schemes. In the final analysis, it opted to declare that broadcasting is not a common carrier,[216] and that "no individual or group has a right to command the use of broadcast facilities."[217] The majority went on to cite Meiklejohn's view that the value worth promoting "is not that everyone shall speak, but that everything worth saying shall be said."[218] It further asserted that a right of access for advertisers would weigh speech in favor of the affluent.[219] The Court did leave the door open for future rule making, however, in stating that Congress or the FCC may, at some date, "devise some kind of limited right of access that is both practicable and desirable."[220]

SUMMARY

The history of access to a variety of forums has been mixed. The government, through its executive, legislative, and judicial branches, has attempted to determine the appropriateness of access requirements based on the differences in forums, speakers, and content of messages, with varying results.

The concept of access to forums can be seen as a continuum. At one extreme, access requirements for newspapers have been held unconstitutional by the Supreme Court. At the other extreme, access rights have been enforced most vigilantly in the traditional public forum. In between, areas of broadcast access, cable access, and nontraditional public forums have had access requirements upheld, while others have been eliminated. Congress and the Federal Communications Commission still endorse reply rights for those personally attacked during a broadcast, and they also maintain that the reasonable access requirement of the Communications Act needs continued enforcement. On the other hand, the FCC and the Supreme Court have taken the position that no one may demand the right to purchase time for commercials, whether they be for products or to espouse controversial positions. Doctrines need to be defined that provide guidance in determining where the demarcation lines have been, and should be, drawn. Chapter 3 examines these precedents to determine distinctions that exist between the various venues of expression. What legal principles are used by courts and policy makers? Can precedent be used to create one cohesive, comprehensive access policy?

NOTES

1. 167 U.S. 43 (1897).
2. *Id.*, at 47–48.
3. Red Lion Broadcasting v FCC, 395 U.S. 367 (1969).
4. F. FRIENDLY, THE GOOD GUYS, THE BAD GUYS AND THE FIRST AMENDMENT 3–5 (1975).
5. *Id.*, at 10.
6. *Id.*, at 44.
7. *Id.*, at 43–60.
8. 418 U.S. 241 (1974). For extensive background on the case, see Powe, *Tornillo*, 1987 SUP. CT. REV. 345.
9. Note, *Reconciling Red Lion and Tornillo*, 28 STAN. L. REV. 563 (1976); Geller, *Does Red Lion Square with Tornillo?* 29 U. MIAMI L. REV. 477 (1975); W. VAN ALSTYNE, INTERPRETATIONS OF THE FIRST AMENDMENT 68, 73–79 (1984). Note 47 contains 26 relevant references.
10. C. SMITH, FREEDOM OF EXPRESSION AND PARTISAN POLITICS 94 (1989).
11. *See* Kahn, *Media Competition in the Marketplace of Ideas*, 39 SYRACUSE L. REV. 737, 745–747 (1988). "Because licenses may be transferred and broadcast operations sold, however, scarcity in broadcasting is not so readily distinguishable from print media." Lively, *Fairness Regulation: An Idea Whose Time Has Gone*, 45 WASH. & LEE L. REV 1379, 1388 (1988). *But cf* Hyde, *FCC Action Repealing the Fairness Doctrine: A Revolution in Broadcast Regulation*, 38 SYRACUSE L. REV. 1175, 1178–1180 (1987) (Red Lion was not based on a scarcity rationale).
12. W. VAN ALSTYNE, *supra* note 9, at 79–81. In broadcasting, it is government that creates the disadvantage to those seeking access, therefore, unlike print, it must provide a remedy.
13. Geller, *supra* note 9.
14. Bollinger, *Freedom of the Press and Public Access: Toward a Theory of Partial Regulation of the Mass Media*, 75 MICH. L. REV. 1 (1976).
15. *Id.*, at 36.
16. B. SCHMIDT, FREEDOM OF THE PRESS VERSUS PUBLIC ACCESS (1976). *But cf.* Note, *In Defense of Monopoly Cable Television Franchising: Defining the First Amendment Rights of the Public and the Cable Operator Under the Public Forum Doctrine and Natural Monopoly Theory*, 13 RUTGERS COMPUTER & TECH. L. J. 137, 224 (1987) ("Although the Tornillo Court never cited Red Lion, it implicitly considered the relevance of the monopoly element of the Red Lion analysis.")

17. CBS v DNC, 412 U.S. 94, 148–161 (1973).

18. One article suggests *Tornillo* refutes the holding in *Red Lion*. *See* Krattenmaker & Powe, *The Fairness Doctrine Today: A Constitutional Curiosity and An Impossible Dream*, 1985 DUKE L. J. 151, 156.

19. *See, e.g.* FCC v League of Women Voters, 468 U.S. 364 (1984) 376–377, n. 11.

20. Those fourteen cases are: Lehman v City of Shaker Heights, 418 U.S. 298 (1974); Buckley v Valeo, 424 U.S. 1 (1976); Virginia Bd. of Pharmacy v Virginia Consumers Council, 425 U.S. 748 (1976); First National Bank of Boston v Bellotti, 435 U.S. 765 (1978); FCC v National Citizens Committee for Broadcasting, 436 U.S. 775 (1978); Houchins v KQED, 438 U.S. 1 (1978); FCC v Pacifica Foundation, 438 U.S. 726 (1978); Herbert v Lando, 441 U.S. 153 (1979); CBS v FCC, 453 U.S. 367 (1981); Metromedia v San Diego, 453 U.S. 490 (1981); FCC v League of Women Voters, 468 U.S. 364 (1984); Dunn & Bradstreet v Greenmoss Builders, 472 U.S. 749 (1985); Pacific Gas & Electric v Public Util. Comm'n., 475 U.S. 1 (1986); Los Angeles v Preferred Communications, 476 U.S. 488 (1986). SHEPARD'S UNITED STATES CITATIONS (through Volume 88–12, May 1990).

21. Lehman v Shaker Heights, 418 U.S. 298, 303, Blackmun's plurality cites Red Lion, Douglas's concurrence cites Tornillo, *Id.*, at 306; Houchins v KQED, 438 U.S. 1, 9, 14, Burger's plurality cites Tornillo, while Stevens's dissent cites Red Lion, *Id.*, at 30; FCC v Pacifica, 438 U.S. 726, 742, Stevens's plurality cites Red Lion, the opinion of the Court used Tornillo, *Id.*, at 748, Powell's concurrence cited Red Lion, *Id.*, at 759, as did Brennan's dissent, *Id.*, at 770.

22. 476 U.S. 488, 492 (1986).

23. 475 U.S. 1 (1986).

24. *Id.*, at 10.

25. *Id.*

26. Omitted from this analysis is Dunn & Bradstreet v Greenmoss Builders, 472 U.S. 749 (1985). Brennan's dissent in the case cites Red Lion and Tornillo merely as two of a litany of cases supporting the proposition that the press is protected to ensure protection of the First Amendment. *Id.*, at 783. As there is no distinguishing, it does not assist this analysis. Likewise omitted is Burger's dissent in Metromedia v San Diego, 453 U.S. 490, 557 (1981). His only purpose in citing the two cases is to demonstrate the Court's tradition in differential treatment for different media.

27. 468 U.S. 364 (1984).

28. *See* Lively, *supra* note 11, at 1387; Labunski, *May It Rest In Peace: Public Interest and Public Access in the Post-Fairness Doctrine Era*, 11 HASTINGS COMM/ENT L. J. 219, 259 (1989).

29. 468 U.S. 364, 376 (1984).

30. *Id.*, at 376–377.

31. *Id.*, at 378–379.

32. "Congress . . . has power to regulate use of this scarce and valuable national resource." *Id.*, at 376.

33. 453 U.S. 367 (1981).

34. 47 CFR Sec. 312(a)(7).

35. 453 U.S. 367, 395.

36. *Id.*, at 396. Emphasis in original.

37. International Ass'n. of Machinists v Street, 367 U.S. 740 (1961). The phrase appeared only twice prior to 1970, appearing another thirty times in the following fifteen years. Farber & Nowak, *The Misleading Nature of Public Forum Analysis: Content and Context in First Amendment Adjudication*, 70 VA. L. REV. 1219, 1221–1222 (1984).

38. Buchanan, *Toward a Unified Theory of Governmental Power to Regulate Protected Speech*, 18 CONN. L. REV. 531, 558 (1986). While the difinition seems simple, a litany of journal articles have been written in an attempt to explain it. *See* Cass, *First Amendment and Access to Government Facilities*, 65 VIRGINIA L. REV. 1287 (1979); Goldberger, *Judicial Scrutiny in Public Forum Cases: Misplaced Trust in the Judgment of Public Officials*, 32 BUFFALO L. REV. 175 (1983); Horning, *The First Amendment Right to a Public Forum*, 1969 DUKE L. J. 931; Kalven, *The Concept of the Public Forum: Cox v Louisiana*, 1965 SUP. CT. REV. 1; Note, *The Public Forum: Minimum Access, Equal Access and the First Amendment*, 28 STANFORD L. REV. 117 (1975); Note, *A Unitary Approach to Claims of First Amendment Access to Publicly Owned Property*, 35 STANFORD L. REV. 121 (1982); Stone, *Fora Americana: Speech in Public Places*, 1974 SUP. CT. REV. 233.

39. 167 U.S. 43 (1897).

40. *Id.*, at 44. The ordinance also covered discharging a cannon or erecting a tent.

41. *Id.*, at 47–48.

42. 303 U.S. 444 (1938).

43. *Id.*, at 451.

44. 307 U.S. 496 (1939).

45. *Id.*, at 515. Justice Butler, one of two dissenters, did not see the distinction, and would have held the ordinance valid. *Id.*, at 533.

46. *Id.*

47. 308 U.S. 147 (1939).

48. The cities with contested ordinances were Los Angeles, Milwaukee, Worcester, Massachusetts, and Irvington, New Jersey.

49. "So long as legislation to this end does not abridge the constitutional liberty of one rightfully upon the street to impart information through speech or the distribution of literature, it may lawfully regulate the conduct of those using the streets." *Id.*, at 160.

50. *Id.*, at 163.

51. 310 U.S. 396 (1940).

52. *Id.*, at 302.

53. *Id.*, at 308.

54. 312 U.S. 569, 574 (1941).
55. Chaplinski v New Hampshire, 315 U.S. 568 (1942).
56. Z. CHAFEE, FREE SPEECH IN THE UNITED STATES 149 (1941).
57. Chaplinski v N.H., 315 U.S. 568, 572 (1942).
58. 318 U.S. 413 (1943).
59. *Id.*, at 416.
60. 319 U.S. 141 (1943).
61. *Id.*, at 147 (emphasis added).
62. 326 U.S. 501 (1946).
63. *Id.*, at 506.
64. 334 U.S. 558 (1948).
65. *Id.*, at 562.
66. 336 U.S. 77 (1949).
67. *Id.*, at 79.
68. *Id.*, at 102.
69. 337 U.S. 1 (1949).
70. *Id.*, at 4.
71. *Id.*
72. *Id.*, at 26–27.
73. Niemotko v Maryland, 340 U.S. 268 (1951).
74. Kunz v New York, 340 U.S. 290 (1951).
75. *Id.*, at 295.
76. 340 U.S. 268, 273.
77. Feiner v New York, 340 U.S. 315 (1951).
78. *Id.*, at 321.
79. *Id.*, at 327, 331.
80. Breard v Louisiana, 341 U.S. 622 (1951).
81. Constitutional questions were also raised regarding due process rights and commerce clause limitations.
82. 341 U.S. 622, 644 (1951).
83. *Id.*, at 650.
84. Public Utilities Commission v Pollak, 343 U.S. 451 (1952).
85. *Id.*, at 463.
86. *Id.*, at 467.
87. 345 U.S. 67 (1952).
88. *Id.*, at 70.
89. 367 U.S. 740 (1961).
90. *Id.*, at 796.
91. Edwards v South Carolina, 372 U.S. 229 (1962).
92. *Id.*, at 237.
93. The second case to explicitly use the phrase "public forum" was Griffin v California, 380 U.S. 609 (1965). As with *Street*, the phrase is used in a dissent, this time by Justice Stewart. "[T]he prosecutor in his argument to the jury explained that a person accused of a crime in a public forum would ordinarily deny or explain the evidence against him if he could truthfully do

so." *Id.*, at 617. Because the case deals with Fifth, rather than First Amendment rights, it is not included in the analysis. Because it is only the second time the phrase is used by any justice in an opinion, it merits mention. Other cases that use the phrase "public forum" but add no information for purposes of this analysis include: Spence v Washington, 418 U.S. 405, 420 (1974) (Rehnquist, J., dissenting); American Radio Assn. v Mobile S.S. Assn., 419 U.S. 215, 230 (1974); Time v Firestone, 424 U.S. 448, 457 (1975); Wolston v Reader's Digest, 443 U.S. 157, 169 (1978); Connick v Meyers, 461 U.S. 138, 152 (1983); Bolger v Young Drug Products Corp., 463 U.S. 60, 76 (1983) (Rehnquist, J., concurring).

94. Brown v Louisiana, 383 U.S. 131 (1966).

95. *Id.*, at 142.

96. *Id.*

97. 385 U.S. 39 (1966).

98. *Id.*, at 47.

99. *Id.*, at 54 (citations omitted).

100. Amalgamated Food Employees Union v Logan Valley Plaza, Inc., 391 U.S. 308 (1968).

101. *Id.*, at 319. "The shopping center premises are open to the public to the same extent as the commercial center of a normal town."

102. 393 U.S. 503 (1969).

103. *Id.*, at 513.

104. *Id.*, at 522.

105. 394 U.S. 111 (1969).

106. *Id.* Justice Black, while concurring, felt the case was not quite so simple. "This I think is a highly important case which requires more detailed consideration than the Court's opinion gives it." *Id.*, at 113.

107. Rowan v U.S. Post Office Dept., 397 U.S. 728 (1970).

108. *Id.*, at 736.

109. *Id.*, at 737.

110. Cohen v California, 403 U.S. 15 (1971).

111. *Id.*, at 21.

112. 407 U.S. 551 (1972).

113. "[W]e must decide whether ownership of the Center gives petitioner unfettered discretion to determine whether or not it will be used as a public forum." *Id.*, at 573 (Marshall, J., dissenting).

114. *Id.*, at 560.

115. *Id.*, at 564.

116. 408 U.S. 92 (1972).

117. *Id.*, at 96.

118. 408 U.S. 104 (1972).

119. *Id.*, at 118 (quoting *Tinker*).

120. 412 U.S. 94 (1973).

121. *Id.*, at 140.

122. Lehman v City of Shaker Heights, 418 U.S. 298 (1974).

123. *Id.*, at 302 (quoting Lord Dunedin).

124. Douglas made an analogy between car cards and newspapers. *Id.*, at 306.

125. *Id.*, at 310.

126. Southeastern Promotions, Ltd. v Conrad, 420 U.S. 546, 555 (1975).

127. Erznoznik v City of Jacksonville, 422 U.S. 205 (1975).

128. *Id.*, at 210.

129. Hudgens v NLRB, 424 U.S. 507 (1976).

130. "The history of this litigation has been a history . . . of considerable confusion, engendered at least in part by decisions of this Court." *Id.*, at 512.

131. *Id.*, at 520.

132. Greer v Spock, 424 U.S. 828 (1976).

133. *Id.*, at 836.

134. *Id.*, at 838.

135. Young v American Mini Theatres, 427 U.S. 50, 65 (1976).

136. *Id.*

137. 429 U.S. 167 (1976).

138. *Id.*, at 179.

139. Hynes v Mayor of Oradell, 425 U.S. 610 (1976).

140. 433 U.S. 119 (1977).

141. Village of Schaumburg v Citizens for Better Environment, 444 U.S. 620 (1980).

142. Pruneyard Shopping Center v Robins, 447 U.S. 74 (1980).

143. Carey v Brown, 447 U.S. 455 (1980).

144. Consolidated Edison v Public Service Commission, 447 U.S. 530 (1980).

145. *Id.*, at 538.

146. *Id.*, at 542.

147. 452 U.S. 640 (1981).

148. *Id.*, at 652–653.

149. U.S. Postal Service v Greenburgh Civic Association, 453 U.S. 114 (1981).

150. *Id.*, at 132.

151. *Id.*

152. 454 U.S. 263 (1981).

153. *Id.*, at 267.

154. Perry Educational Assn. v Perry Local Educators Assn., 460 U.S. 37 (1983).

155. "Although a State is not required to indefinitely retain the open character of the facility, as long as it does so it is bound by the same standards as apply in a traditional public forum." *Id.*, at 46.

156. *Id.*

157. U.S. v Grace, 461 U.S. 171 (1983).

158. *Id.*, at 178.

159. Minnesota State Bd. for Community Colleges v Knight, 465 U.S. 271 (1984).

160. *Id.*, at 280.

161. City Council v Taxpayers for Vincent, 466 U.S. 789 (1984).

162. *Id.*, at 814.

163. Clark v Community for Creative Non-Violence, 468 U.S. 268 (1984).

164. *Id.*, at 313.

165. 473 U.S. 788 (1985).

166. *Id.*, at 801.

167. *Id.*, at 805–806.

168. *Id.*, at 808.

169. *Id.*, at 809.

170. For histories of cable regulation, see generally Hollinrake, *Cable Television: Public Access & The First Amendment*, COM. & L. 3, 5–11 (Feb. 1987); Grow, *Cable Television: Local Governmental Regulation in Perspective*, 7 PACE L. REV. 81, 86–103 (1986); Note, *Access to Cable, Natural Monopoly & the First Amendment*, 86 COLUM. L. REV. 1663, 1664–1669 (1986).

171. CATV & TV Repeater Services, 26 FCC 403, 427–431 (1959).

172. First Report & Order, 38 FCC 683, 715 (1965).

173. U.S. v Southwestern Cable, 392 U.S. 157, 178 (1968).

174. First Report & Order, 20 FCC 2d. 201 (1969). 47 CFR 74.111(a) (1970) (repealed 1974).

175. LaPierre, *Cable Television and the Promise of Program Diversity*, 42 FORDHAM L. REV. 25, 85 (1973).

176. U.S. v Midwest Video, 406 U.S. 649 (1972).

177. *Id.*, at 670.

178. Second Report & Order, 23 FCC 2d. 816, 820 (1970).

179. Cable Television Report & Order, 36 FCC 2d. 143, (1972) *modified* 59 FCC 2d. 294 (1976).

180. *Id.*, at 190.

181. *Id.*, at 240–241.

182. FCC v Midwest Video Corp., 440 U.S. 689 (1979).

183. *Id.*, at 700.

184. *Id.*, at 708.

185. Cable Communications Policy Act, 47 USC (1985) Sec. 541(c).

186. *Id.*, Sec. 611.

187. Cook, *Cable TV: The Constitutional Limitations of Local Government Control*, 15 SW UNIV. L. REV. 181, 185–186 (1984).

188. 47 CFR Sec. 612(b)(1).

189. On remand, the District Court found the requirement of six access channels unconstitutional. *Judge Says LA Erred in Refusing Second Cable Franchise*, BROADCASTING, Jan. 15, 1990, at 58.

190. Hollinrake, *supra* note 170, at 33–35.

191. Berkshire Cablevision v Burke, 571 F. Supp. 976 (D.R.I. 1983).

192. Minneapolis Star & Tribune v Minnesota Comm'r. of Revenue, 460 U.S. 575 (1983). *See* note, *supra* note 170, at 1665.

193. Memorandum Opinion & Order in Docket 16574, 8 FCC 2d. 721 (1967). C. SMITH, FREEDOM OF EXPRESSION AND PARTISAN POLITICS 92 (1989).

194. *See* Martin, *FCC Adheres to Fairness "Corollaries,"* BROADCAST ENGINEERING, July 1990, at 8.

195. 47 CFR Sec.79.1920.

196. D. TUCKER, LAW, LIBERALISM AND FREE SPEECH 100 (1985).

197. 47 USC Sec. 312(a)(7).

198. Note, *Reexamining the Reasonable Access and Equal Time Provisions of the Federal Communications Act: Can These Provisions Stand if the Fairness Doctrine Falls?* 74 GEORGETOWN L. J. 1491, 1493 (1986).

199. 453 U.S. 367 (1981).

200. For a thorough review of the case, *see* Geller & Yurow, *The Reasonable Access Provision of the Communications Act: Once More Down the Slippery Slope,* 34 FED. COM. L. J. 389 (1982).

201. ABC offered to sell the time one month later than requested; CBS offered to sell them five-minute time slots. Carter-Mondale, 74 FCC 2d. 623–624 (1979).

202. 453 U.S. 367, 389 (1981). Emphasis in original.

203. Comment, *Access Rights to the Media After CBS v DNC*, 25 HOWARD L. J. 825, 835 (1982).

204. It is asserted that the "individual basis" directive of the Supreme Court forbids stations from creating blanket rules or uniform policies. Note, *CBS, Inc. v FCC: Recognition of Candidates' Right of Access to Broadcasting Facilities,* 1982 UTAH L. REV. 641, 649.

205. Geller & Yurow, *supra* note 200, at 399–414.

206. 453 U.S. 367, 418–419 (1981) (Stevens, J., dissenting).

207. According to the commission, broadcasters' opinion should weigh heavily. The FCC is committed to "defer to the reasonable, good faith judgment of licensees as to what constitutes reasonable access." *In re* Commission Policy Enforcing Sec. 312(a)(7), 68 FCC 2d. 1079 (1978).

208. "NAB Opposes Academic Panel's Proposal for 'Free' Political Airtime" TV TODAY (NAB Newsletter) (Mar. 12, 1990) p. 1.

209. Koppel, *The Applicability of the Equal Time Doctrine and The Reasonable Access Rule to Elections in the New Media Era,* 20 HARVARD J. ON LEGIS. 499, 538 (1983).

210. Lorain Journal Co. v U.S., 342 U.S. 143 (1951).

211. Nadel asserts this right to refuse advertising is based not on any First Amendment right, but on a Fifth Amendment property right of the media owners. Nadel, *A Unified Theory of the First Amendment: Divorcing the Medium from the Message,* 11 FORDHAM L. REV. 163, 179 (1982).

212. 15 USC Sec. 1–7 (1982).

213. *E.g.*, Miami Herald v Tornillo, 418 U.S. 241, 255 (1974) (no general right of access to media exists).

214. *See* Balsam, *The Media's Right to Refuse Advertising*, 1985 ANN. SURVEY AM. L. 699. Balsam also contends there is an enforceable right of access for advertising when the state owns the medium. His evidence, however, is quite limited, based largely on a Seventh Circuit decision involving a college newspaper. Lee v Bd. of Regents, 441 F.2d. 1257 (7th Cir. 1971). The court in that case required the paper to accept ads regarding the Vietnam War. More recently, however, the Fifth Circuit ruled that school newspapers were not required to provide access to a group of gays. Mississippi Gay Alliance v Goudelock, 536 F.2d. 1073 (5th Cir. 1976).

215. 412 U.S. 94 (1973).

216. *Id.*, at 108–109.

217. *Id.*, at 113.

218. *Id.*, at 122.

219. *Id.*, at 123.

220. *Id.*, at 131.

3 LEGAL PRINCIPLES AND APPROACHES APPLICABLE TO MEDIA ACCESS

To determine whether adequate access to the media exists, and whether government-imposed access obligations are appropriate, it is first necessary to examine the legal principles directing these determinations. What existing legal doctrines guide our understanding of this issue?

TRADITIONAL BROADCAST/PRINT DISTINCTIONS

"The divergent approach to mass communications media [regulation] in the United States rests on the belief that print and broadcast media are fundamentally different."[1] Limited rights of access have been found constitutional in broadcast media, while analogous claims have not been accepted for print media. Several propositions put forward a print/broadcast distinction in the regulatory scheme. Most of these revolve around the original necessity of enacting the Radio Act of 1927.[2] The argument is that if anyone who wished to broadcast were allowed to do so, no one could be effectively heard.[3] Interference from stations would be so great that fewer stations could successfully reach the public. A system was therefore devised allowing only certain people to receive licenses to broadcast on allotted channels with specified power.[4] In order to serve the best interests of all, licenses are issued on a limited basis to competing applicants.[5] Since it was not possible to allot everyone who wanted one a frequency to use, a selection process was devised. Nearly fifty years ago, the Supreme Court upheld the right of the Federal Communications Commission (FCC) to select licensees from among applicants based on a variety of criteria intended to serve the public interest. The decision in *National Broadcasting Co. v U.S.*[6] held that the FCC was more than simply the "traffic cop" of the airwaves, but was also responsible for the "burden of determining the composition of that traffic."[7] The granting of licenses can be analogized in this narrow regard to permit requirements for speakers wishing to use the public streets. In *Cox v New Hampshire*,[8] the Court held permit requirements for public streets constitutional, otherwise "liberty itself would be lost in the exercise of unrestrained abuses."[9] The process requires that broadcasters serve the "public interest, convenience and necessity."[10] Licenses are distributed for a limited time to those thought most likely to serve the public.[11]

Distinction I: Scarcity

The Supreme Court has justified differing approaches to print and broadcast regulation thus: "The fundamental distinguishing characteristic of the new medium of broadcasting that, in our view, has required some adjustment in First Amendment analysis is that broadcast frequencies are a scarce resource that must be portioned out among applicants."[12]

The scarcity rationale has been questioned in recent years due to the surge in the number of stations on the air, and to the prospect for additional channels provided by new technologies.[13] Former FCC Chairman Mark Fowler and others believe that new broadcast technologies (such as direct broadcast satellites and low power television) will provide expanded opportunities for divergent voices in the marketplace.[14] Arguments that increased broadcast voices provide greater diversity for the listener consider the question of scarcity from a listener's perspective. This approach to the First Amendment leads to the conclusion that the rights deserving of greatest protection in balance are those of the listener, rather than those of the speaker.[15]

A definitional problem exists in differentiating scarcity from diversity.[16] If scarcity means "limited voices," clearly scarcity as a rationale for regulation seems more appropriate for print than for broadcast media. The number of daily newspapers in the United States is less than one-sixth the number of conventional radio and television outlets.[17] If, on the other hand, scarcity is defined as the inability of individuals seeking use of a medium to obtain it, or a portion of it, then broadcasting is still the medium of scarcity.[18]

Arguments to discredit the scarcity rationale often cite the diversity of media voices existing today. The claim is made that many more voices can be heard today than years ago.[19] The problem with such thinking is simply the confusion of scarcity and diversity. Lack of diversity exists when there are relatively few voices for any individual to hear. Scarcity exists, on the other hand, when those desiring access are denied it due to lack of space.[20] Powe claims one reason for abandoning a scarcity rationale is the ability of advancing technology to increase the number of stations.[21] This ignores current conditions, and emphasizes increased outlets rather than the ratio of available frequencies to those desiring them. Powe attributes this excess demand to the fact that licenses are given free by the government.[22] The distinction here has caused confusion for the courts and the FCC. In *Telecommunications Research and Action Center v FCC*,[23] Judge Bork discounted scarcity by citing the abundance and diversity of today's media marketplace. In eliminating the fairness requirement for broadcasters, the FCC claimed scarcity no longer exists, when in fact it was the increased diversity of outlets they were describing.[24] The definition of scarcity as diversity is clearly inappropriate, otherwise the *Red Lion* and *Tornillo* cases would have to have been decided differently. Even in 1969 when *Red Lion* was decided, broadcast stations outnumbered daily newspapers more than four to one. Scarcity in this context must be taken to mean a limitation on entry to the means of communication.[25]

Fowler and Brenner point out that broadcast scarcity could be virtually eliminated if modifications were made in the spectrum.[26] Examples they cite include decreasing the bandwidth for existing services, reallocating portions of the spectrum that are currently reserved for nonbroadcast uses, and revising rules to tolerate increased interference so that stations may be positioned more closely, geographically and on the spectrum.

While the above proposals are valid means for increasing availability, they do not eliminate the existing scarcity of broadcasting opportunities. In the past decade, all three of the means above for "shoe horning" additional stations have been proposed, and two of the three have been implemented. The commission discussed a proposal to decrease the bandwidth for AM radio stations from 10 to 9 kHz, which would have increased the number of AM allocations available to allow for hundreds of new AM stations. It was rejected because the cost to broadcasters and listeners was seen as too high.[27]

In a different area, the commission was successful in increasing the frequencies available for AM stations by expanding the AM band at the upper end, allowing for the addition of ten new channels.[28] The rules were also modified to allow for "drop in" of stations formerly thought too close to existing stations to be technically acceptable.[29] The fact that these allocations were in such high demand and sought by far more applicants than could possibly be accommodated ought to provide increased evidence of the scarcity of such channels. It has further been asserted that the selling price of broadcast stations is evidence of scarcity.[30]

Fowler and Brenner also assert that scarcity is not appropriate because the entire available speech opportunities, rather than simply the broadcast options, should be considered when determining scarcity.[31] They cite not only newspapers, but cable and video cassettes as viable speech options. This rationale seems inappropriate in light of repeated reminders by the Supreme Court that expression should not be denied in one area because it is available elsewhere.[32] It also seems inconsistent with repeated admonitions that differing media demand different legal analysis.[33] Perhaps Fowler and Brenner know the commission better than does the Court, because in 1987 the FCC asserted that despite differences in media "their roles in society are identical, and we believe that the same First Amendment principles should be equally applicable to both."[34] The decision has been seen as a rejection by the commission of a scarcity distinction for regulating broadcast.[35]

Distinction II: The Spectrum as Public Resource—The Trusteeship Model

In addition to the argument of the scarcity of the spectrum, or sometimes in place of it, is the proposition that the broadcast spectrum is a national resource. "The communication frequencies that constitute the radio spectrum are a natural resource essential to living in the modern world."[36] President Kennedy referred to the spectrum as a "critical natural resource."[37] Its use by individuals for their own purposes encumbers them with some sort of requirement to act at least responsibly, perhaps in the public interest, in the use of that frequency.[38] This rationale asserts that broadcasters are trustees of this valuable resource and can be expected to act according to the dictates of those allowing them use of this commodity.[39] This rationale has been supported by Congress,[40] the executive branch (through the NTIA),[41] and by the Supreme Court.[42] The trusteeship model is not unique to broadcast regulation, but has been the standard in natural resource law for some time.[43]

According to Lucas Powe, the trusteeship model is inappropriate because it rests on the flawed assumption that government ownership entitles it to violate individual rights.[44] Because the government is precluded from requesting a citizen's constitutional rights as a condition of other benefits (such as employment or welfare payments), he concludes that the forfeiture of full First Amendment rights by broadcasters is unconstitutional.[45] While his argument has much to recommend it, he is incorrect in stating that the Supreme Court has never used the trusteeship rationale for regulation.[46]

While noble in purpose, many contend that due to the profit incentive inherent in American broadcasting, the trusteeship model of broadcasting has never been anything more than an idealization.[47] Famed broadcast policy critic Henry Geller contends the failure has been primarily due to lack of enforcement by the FCC.[48] Regardless of where the fault lies, it is difficult to assert a public trusteeship model for broadcast given current realities. Geller postulated that the elimination of the Fairness Doctrine would "unravel" the entire public trustee concept.[49]

Distinction III: Interference

It has already been well established that broadcast stations occupy spectrum space, and in so doing they preclude use by others on that same frequency in that same locale. Sometimes this is interpreted as part of a physical scarcity argument, but it is separable.[50] Bollinger asserts that in *Red Lion* the Supreme Court devised the new principle "that when only a few interests control a major avenue of communication, those able to speak can be forced by the government to share."[51] In fact, the interference rationale has a longer history. As justification for broadcast regulation, the Supreme Court stated that "[f]reedom of utterance is abridged to many who wish to use the limited facilities of radio."[52] Although stated in terms of limited facilities, the dictum also speaks of abridgement to many. One wonders whether, if an infinite supply of spectrum were available, the selection of one speaker over another would still cause consternation for the Court. While both scarcity and interference were asserted in *Red Lion*,[53] they need not be connected. Their connection in broadcast contexts is quite understandable, as the spectrum may be subject to both scarcity and interference, but interference claims can be asserted when there is no physical scarcity. In fact, interference has been used in cases involving print media and public forums as rationale for regulation.

In *Associated Press v U.S.*,[54] the Supreme Court ruled that news media could be prevented from interfering with the speech rights of others. The *Red Lion* Court cited the *Associated Press* decision[55] as support for the proposition that "the right of free speech . . . does not embrace a right to snuff out the free speech of others."[56]

The *Red Lion* Court also refers to the appropriateness of regulating noise from sound trucks in order to prevent the interference that would result. The decisions in *Saia*[57] and *Kovacs*[58] were primarily decided on other grounds, but the Supreme Court's extension of the interference approach is enlightening. The Court seems to justify regulation not wholly on the scarcity argument, but also on the premise that use of the forum by one speaker necessarily precludes the use by another. In situations where such a condition exists (as in broadcasting) some sort of regulation is appropriate.

Distinction IV: Pervasiveness and Power

Finally, several Supreme Court decisions and legal treatises have suggested that it is appropriate to distinguish between print and broadcast media because of the latter's place in American society. While newspapers have traditionally been powerful influences on public opinion, more people rely on television as their primary source of news and information.[59] As one commentator stated, "we may well speculate that scarcity is not the real concern of regulators, but what they are really troubled by is the power of communicators."[60] Another asserted that "the pervasive nature of radio and television have prevented those media from gaining" First Amendment rights similar to those of other communications.[61]

This was the rationale employed by the Court in its *Pacifica* decision.[62] "[T]he broadcast media have established a uniquely pervasive presence in the lives of all Americans."[63] The Court seemed to exhibit concern that the communication at issue could pervade the home, yet as the dissent in the case points out, the privacy rights of the receiver are no more involved than in prior cases involving offensive speech.[64] Justice Brennan's argument makes a good deal of sense. It is interesting to speculate whether the Court would have found Cohen guilty as a public nuisance if he had worn his offensive jacket to solicit signatures door-to-door.[65] Fowler and Brenner point out that the Court was mistaken in asserting pervasiveness because the one station at issue was not pervasive. The unit of regulation was not all of broadcasting, but should instead have been the one Pacifica station, which in fact was a rather small, not-for-profit radio station.[66] Brenner further cautions that power can be interpreted either as market power (as with oligopolies) or as the inherent power in media (as in Pacifica's case).[67] Spitzer argues that indecency concerns are justified for broadcasting in light of children who could be in the audience, yet less restrictive means could be devised, such as receivers with "adults only" bands.[68]

Van Alstyne presents a persuasive argument, asserting that pervasiveness and power could not possibly be a print/broadcast regulatory distinction. Comparing *Red Lion* and *Tornillo*, Van Alstyne claims the cases should have been resolved differently. WGCB was one of many radio stations available in Red Lion, while the *Herald* was the only daily newspaper in Miami. Clearly, the paper was more pervasive and powerful in Miami than the radio station was in Red Lion.[69] Powe echoes Van Alstyne's criticism and also asserts that the pervasive and powerful criteria are vague and have no rational basis for distinguishing media.[70] Exactly how is a radio station more powerful than the *New York Times*? What yardstick is used to determine pervasiveness? Bollinger also rejects what he terms the "impact thesis" because there is no justification or evidence for such a regulatory differentiation.[71] Former FCC Chairman Mark Fowler obviously saw no appropriate differentiation when he referred to television as "just another appliance . . . a toaster with pictures."[72]

PUBLIC FORUM DOCTRINE

The history and evolution of cases defining the public forum has already been discussed at length. This section identifies those legal tenets established in public forum cases that further an understanding of the general principle of access.

Although not the most recent decision, the Supreme Court still relies on the distinction created in *Perry* in defining a forum.[73] In that case, the Court defined three different forums for state-owned property, each one deserving a different level of analysis to determine whether governmental restrictions on speech are permissible. Clearly, simply determining that a forum is public does not immediately guarantee access.[74]

Traditional Public Forum: In forums where speech has been long understood as part and parcel of that venue, speech is entitled to the greatest protection.[75] Streets and parks fall into this category.[76] Regulation of speech in traditional forums requires a compelling state interest and must be narrowly drawn.[77] Time, place, and manner restrictions are appropriate.

Designated Public Forum: Government property that does not have a tradition of permitting free speech, but where the state has opened it for such a use, is the second category under *Perry*.[78] The Court points out that the government need not keep these forums open indefinitely, but so long as they remain open, the government is limited as it would be under traditional public forum analysis. There is, however, no guaranteed right of access to a nontraditional forum.[79] It is also appropriate for the state to limit the sorts of discussion that are provided access, thus the term, "limited public forum."[80] University meeting rooms fit this designation,[81] as do open school board meetings[82] and municipal auditoriums.[83]

Nonpublic Forum: If state-owned property is neither traditionally nor by designation a public forum, then it is nonpublic, in which case, government may impose reasonable regulations that do not attempt to suppress speech with which the government disagrees.[84] The Court has asserted that school newspapers,[85] bus card advertising,[86] military bases,[87] and jailhouse grounds[88] are nonpublic forums. The Supreme Court has avoided the question of whether an airport terminal is a public forum.[89]

Buchanan claims that although there are two types of public forum, regulation that is content neutral or content selective has resulted in four combinations of regulation, creating a hierarchy of judicial scrutiny.[90] From greatest to least scrutinized, they are

1. Content selective regulation of a traditional public forum must serve a compelling state interest and be narrowly drawn to achieve that end.
2. Content neutral regulation of a traditional public forum (time, place, and manner rules) must be narrowly tailored and serve a significant government interest.
3. Content selective regulation of a nontraditional public forum is subject to "careful" scrutiny.
4. Content neutral regulation of a nontraditional public forum must be only reasonable.[91]

In deciding which of the above analyses is appropriate, the Court in *Cornelius* instructs us that it is appropriate to determine the access being sought.[92] For example, persons seeking access to a school's internal mail system are not seeking access to the broader forum of the school. Likewise, access sought to advertising cards on buses did not require the Court to consider the entire bus as the forum. This rationale may provide the analysis for an understanding of *Grace*: the sidewalks surrounding the Supreme Court were not a part of the larger traditional forum of the sidewalks of Washington, D.C.[93] If this narrowing approach is applied in the future to other, traditional public forums, one wonders whether the Court might allow restrictions on speech that would otherwise be unconstitutional. It is conceivable that a court could rule that while a park's speaker's corner is a traditional public forum, the rest of the park would not be, and could be treated as a nonpublic forum. Such an application would relegate public forums to very limited areas.

One of the difficulties in applying public forum doctrine to recent cases is the changing nature of expression and its venues in the twentieth century. "[S]ocioeconomic changes have shifted the focus of community life from these traditional public forums to privately owned forums, such as shopping centers, airports, and corporate office complexes."[94] The appropriate application of public forum analysis to private property ought to be that provided by the Court more than forty years ago in *Marsh*: "the more an owner, for his advantage, opens up his property for use by the public in general, the more do his rights become circumscribed by the statutory and constitutional rights of those who use it."[95]

The courts have not, however, seen the dicta in *Marsh* as a formula for application of the public forum doctrine. Shopping centers provide the venue where courts have had the greatest opportunity to comment. In a series of three cases, the Supreme Court took a position, modified that position, then reversed itself. The first of the so-called shopping mall cases was *Amalgamated Food Employees Union v Logan Valley Plaza, Inc.*[96] The case involved the union's right to picket in a privately owned shopping center. The Court applied the thinking from *Marsh*, finding the shopping center the functional equivalent of the streets of a company-owned town.[97] As such, prohibitions on free speech were state action, a violation of First Amendment rights. This created great difficulty for jurisdictions across the country attempting to define public and private forums.[98]

In *Lloyd Corp. v Tanner*,[99] the Court realized that the precedent it had established in *Logan Valley* was limited and needed redefinition.[100] The Court distinguished *Lloyd* from *Logan Valley* by considering the nature of the communication. The Court held that free speech did not have to be provided in *Lloyd* because the communication did not have any relationship to the business being conducted at the shopping center (the leaflets dealt with antiwar issues).[101] The Court was protecting the property rights of the shopping center owners. Writing for the Court, Justice Powell stated that "Fifth and Fourteenth Amendment rights of property owners, as well as First Amendment rights of all citizens, must be respected and protected."[102] Four years later, the Court took another opportunity to clarify the situation.[103]

Hudgens v NLRB[104] was the Supreme Court's attempt to resolve the shopping mall forum question. The Court held that *Logan Valley* was overruled by *Lloyd*, and that prohibitions by shopping center owners could not be considered state action.[105] It was a recognition that private property rights were as protected as First Amendment rights, and that one did not have to give way for the expression of other.[106]

Since *Hudgens*, the question of shopping malls has for the most part been decided differently in different states based on provisions of each state's constitution. In *Pruneyard*,[107] the Court upheld a right of access to a privately owned shopping center based on a state constitution provision. Thus shopping centers may be subject to public forum analysis in California,[108] Washington,[109] and Massachusetts.[110] Conversely, cases decided in Michigan,[111] New York,[112] and Connecticut[113] found no state-required right of access to private property.[114]

There is disagreement whether a public forum analysis would be appropriate for electronic media. Cable television, it is argued should not as a whole be subject to public forum analysis because the physical conditions are quite different, and such an approach merely "clouds the real [F]irst [A]mendment issues."[115] It is further asserted that inadequate state action exists to claim cable as a public forum.[116] However it can be argued quite convincingly that cable public access channels are designated public forums, and their regulation should be subject to the same scrutiny as university meeting rooms and civic auditoriums.[117]

A unique application of the public forum doctrine is its use in broadcast contexts. Others have drawn parallels between public forum regulation and broadcasting,[118] but most center on the station as forum rather than the entire spectrum. The claim is not that stations themselves were public forums,[119] but rather the spectrum in its entirety: a sort of reversal of the *Cornelius* approach. Because the spectrum has been "traditionally" used as a venue for free expression, it should be viewed as a traditional public forum. Those areas of the country where there are frequencies not in use should allow them to be used by anyone wishing to do so.[120] Regulation of these speakers could not be premised on an interference rationale, because they would be operating on unused, noninterfering frequencies.

THE MARKETPLACE APPROACH

One of the values stated for protecting free expression is the belief that free discussion is necessary for the purpose of self-governance.[121] This is consistent with the Miltonian "marketplace of ideas" approach: the belief that in open competition, truth ultimately prevails over falsity.[122] It is also an affirmation that there is no absolute truth; the best that can be hoped for is that understandings of truth continues to evolve. Of course, the marketplace of ideas rests on the questionable assumptions that truth is discoverable,[123] and that conflicts of values among people do not disrupt this search for truth.[124] This fits the popular romantic notion of democracy.[125]

In keeping with the trend toward deregulation of industry, the Federal Communications Commission has, in recent years, adopted a marketplace metaphor. It has long been believed that as electronic communication outlets increased, regulatory need might be inversely proportional.[126] Former FCC Chairman Mark Fowler has often spoken of a marketplace that would provide all the necessary opportunities.[127] The irony of this is that given economic considerations, without some government control or supplementation, the marketplace cannot facilitate all the needs of a First Amendment right.[128]

The economic marketplace and the marketplace of ideas are not the same. Whether economic competition can result in diversity in the intellectual marketplace is questionable.[129] Often, the best way of protecting the marketplace of ideas is to regulate the economic marketplace. By definition, economic marketplaces are efficient when one person uses the full extent of the availability (a monopoly). This may account for the vast percentage of communities that are one-newspaper cities.[130] Problems of access due to concentration of media ownership may also discourage citizen participation in public affairs.[131] In a marketplace of ideas, however, nothing could be more repugnant than a monopoly on thought. "Ironically, it is only through escape from competitive pressure that the press will perform the functions that conventional first amendment doctrine thrusts upon it."[132] The problem is compounded in broadcasting because technological considerations cause modifications in the way the spectrum is perceived. As one broadcast engineer stated, "the broadcasting marketplace is not driven by economic forces alone."[133] A number of broadcasters have expressed concern that as increased emphasis is placed on market forces, inference from other stations will increase.[134]

It would be economically efficient for anyone using the airwaves to be charged a fee, but this would result in free speech rights only for the wealthy.[135] This "user fee" could raise funds necessary for administration, and also aid in gauging public demand.[136] However, social disparity, even if "inexpensive," would be intolerable if it were to result in adverse distributive impact on such rights as free speech.[137]

Moreover, the economic marketplace suggests that "products" (for speech, this means "ideas") that are acceptable to the majority will survive, while those supported by the minority will not be viable. Popularity is an inappropriate means for determining acceptability if free speech is intended to allow minority viewpoints.[138]

While the Supreme Court has not called into question a market-oriented First Amendment policy,[139] it has realized that the market is an inadequate regulator for political campaigns. The Court has held that limits on corporate contributions to political campaigns are constitutional.[140] In a decision a decade earlier, the Court found some of the provisions of the Federal Election Campaign Act acceptable; others were constitutionally suspect.[141] The limitations on expenditures by candidates was found invalid, but individual contribution limits were acceptable. Clearly, the ability of the marketplace to protect franchise rights is questionable.

If a central intent in advocating a marketplace metaphor for speech is the desire to bring about social and political change, how does one explain Supreme Court decisions regarding obscenity?[142] The Court has characterized the state interest in preventing obscenity as protecting "the community environment."[143] The FCC has also been unwilling to let the marketplace decide in the area of indecency regulation.[144] Baker also contends that differing treatment for plaintiffs in libel suits is demonstration by the Court that the marketplace is not adequate for righting wrongs.[145]

SPEAKER RIGHTS VERSUS LISTENER RIGHTS

Frequently, constitutional claims for free speech must be weighed in light of other constitutional rights: "balanced," as the Supreme Court calls it. In some cases, free speech must be contrasted with the right to a fair trial, while in other instances, expression may face opposition from the government's right to maintain national security. There are, however, many instances where the right claimed against the First Amendment is the First Amendment itself.

Free expression conflicts must be resolved in one of three ways:

- The rights of one speaker are given precedent over the rights of another speaker;
- The rights of the speaker are given precedent over the rights of the listener; or

- The rights of the listener are given precedent over the rights of the speaker.

Following is an explication of each of these conflicts and their applicability to free speech cases. In most instances the cases are not seen simply as the preference of one right over another, but that, in effect, is the result. Ideally, it would be advantageous to protect the rights of both the speaker and listener.[146] After all, Justice Marshall stated that speaking and hearing are two sides of the same coin.[147]

Speaker versus Speaker

When the rights of one person to speak freely conflict with the rights of another to speak freely, legal theory must provide for some remedy to determine which of the two has the more legitimate claim. In many cases, this involves an ad hoc balancing by the courts. In some specific areas, legal theory provides rules that have been codified.

Copyright law, based in the Constitution and first codified in 1790[148] and most recently by the Copyright Revision Act of 1976, is perhaps this country's first example of a scheme to provide preference for one type of speaker over another. In the interest of promoting intellectual, creative activity, Congress has the authority to grant patents and copyrights. The theory is that more people will pursue creative activities if a system protecting their ability to profit from their efforts exists. If, after creating a work, writers lost all rights of copy, there would be very little profitability in writing. The Supreme Court has claimed the purpose is to encourage creative work, "but private motivation must ultimately serve the cause of promoting broad public availability of literature, music and the other arts."[149]

In spite of Supreme Court allusions to public needs, copyright laws have weighted the balance in favor of the rights of one speaker over another. It grants to the original author of a work the right to prohibit its use by others, even in limited forms.[150] The concept of protecting the copyright holder even entitles him the right to deny use of his composition at any price.[151] Thus, rights of one speaker are protected against infringement by others.[152]

Early in this century, businesses expressed concerns that claims made by competitors were invalid, resulting in unfair business practices. Originally, regulations regarding deceptive advertising were attempts to protect the rights of one speaker against those of another.[153] If a marketplace approach were adopted, unfair or deceptive advertising would not need regulating, as consumers would be capable of discerning truth and making their purchases accordingly. Instead, a philosophical approach was adopted, based on the premise that businesses need to be protected from unfair competition resulting from unfair speech. While later regulation was based on assumptions that the consumer (i.e., listener) needs the protection,[154] that was never the case in early legislation. Speakers, unable to overcome the influence of inappropriate messages, need state protection.

Early advertising law demonstrates a willingness by the government to stifle the speech of one speaker in order to protect the rights of others. This theme is continued in a Supreme Court decision involving the Federal Election Campaign Act. In *Buckley v Valeo*, the Court upheld regulations limiting contributions to a political candidate but found expenditure limits unconstitutional.[155] The Court's reasoning included the assertion that contributions are only "indirect or symbolic speech,"[156] while expenditures are more directly related to political speech. In limiting contributions, the Court claims to be limiting the ability of individuals and groups to curry favor from politicians. It is difficult to distinguish this concern from a similar concern that individuals will make independent expenditures in support of a candidate in hopes of being just as favored. Furthermore, the claim that contributions directly to the candidate are not speech, while the same amount spent to support the candidate without his direct approval becomes speech, seems unfounded.

Regardless, the Supreme Court claimed it was not limiting anyone's free speech to protect the rights of other speakers. "[T]he concept that government may restrict some elements of our society in order to enhance the relative voice of others is wholly foreign to the First Amendment."[157] Despite the rhetoric, the result of the decision was precisely that: to restrict some speakers in order to strengthen the position of other speakers.

In another area of campaign expression, legislation exists primarily to restrict the speech of one type of speaker in favor of another type of speaker. Broadcasters are obligated by act of Congress to provide reasonable access to candidates for federal office,[158] with the federal government empowered to make determinations about whether access has been reasonable,[159] and the rates charged these candidates are regulated.[160] The government has made a clear determination that the rights of one type of speaker take precedent over the rights of another type of speaker.

Preference of the Speaker over the Listener

Assertions that the right of the speaker are tantamount stem from a philosophical approach that sees free expression as part of the process of self-actualization. This is the approach taken by Dworkin.[161] Viewing the rights of the speaker as more important than those of the listener sees expression as an end in itself.

[W]hen we look upon freedom of speech as a speaker's interest, the core of the theory has much more to do with individual dignity and equality, the moral right of equal participation, than it does with any notion of electoral sovereignty, or even with any pragmatic or utilitarian calculation of how government may function most effectively.[162]

Proponents of a right of access to the media adopt this approach. Speakers must be provided access, it is argued, because it is the only way they can have adequate opportunity to speak freely. The content of the message is irrelevant; the opportunity to speak freely, regardless of intent, intellect, or number of supporters is correlative to being human and must be protected. Ironically, valuing editorial autonomy is also predicated on the right of the speaker. Freedom of the press is often characterized as the speaker's right.[163]

The Prime Time Access Rule, created by the FCC, is an example of a government affirmative action intended to protect speakers' rights. The rule prohibits stations in the top fifty markets from airing more than three hours of network programming during prime time.[164] The rule was created to enable access to major markets by new producers of television programs. The fact that the rule functions only in the largest markets demonstrates the desire not to increase diversity (which would seem to need the greatest push in smaller markets) but rather to afford opportunities for new "speakers" where none presently exist.

Access proponents are not the only people who support the rights of speakers over those of listeners. Cases revolving around pugnacious speech often afford the opportunity for analysis of doctrines supporting the speaker's rights. In *Cohen v California*, the Supreme Court upheld the right of an individual to wear clothing emblazoned with the words "fuck the draft" for all to see.[165] The Court did not accept the argument that the language was offensive to most and should be prohibited. Instead, the Court advised those who were offended to simply "avert their eyes" to avoid the speech. The right of the speaker to speak freely took precedent over the listener's right not to be offended.

A decade later, a Chicago suburb had to tolerate a march by Nazis. Skokie, a predominantly Jewish community, had to tolerate speech that it found abhorrent, on the premise that the rights of the speaker were entitled more consideration than those of the listener.[166]

Most recently, the Supreme Court decided a Texas case that permitted the burning of the American flag as an act of symbolic speech. In a very unpopular decision, the Court narrowly decided the rights of the speaker were due greater consideration than those of the listener.[167]

In all three of the preceding cases, the speech was offensive to an overwhelming majority of local citizens. Had the decisions been reached by popular vote rather than by Supreme Court decision, it is safe to say all three would have been decided in favor of the listener.[168] Instead, the Supreme Court chose to defend the speakers' rights over the rights of the listeners.

Preference of the Listener over the Speaker

From a philosophical perspective, the rights of the listener are protected whenever there is an interest in the diversity of voices. Diversity is arguably a value for the democratic process, thus the rights of listeners should be favored in speech contributing to the political process.[169] Obviously, a Meiklejohnian approach to regulation of speech accepts this perspective.[170] This may be the approach with which most constitutional lawyers find comfort.[171] Ironically, however, regulations attempting to protect the sensitivities of the audience are also promulgated in the listener's interest. Thus, regulations attempting to make more speech available to the public, as well as regulations intended to restrict certain speech from the public, can both be claimed as being in the listener interest. Since most Americans view themselves as listeners rather than speakers, the general public tends to approach free expression from a listener's right.[172]

The famous *Red Lion* case is an example of protecting the listeners' rights in the interest of diversity.[173] The case has been used to support the proposition that listeners' rights occupy a privileged position in broadcasting.[174] The Supreme Court explicitly stated that "[i]t is the rights of the viewers and listeners which is paramount."[175] The Fairness Doctrine, which was at issue in that case, was a rule promulgated with diversity as a goal. The doctrine was not enacted so that everyone would have access to the airwaves, but rather so that "everything worth hearing" would be said,[176] clearly protecting the interest of those doing the hearing.[177]

While *Red Lion* established the listener's right to hear everything it should, *Pacifica* determined that regulations could prohibit the airing of material the audience shouldn't have to hear.[178] The Supreme Court upheld FCC regulations regarding indecent broadcasts, primarily on the premise that audience members should not have to be subjected to "that kind" of communication. While the disputed language in *Pacifica* was identical to that used in *Cohen*, the Court chose to distinguish the cases. If averting one's eyes was good enough in *Cohen*, why not averting one's ears in *Pacifica*? A simple distinction is that Cohen's words were printed while Carlin's were broadcast, but that is circular reasoning: why the distinction? The essential difference in the two appears to be in the venue of the listeners. While Cohen's speech was only visible to those who had wandered into a public place, Carlin's speech permeated every nook and cranny, even into private homes "where the individual's right to be let alone plainly outweighs the First Amendment rights of the intruder."[179] This ruling suggests that rights of access, if asserted as a preference for a speaker's right over the interest of the listeners, will not pass constitutional muster.

It appears the Court is especially sensitive to the rights of the listener in situations where the audience has no alternative but to listen. In situations where there is a captive audience, the Court is likely to prefer the rights of listeners over the rights of speakers. First articulated by Justice Black in his concurrence in *Cox v Louisiana*,[180] the principle is that people should not be forced to listen "against their will to speakers they did not want to hear."

While people may not be "forced to hear" the words of offensive speakers, they may in fact be forced to listen to face-to-face confrontational provocations, which the Court has ruled can be prohibited. The fighting words doctrine makes it permissible to protect the speaker in an odd way. Fighting words can be prohibited on the premise that they could invoke an attack on the speaker by the listener. It appears at first glance to protect the speaker. Why then does such protection result in the stifling of the expression? If the doctrine's intent were to protect the speaker, it would appear appropriate to provide protection for the speaker, or at least to threaten the listener with legal action should the listener choose to become violent. Instead, the listener is not compelled to hear speech that may provoke him, and the speaker's vitriolic commentary is ceased. While the fighting words doctrine has been greatly narrowed in subsequent decisions, the legal argument remains the same: it protects the rights of the listener over the rights of the speaker.

It can also be asserted that regulation of advertising is promulgated in the interest of the listener.[181] While early advertising regulations may have intended to protect businesses from unscrupulous competitors, current rules and enforcement are couched in a desire to protect consumers.

SUMMARY

Despite a plethora of rhetoric, regulation of broadcasting has been differentially viewed from print regulation. The rationales for the differentiation are many, but can be broadly categorized into four separate generalizations. Broadcasting has been regulated more than print on the premise, first and foremost, that broadcast frequencies are scarce. While many argue that scarcity no longer exists, they confuse the true meaning of scarcity. There still exists a high ratio of people desiring broadcast facilities to those granted their operation by the federal government, especially in major markets. Broadcasting is also regulated due to its use of a public resource, that is, the spectrum. While other acceptable means of rationing the spectrum could have been adopted, the government chose a public trusteeship model, whereby those allocated the resource have a public service obligation. In addition, users of the spectrum interfere with other uses, requiring regulation. Finally, a number of judgments suggest regulation of broadcasting because it is more pervasive and/or powerful than other media (particularly print).

While recent administrations have attempted to implement a marketplace approach to broadcast regulation, by and large its implementation has been limited. The rhetoric constantly confuses the marketplace of ideas with the economic marketplace. Further, true implementation of market forces would require a radical departure from our current system, including the elimination of existing band designations.

Legal decisions require a constant balance between conflicting rights. In addition to conflicting with rights of privacy or fair trial, expression rights often conflict with one another. Courts must constantly choose the rights of one speaker over another, and determine whether the speaker or the listener deserves greater consideration. Existing cases and laws demonstrate the value of protecting each, but in the interest of protecting listeners, the rights of speakers exercising self-expression should not be slighted. The rights of individual speakers need to be considered at least as important as the rights of listeners.

Chapter 4 examines some of these theoretical problems in a realistic framework. Current conditions in the communications environment are not those that existed a decade ago. What are the technological, economic, and regulatory realities that exist in America today? How do these realities impact access opportunities for self-expression?

NOTES

1. Schmidt, *Pluralistic Programming and Regulation of Mass Communications Media* in COMMUNICATIONS FOR TOMORROW 191, 193 (1978).
2. The Radio Act established the Federal Radio Commission, empowered with licensing broadcasters in the public interest. Prior to the Radio Act's passage, the secretary of commerce granted radio licenses, but was denied the power to regulate radio. U.S. v Zenith Radio Corp., 12 F.2d. 614 (N.D. Ill. 1926). More than two hundred new stations were licensed in 1926, causing a great deal of interference, especially in metropolitan areas. Congress responded in 1927 by passing the Radio Act. *See* L. Benjamin, Radio Regulation in the 1920s: Free Speech in the Development of Radio and the Radio Act of 1927 (1985) (dissertation, University of Iowa, Journalism & Mass Communication).
3. Red Lion Broadcasting v FCC, 395 U.S. 367, 376 (1969).
4. For concise histories of broadcasting's regulatory development, see E. BARNOUW, A HISTORY OF BROADCASTING IN THE UNITED STATES (1966) and C. STERLING & J. KITTROSS SAY TUNED 94–194 (1978).
5. NBC v U.S., 319 U.S. 190 (1943) (rules regulating chain broadcasting within FCC jurisdiction).
6. *Id.*
7. *Id.*, at 216.
8. 312 U.S. 569 (1941) (upholding license requirement for use of streets for expression, provided law is strictly limited). *See also* Consolidated Edison v Public Serv. Comm'n., 447 U.S. 530, 546 (1980) (Stevens, J., concurring) (restriction on inserts in utility bill envelopes found invalid).
9. *Id.*, at 574.
10. The standard is vague. *See* Volner, *Broadcast Regulation: Is There Too Much "Public" in the Public Interest?* 43 U. CINN L. REV. 267 (1974). The problem is not only one of definition. Much confusion revolves around the question of who is best suited to be the determiner of the public interest: the FCC, the broadcaster, or special interest groups.
11. League of Women Voters v FCC, 468 U.S.364, 377 (1984) (Congress may promulgate rules that promote efficient use of the spectrum).
12. *Id.*
13. Commerce Department Study, *Print and Electronic Media: The Case for First Amendment Parity*, S. Print 98–50, 98th Congress (May 3, 1983);

Bazelon, *The First Amendment and the "New Media,"* 31 FED. COM. L. J. 201, 207–209 (1979).

14. Fowler & Brenner, *A Marketplace Approach to Broadcast Regulation.* 60 TEX. L. REV. 207 (1982).

15. Note, *Access to the Press: A Teleological Analysis of a Constitutional Double Standard,* 50 GEO. WASH. L. REV. 430, 436 (1982). In the broadcast realm, the right of the listeners has been thought to outweigh that of the speaker in most cases. The right of viewers and listeners is "paramount." Red Lion Broadcasting v FCC, 395 U.S. 367, 390 (1969). There is, however, some indication otherwise. "[I]t is through the protection of the rights of speakers that the interest of society as a whole will best be protected." Fairness Doctrine Inquiry, 102 FCC 2d. 145, 154 n. 39 (1985). For more on speaker versus listener rights, *see infra* notes 146–180 and accompanying text.

16. Although diversity is valued, it has not been asserted as a reason for distinguishing between print and broadcast regulation. In fact, the myriad of regulatory institutions may be undermining the system. "The value of diversity is lessened where some form of coordination is lacking." Symons, *The Communications Policy Process* in 1 NEW DIRECTIONS IN TELECOMMUNICA-TIONS POLICY 275, 297 (P. Newberg ed. 1989). As an example of the lack of diversity that exists, see Hammond, *Meeting Minority Concerns: Structural Versus Regulatory Approaches to Broadcasting* in PROCEEDINGS OF THE SIXTH ANNUAL TELECOMMUNICATIONS POLICY RESEARCH CONFERENCE 89 (H. Dordick ed. 1979).

17. Although the actual numbers change virtually every week, daily newspapers have totaled approximately 1,700 for the past decade, while radio and television stations total more than 12,000. In fact, despite a drop to 1,646 dailies in 1986, there were 1,773 dailies in 1989. STATISTICAL ABSTRACT OF THE UNITED STATES 555 (1990). As of 1990, there were 10,688 radio stations and 1,448 TV stations. *Summary of Broadcasting and Cable,* BROADCASTING, June 11, 1990, at 86.

18. Theoretically, every city in America could tolerate another daily paper, provided there were individuals willing to fund them. In practice, however, most cities may have natural monopolies. J. BUSTERNA, DAILY NEWSPAPER CHAINS AND THE ANTITRUST LAWS 25–29 (Journalism Mono-graphs 110, 1989). While in some cities some frequencies are available, most of the preferred channels have already been assigned. In the entire United States, only thirty-four commercial VHF channels were available, not one of them in the fifty largest markets. Only thirty-two commercial UHF stations remained unassigned in those cities. Fairness Doctrine Inquiry, 102 FCC 2d. 145, 207 (1985). This means no television stations were available in at least eighteen of the nation's fifty largest cities. The problem was exacerbated by the FCC decision to freeze UHF applications in the thirty largest markets to decide whether some channels should be reassigned for other broadcast purposes including high-definition television. Hughes, *FCC Eyes HDTV, UHF CPS Frozen,* 5 TV TECHNOLOGY 1 (Sept. 1987). *Cf,* Fowler & Brenner,

supra note 14, at 223. "Except in the largest cities . . . advertising support or subscriber dollars restrict broadcast opportunities more than does the number of channels." What the authors fail to recognize, or ignore, is that policy affecting only the five largest markets in the country impacts more than 20 percent of the nation's population. But "[b]ecause licenses may be transferred and broadcast operations sold, however, scarcity in broadcasting is not so distinguishable from scarcity in the print media." Lively, *Fairness Regulation: An Idea Whose Time Has Gone*, 45 WASH. & LEE L. REV. 1379, 1388 (1988). In fact, 65 percent of stations surveyed in 1983 were owned by someone other than the original grantee. Webbink, *Radio Licenses and Frequency Spectrum Use Property Rights*, COM. & L. 3, 6 n. 10 (June 1987).

19. C. SMITH, FREEDOM OF EXPRESSION AND PARTISAN POLITICS 93 (1989). Smith additionally provides a historical argument that the framers were obviously not concerned with scarcity, because there were only eight daily newspapers in 1791.

20. Spitzer identifies five versions of scarcity: static technological, dynamic technological, excess demand, entry, and relative. Spitzer, *Broadcasting and the First Amendment* in 1 NEW DIRECTIONS IN TELECOMMUNICATIONS POLICY 155, 169 (P. Newberg ed. 1989).

21. L. POWE, AMERICAN BROADCASTING AND THE FIRST AMENDMENT 202 (1987).

22. *Id.*, at 203.

23. 806 F. 2d 1115 (1986).

24. *In re* Complaint of Syracuse Peace Council, 4 FCC Rcd. 5045–5055 (1987).

25. *Accord*, Labunski, *May It Rest in Peace: Public Interest and Public Access in the Post-Fairness Doctrine Era*, 11 HASTINGS COMM/ENT L. J. 219 (1989) (primary justification for regulation is physical limitation coupled with higher demand than can be accommodated); R. HORWITZ, THE IRONY OF REGULATORY REFORM 249 (1989) ("The bottom-line legal rationale for the regulation of broadcasting is the scarcity of the electromagnetic spectrum.")

26. Fowler & Brenner, *supra* note 14, 222–223.

27. 9 kHz Channel Spacing for AM Broadcasting, 88 FCC 2d. 290 (1981).

28. *Extended AM Band: Problem or Solution?* BROADCASTING, p. 47 (Aug. 28, 1989).

29. *FCC Approves FM Short Spacing*, BROADCASTING, p. 51 (Dec. 19, 1988).

30. Labunski, *supra* note 25, at 271.

31. Fowler & Brenner, *supra* note 14, 15 225–226.

32. City Council v Taxpayers for Vincent, 466 U.S. 789, 812 (1984); U.S. v Grace, 461 U.S. 171, 180–184 (1983); Linmark Associates v Willingboro, 431 U.S. 85, 93 (1977); Schneider v State, 308 U.S. 147, 163 (1939).

33. *See* Metromedia v City of San Diego, 453 U.S. 490, 501 n. 8 (1981); FCC v Pacifica Foundation, 438 U.S. 726, 744–746 (1978); Red Lion Broadcasting v FCC, 395 U.S. 367, 386 (1969).

34. Syracuse Peace Council, Memorandum Opinion & Order, 2 FCC Rcd. 5043, paragraph 99 (1987).

35. Spitzer, *supra* note 20.

36. H. LEVIN, THE INVISIBLE RESOURCE 1 (1971).

37. *Id.*, at 3 (citing Executive Order 10995, Feb. 16, 1962).

38. W. FREEDMAN, FREEDOM OF SPEECH ON PRIVATE PROPERTY 65 (1988).

39. Wilson, *Minority and Gender Enhancements: A Necessary and Valid Means to Achieve Diversity in the Broadcast Marketplace*, 40 FED. COM. L. J. 89 (1988).

40. Broadcast Regulation Reform 1983: Hearings Before the Subcomm. on Telecommunications, Consumer Protection & Finance of the House Committee on Energy & Commerce, 98th Cong., 1st Sess. (1983).

41. Comprehensive Policy Review of Use and Management of the Radio Frequency Spectrum, 54 Fed. Reg. 50694, 50695 (NTIA Request for Comments Dec. 8, 1989).

42. Red Lion Broadcasting v FCC, 395 U.S. 367, 375–377, 394 (1969); FCC v Pottsville Broadcasting, 309 U.S. 134 (1940).

43. *See* Lazarus, *Changing Conceptions of Property and Sovereignty in Natural Resources*, 71 IOWA L. REV. 631, 633–641 (1986).

44. L. POWE, *supra* note 21, at 199.

45. *Id.*

46. *See supra* note 42.

47. McGill, *The Market for Corporate Control in the Broadcasting Industry*, 40 FED. COM. L. J. 39, 84 (1988).

48. Geller, *The Role of Future Regulation: Licensing, Spectrum Allocation, Content, Access, Common Carrier and Rates* in VIDEO MEDIA COMPETITION: REGULATION, ECONOMICS, AND TECHNOLOGY 283, 296 (E. Noam ed. 1985).

49. Geller, *Broadcasting* in 1 NEW DIRECTIONS IN TELECOMMUNICATIONS POLICY 125, 136 (P. Newberg ed. 1989).

50. *See* Note, *In Defense of Monopoly Cable Television Franchising: Defining the First Amendment Rights of the Public and The Cable Operator Under the Public Forum Doctrine and Natural Monopoly Theory*, 13 RUTGERS COMP. & TECH. L. J. 137, 215–219 (1987).

51. Bollinger, *Freedom of the Press and Public Access: Toward a Theory of Partial Regulation of the Mass Media*, 75 MICH. L. REV. 19 (1976).

52. NBC v FCC, 319 U.S. 190, 226 (1943).

53. 395 U.S. 367 (1969).

54. 326 U.S. 1 (1945).

55. 395 U.S. at 387.

56. *Id.*

57. 334 U.S. 558 (1948).

58. 336 U.S. 77 (1949).

59. Television Information Office/Roper, *America's Watching: Public Attitudes Toward Television* 4 (1987). Sixty-six percent of those surveyed cited television as a main source of news; only 36 percent cited newspapers.

60. D. TUCKER, LAW, LIBERALISM AND FREE SPEECH 149 (1985).

61. C. SMITH, *supra* note 19, at 89. *Accord*, Cohn, *Who Really Controls Television?* 29 U. MIAMI L. REV. 482, 486 (1975) (broadcasting no longer private enterprise).

62. FCC v Pacifica Foundation, 438 U.S. 726 (1978).

63. *Id.*, at 748.

64. *Id.*, at 764–766 (Brennan, J., dissenting).

65. A recent decision might suggest the Court would find in favor of the privacy right over the expression right. A Wisconsin ordinance prohibiting picketing around private homes in order to protect citizens' privacy was found not facially invalid. Frisby v Schultz, 56 U.S.L.W. 4785 (1988).

66. Fowler & Brenner, *supra* note 14, at 228.

67. Brenner, *Toward a True Marketplace for the Marketplace of Ideas* in FREE BUT REGULATED 272, 275 (D. Brenner & W. Rivers eds. 1982).

68. Spitzer, *supra* note 20, at 167.

69. W. VAN ALSTYNE, INTERPRETATIONS OF THE FIRST AMENDMENT 78 (1984).

70. L. POWE, *supra* note 21, at 209–212.

71. Bollinger, *supra* note 51, at 13.

72. Mayer, *FCC Chief's Fears: Fowler Sees Threat in Regulation*, WASH. POST, Feb. 6, 1983, at K6, col. 4, cited in Stern, Krasnow, & Sendowski, *The New Video Marketplace and the Search for a Coherent Regulatory Philosophy*, 32 CATH U. L. REV. 529, 602 (1983).

73. Perry Education Assn. v Perry Local Educators' Assn., 460 U.S. 37 (1983).

74. Cornelius v NAACP Legal Defense Fund & Ed. Fund, 473 U.S. 788, 799 (1985).

75. Perry, at 45.

76. Hague v CIO, 307 U.S. 496, 515 (1939).

77. Boos v Barry, 56 U.S.L.W. 4254, 4257 (1988) (a statute found unconstitutional that prohibits signs that would tend to bring foreign governments into "public odium" within five hundred feet of foreign embassies.)

78. Perry, at 45–46.

79. Buchanan, *Toward a Unified Theory of Governmental Power to Regulate Protected Speech*, 18 CONN. L. REV. 531, 569 (1986).

80. Heffron v International Society for Krishna Consciousness, Inc., 452 U.S. 640, 655 (1981).

81. Widmar v Vincent, 454 U.S. 263, 267 (1981).

82. Madison Joint School District v Wisconsin Employment Relations Comm'n., 429 U.S. 167, 174 n. 4 (1976).

83. Southeastern Promotions Ltd. v Conrad, 420 U.S. 546, 555 (1975).

84. Perry, at 49.

85. Hazelwood School District v Kuhlmeyer, 108 S. Ct. 562, 569 (1988). *Contra* Buss, *School Newspapers, Public Forum, and the First Amendment*, 74 IOWA L. REV. 505, 509–510 (1989).

86. Lehman v City of Shaker Heights, 418 U.S. 298 (1974).

87. Greer v Spock, 424 U.S. 828 (1976).

88. Adderly v Florida, 385 U.S.39 (1966).

89. Bd. of Airport Comm'ners. V Jews for Jesus, 55 USLW 4855 (1987).

90. Buchanan, *supra* note 79.

91. *Id.*, at 576–577.

92. Cornelius, *supra* note 74, at 801.

93. *See* Note, *The Public Forum and the First Amendment: The Puzzle of the Podium*, 19 NEW ENG. L. REV. 619, 635–641 (1984).

94. W. FREEDMAN, *supra* note 38, at 3.

95. Marsh v Alabama, 326 U.S. 501, 506 (1946). *Accord* D. TUCKER, *supra* note 60, at 68. "[W]e must allow that once the public are admitted on an indiscriminate basis, whatever right to communicate they would enjoy in a public place controlled by a governmental authority ought also to be enjoyed when the property is privately owned."

96. 391 U.S. 308 (1968).

97. *Id.*, at 319. "The shopping center premises are open to the public to the same extent as the commercial center of a normal town."

98. Two examples are illustrative. First, in Central Hardware Co. v NLRB, 439 F.2d 1331, *vacated* 407 U.S. 539 (1972), the National Labor Relations Board and the Eighth Circuit Court of Appeals cited *Logan Valley* and found Central Hardware's no soliciting rule a violation of employee's organizational rights under the National Labor Relations Act, Sec. 7. The Supreme Court vacated and remanded, saying *Logan Valley* was not applicable to the case. In Lloyd Corp. v Tanner, 446 F.2d 545, *rev'd*, 407 U.S. 551 (1972), the Oregon District Court and the Ninth Circuit Court of Appeals held a prohibition on handbilling in a shopping mall was a violation of the First Amendment right of the handbillers, using *Logan Valley* as determinative. The Supreme Court distinguished the case, reversed and remanded.

99. 407 U.S. 551 (1972). Individuals wanting to distribute leaflets in a shopping center were prohibited from doing so. The Supreme Court held the handbilling was unprotected because the handbills were unrelated to any activity within the shopping center.

100. *Id.*, at 560. "The Court noted that the scope of its holding was limited, and expressly reserved judgment on the type of issues presented in this case."

101. *Id.*, at 564.

102. *Id.*, at 570.

103. Even the Supreme Court noted the confusion. In Hudgens v NLRB, 424 U.S. 507 (1976), the Court wrote the case "has been a history, in short, of considerable confusion, engendered at least in part by decisions of this

court." *Id.*, at 512. A variety of cases that used *Lloyd* were reversed on appeal. *E.g.*, Connecticut S. Fed. of Tchrs. v Bd. of Ed. Members, 538 F.2d 471, 481 (2d Cir. 1976). The Connecticut District Court granted summary judgment for the plaintiffs, which was remanded in part with directions (availability of alternative means of communication relevant when balancing First Amendment and government interests); Illinois Migrant Council v Campbell Soup Co., 519 F.2d 391, 395 (7th Cir. 1975). Reversed and remanded a Northern District of Illinois decision. The District Court believed a company town could refuse access to a nonprofit council, since it had maintained its private character. The Appeals Court ruled the town was more like a shopping center.

104. 424 U.S. 507 (1976).

105. *Id.*, at 518–519.

106. "[I]n the case of shopping centers, malls, and the like, the Court has determined that property rights outweigh First Amendment rights." Emerson, *The Affirmative Side of the First Amendment*, 15 GA. L. REV. 795, 811 (1981).

107. Robins v Pruneyard Shopping Center, 447 U.S. 74 (1980).

108. *Id.*

109. Alderwood Assoc v Washington Environmental Council, 635 P.2d 102 (1981).

110. Batchelder v Allied Stores Int'l., 445 N.E. 2d 590 (1983).

111. Woodland v Michigan Citizens Lobby, 378 NW2d 337 (Mich. 1985).

112. Shad Alliance v Smith Haven Mall, 488 NE2d 1211 (N.Y. 1985).

113. Cologne v Westfarms Associates, 469 A2d 1201 (Conn. 1984).

114. *See* W. FREEDMAN, *supra* note 38, at 50–52; Sedler, *The State Constitutions and the Supplemental Protection of Individual Rights*, 16 U. TOL. L. REV. 465, 490 (1985).

115. Brunelli, *Why Courts Should Not Use Public Forum Doctrine in Considering Cable Operators' Claims Under the First Amendment*, 24 AM. BUS. L. J. 541, 552–565 (1986).

116. P. PARSONS, CABLE TELEVISION AND THE FIRST AMENDMENT 123–128 (1987).

117. Note, *Controversial Programming on Cable Television's Public Access Channels: The Limits of Governmental Response*, 38 DE PAUL L. REV. 1051, 1095–1105 (1989).

118. *See, e. g.*, Canby, *The First Amendment Right to Persuade: Access to Radio and Television*, 19 UCLA L. REV. 723, 746–754 (1972).

119. Courts have rejected the premise that broadcast stations are public forums, even if they happen to be state owned. *See* Muir v Alabama Educational Television Comm'n., 688 F.2d 1033 (5th Cir. 1982).

120. W. VAN ALSTYNE, *supra* note 69, at 122, n. 57.

121. T. EMERSON, THE SYSTEM OF FREEDOM OF EXPRESSION 7 (1970).

122. J. MILTON, AREOPAGITICA 59 (W. Haller ed. 1927).

123. This is an internal contradiction. A marketplace theory's goal is truth, yet it simultaneously argues that one can never know the truth. Redish, *The Value of Free Speech*, U. PA. L. REV. 591, 617 (1982).

124. Baker, *Scope of the First Amendment Freedom of Speech*, 25 UCLA L. REV. 964, 967 (1978).

125. Francois, *Media Access: Romance and Reality*, AMERICA, Sept. 22, 1973 at 186.

126. *See, e.g.*, Note, *Regulation of Radio Broadcasting: Competitive Enterprise or Public Utility*? 27 CORNELL L. REV. 249 (1942).

127. Fowler & Brenner, *supra* note 14. In the utopia they propose, the interests of listeners and broadcasters converge to produce services for the benefit of all. *Id.*, at 239.

128. *Id.*, at 254. "Creation of a limited right of access during certain hours on television for individual speakers as well as documentary and entertainment program producers would bring the public forum, long a tradition in American society, to the medium of broadcasting, which has functioned in many ways as the modern equivalent of the soap box in the town square." Thus, even Fowler, a strong proponent of an economic marketplace as the method of regulating (or not regulating) broadcasting, sees problems that an economic marketplace would not solve. Before media ownership concentration was at its present level, Zechariah Chafee noted, "We must do more than remove the discouragements to open discussion. We must exert ourselves to supply active encouragements. . . . We must take affirmative steps to improve the methods by which discussion is carried on." Z. CHAFEE, FREE SPEECH IN THE UNITED STATES 559 (1941). What is needed is an understanding of the "reformist marketplace theory" that acknowledges that the debate is related to people's ability to participate. Baker, *Unreasoned Reasonableness*, 78 N.W.U. L. REV. 937, 944 (1983). The marketplace is dysfunctional when participation is limited.

129. Kahn, *Media Competition in the Marketplace of Ideas*, 39 SYRACUSE L. REV. 737, 738 (1988).

130. *Id.*, at 757. *See also* Barnett, *Newspaper Monopoly and the Law*, 30 J. COM. 72 (1980); Rosse, *The Decline of Direct Newspaper Competition*, 30 J. COM. 65 (1980).

131. Garry, *The First Amendment and Freedom of the Press: A Revised Approach to the Marketplace of Ideas Concept*, 72 MARQUETTE L. REV. 187, 194 (1989).

132. *Id.*, at 742.

133. Rudman, *The Marketplace Model: Fixing Something That's Broken*, BROADCASTING MANAGEMENT/ENGINEERING 82 (Jan. 1989).

134. Taylor, *Public Interest vs. Marketplace*, RADIO WORLD 17 (Apr. 26, 1989).

135. Note, *Broadcasting's Fairness Doctrine: An Illogical Extension of the Red Lion Concept*, 6 U. RICH. L. REV. 448, 453 (1972). Charging a fee for expression of a viewpoint would result in only the views of those with economic means being aired. At the very least, there would be substantial imbalance.

136. Neisser, *Charging for Free Speech: User Fees and Insurance in the Marketplace of Ideas*, 74 GEO. L. J. 257, 279 (1985). Use fee theory holds that when people receive a good for free, they are more inclined to use goods they may not need or want. If a fee is charged, only those who truly want the good will acquire it.

137. *Id.*, 313–315, 329–349. However, Neisser suggests fees might be assessed, provided indigents are exempted. The only way to achieve this would be either by burdensome administration, or through the filing by the applicant of an "affidavit of indigency."

138. Note, *Resolving the Free Speech—Free Press Dichotomy: Access to the Press Through Advertising*, 22 U. FLA. L. REV. 293, 310 (1969). *See also* Martin v City of Struthers, 319 U.S. 141, 143 (1943) (ordinance prohibiting canvassing unconstitutional as applied to person distributing notices of a religious meeting); Bond v Floyd, 385 U.S. 116 (1966) (legislator critical of nation's Vietnam policy could not be denied membership in state House of Representatives).

139. Kahn, *supra* note 129, at 740. In one case, the Court asserted that the marketplace of ideas is the central concept of the first amendment. Dennis v U.S., 341 U.S. 494, 503 (1951).

140. Federal Election Comm'n. v Massachusetts Citizens for Life, 107 S. Ct. 616, 631 (1986).

141. Buckley v Valeo, 424 U.S. 1 (1976).

142. Baker, *supra* note 124, at 971.

143. Paris Adult Theatre v Slaton, 413 U.S. 49, 58 (1972).

144. *See In re* Infinity Broadcasting Corp., *In re* Pacifica Foundation, Inc., *In re* Regents of Univ. of Cal., Memorandum Opinion & Order, 3 FCC Rcd. 930 (1987), cited in Labunski, *supra* note 25, at 220–221.

145. Baker, *supra* note 124, at 973.

146. Hodge would suggest the phrase freedom of communication rather than freedom of expression. He asserts that expression puts too much emphasis on the speakers. Communication implies both speakers and listeners. Hodge, *Democracy and Free Speech: A Normative Theory of Society and Government* in THE FIRST AMENDMENT RECONSIDERED 148, 152 (B. Chamberlain & C. Brown eds. 1982).

147. Kleindienst v Mandel, 408 U.S. 753, 775 (1972) (Marshall, J. dissenting). *See also* Z. CHAFEE, GOVERNMENT AND MASS COMMUNICATIONS 21 (1947) (communication is a two-way process). This approach is the same as that asserted in philosophy of language debates. *See* Chevigny, *Philosophy of Language and Free Expression*, 55 N.Y.U. L. REV. 157, 183 (1980).

148. 1 Stat. 124 (1790).

149. Twentieth Century Music Corp. v Aiken, 422 U.S. 151, 156 (1975).

150. Harper & Row, Publishers, Inc. v Nation Enterprises, Inc., 471 U.S. 539 (1985).

151. The one anomaly to this principle is in the area of local over-the-air television broadcasting, which is required to provide its product to cable

systems whether or not the stations want to. This compulsory copyright provision comes complete with its own schedule for remuneration, preempting the ability of both the broadcast and the cable system to attempt to negotiate a better deal. *See* Goldstein, *Copyright Law and Policy* in 2 NEW DIRECTIONS IN TELECOMMUNICATIONS POLICY 70, 85–87 (P. Newberg ed. 1989).

152. Exemptions do exist to the copyright law, most notably the doctrine of fair use. Copyright Revision Act Sec. 107. Fair use further typifies the preference of one speaker's rights over those of another. Copyright holders do have preference, except in cases where the speaker in opposition makes an adequate claim of fair use, in which case a court must make an ad hoc determination on the merits. For a discussion of fair use, *see* K. MIDDLETON & B. CHAMBERLAIN, THE LAW OF PUBLIC COMMUNICATION 238–251 (1988).

153. FTC v Raladam Co., 283 U.S. 643 (1931) (misleading ads that hurt only consumers beyond FTC jurisdiction).

154. *See, e.g.* the Wheeler-Lea amendments to the Federal Trade Act, 15 U.S.C.A. Sec. 45 (a)(1).

155. 424 U.S. 1 (1976).

156. *Id.* at 20.

157. *Id.* at 48.

158. 47 U.S.C. Sec. 312(a)(7).

159. *See* CBS v FCC, 453 U.S. 367 (1981) (network refusing to sell half-hour time slot during prime time did not provide reasonable access).

160. 47 U.S.C. Sec. 315(b).

161. *See* D. TUCKER, *supra* note 60, at 27; R. DWORKIN, A MATTER OF PRINCIPLE 381–397 (1985).

162. F. SCHAUER, FREE SPEECH: A PHILOSOPHICAL INQUIRY 42 (1982).

163. W. HOCKING, FREEDOM OF THE PRESS 79–134 (1947).

164. 47 CFR 73.658(k).

165. 403 U.S. 15 (1971).

166. Village of Skokie v National Socialist Party, 373 N.E. 2d 21 (1978).

167. Texas v Johnson, 57 USLW 4770 (1989).

168. Polls immediately after the *Johnson* decision indicated overwhelming disagreement with the decision. *See e.g.*, *A Fight for Old Glory*, NEWSWEEK July 3, 1989, p. 18 (71 percent support amendment making flag burning illegal) *and Poll: 69% Want Flag Protected*, USA TODAY June 23, 1989, p. 1A.

169. F. SCHAUER, *supra* note 162.

170. *See* D. TUCKER, *supra* note 60, at 27.

171. R. DWORKIN, *supra* note 161, at 385.

172. J. IIMMERWAHR, J. JOHNSON, & J. DOBLE, THE SPEAKER AND THE LISTENER: A PUBLIC PERSPECTIVE ON FREEDOM OF EXPRESSION 23 (1980).

173. Red Lion Broadcasting v FCC, 395 U.S. 367 (1969).

174. Note, *The Listener's Right to Hear in Broadcasting*, 22 STANFORD L. REV. 863 (1970).

175. *Id.*, at 390.

176. This is the proposition first enunciated by Alexander Meiklejohn. "What is essential is not that everyone shall speak, but that everything worth saying shall be said." A. MEIKLEJOHN, POLITICAL FREEDOM 26 (1965). For criticism of the doctrine's fulfillment of this goal, *see* Chamberlain, *The FCC and the First Principle of the Fairness Doctrine: A History of Neglect and Distortion*, 31 FED. COM. L. J. 361 (1979); F. ROWAN, BROADCAST FAIRNESS (1984).

177. The doctrine has been misunderstood to provide access rights for interest groups. *See, e.g.,* H. DONAHUE, THE BATTLE TO CONTROL BROADCAST NEWS 179 (1989) ("core belief among Fairness Doctrine supporters that each interest group owns a First Amendment right to the airwaves of every broadcaster"). While the doctrine was in effect, broadcasters always had the authority to select who would present various sides of controversial issues. 47 CFR 73.1910 (1985).

178. FCC v Pacifica Foundation, 438 U.S. 726 (1978).

179. *Id.*, at 748.

180. 379 U.S. 536 (1965).

181. J. COHEN & T. GLEASON, SOCIAL RESEARCH IN COMMUNICATION AND LAW 70 (1990).

4 CURRENT REALITIES IMPACTING MEDIA ACCESS

Discussing access in terms of conditions that existed in this country hundreds of years ago, during the framing of the Bill of Rights and its ratification is of little value. Increasingly, conditions of only a decade ago lose meaning in a rapidly changing communications environment. In order to consider free expression opportunities as they exist, it is necessary to consider the current technical, economic, and regulatory conditions. This chapter examines current realities of the communications environment and how they relate to the individual's ability to access it.

TECHNICAL REALITIES

Spectrum scarcity is a concept created more than sixty years ago, when spectrum users were far fewer. A variety of means have been devised for "stretching" the broadcast spectrum to cram ever-more signals into the same spectrum that existed when radio was first used. Technological advances have, for the most part, been able to add segments of the spectrum for broadcast uses.[1] Initially, radio was an amplitude modulated medium that existed only between 500 and 1700 kHz. When the Federal Communications Commission (FCC) added frequency modulated broadcasts, one hundred channels immediately became available in the higher band between 80 and 110 MHz.[2] A similar sort of "band expansion" occurred with the addition of UHF channels to the existing VHF band for television.

Technological advances have also enabled use of less bandwidth per channel. Land mobile services are now capable of carrying eight channels in the 100 kHz that was occupied by only one channel fifty years ago.[3] Accommodating added users by decreasing bandwidth has met with great resistance in at least one case. Consideration had been given to changing the channel spacing for AM stations from 10 to 9 kHz per channel, which would allow twelve additional AM channels, resulting in another potential five hundred stations. Opposition resulted mostly from the fact that all broadcasters then transmitting would need to reconfigure their equipment to adapt to the smaller bandwidth, resulting in great expense (and increased competition).[4]

Another technological advance that increased the number of broadcast spectrum users is the improvement in transmission and reception technology. Multiplexing, allowing for multiple users of the same frequency, has facilitated the doubling of available satellite transponders and allows for the use of sub-carrier services such as Muzak.[5] Transmitters "wander" much less than they did years ago, requiring less separation between channels. Similarly, receivers are now more capable of filtering out unwanted frequencies. An example of the exploitation of these improvements is the "dropping in" of additional FM stations to the FM assignments table.[6] The drop-ins are the result of improved transmitting methods, and have created the potential for hundreds of new FM stations.[7]

Hence, although spectrum scarcity is not a novel concept, its meaning has changed considerably in the twentieth century. Whereas a few hundred stations "crowded" the available spectrum only fifty years ago, now several thousand stations "crowd" that very same spectrum.[8]

Technological advances spawning new communication media may have been the most influential force behind the deregulation movement.[9] This is consistent with thinking that asserts that new media provide a force for undermining state control and authority.[10] If government control is weakened by new media, where better to see this than in regulation of those media themselves?

In addition to the technical concerns for the spectrum, trade issues are involved. Beyond concerns of free expression, "spectrum resource allocation ha[s] a direct effect on our international trade balance in telecommunications equipment and services."[11] It is naive to view spectrum management purely as a technological consideration: trade implications and the value of electromagnetic spectrum make it also an economic consideration.

ECONOMIC REALITIES

Any mass medium is a big business,[12] as electronic communication certainly exemplifies.[13] Broadcast stations are capital intensive, and require huge investments.[14] Television stations customarily sell for tens of millions of dollars[15] and have sold for amounts in excess of one-half billion dollars.[16] Radio stations, somewhat less expensive, often command million dollar price tags, with even the smallest bringing in six figures.[17] "The escalating price of stations, while leveling off recently, is testimony to the confidence of investors in the industry and to recognition that very few good frequencies are ever available."[18] Clearly a portion of the value of the stations is attributable to the reserved frequency they occupy.[19] FCC Chairman Alfred Sikes estimated the value of one block of 200 MHz (less than is currently allocated exclusively to UHF television) could be as high as $100 billion.[20]

Due in part perhaps to the expense associated with station ownership, broadcast properties are owned primarily by large corporations.[21] The majority of broadcast stations are actually owned by someone other than the entity to which the government originally awarded the license.[22] "The government may give the license away initially, but thereafter a free marketplace reigns."[23] This is despite the fact that it is rare for the FCC to revoke or deny renewal of a license.[24] In recent years, mergers, buyouts, and takeovers have increased the concentration of broadcast owners.[25] Concentration of ownership is seen as frustrating to a marketplace of ideas.[26] Two recent regulatory changes have encouraged increased concentration. First, more broadcast properties can now be owned by one entity than was ever possible before. The maximum number of stations that can be owned by any individual or corporation has expanded from twenty-one to 36.[27] Second, individuals and corporations are now able to purchase a station and resell it without the antitrafficking rules that existed in past years, which some speculate has increased the recent station sales activity.[28] The amount spent annually on television station purchases increased 800 percent from 1982 to 1986.[29] In 1986, 145 TV stations were sold, along with 522 FM stations and 617 AM stations.[30]

Despite the increasing cost of broadcast stations and concentration of ownership, evidence strongly suggests that entry into the broadcasting marketplace is easier to achieve economically than entry into the newspaper market.[31] While legal barriers may be greater for entry into the broadcast market, establishing a daily newspaper is "all but an economic impossibility," especially in communities where a daily newspaper already exists.[32] It is the belief of many that "daily newspapers are considered to be 'natural monopolies' in their local markets."[33]

Cable franchise ownership has followed a path similar to broadcast ownership, with ownership increasingly concentrated into fewer hands.[34] Most cable franchise owners, like broadcast property owners, are conglomerates, simply because the cost of cable ownership has become so great.[35] Larger companies can vertically integrate themselves, thus improving their profitability.[36] Vertical integration is also an effective way to discourage competition.[37] Cable television systems are the nearest thing to a perfect monopoly of any media industry.[38] The monopolistic situation is likely to continue, because municipalities receive revenues based on the local cable franchise's revenues: the more the cable company earns, the more the community receives in revenue from franchise fees assessed as a percentage of the system's income. "Monopoly will be tolerated as long as it can be milked."[39]

There are a variety of reasons for the recent attractiveness of broadcast properties to investors. According to investment banker Joel Hartstone, they can be characterized as follows:

1. Ownership is limited by the FCC, therefore competition is limited. Also, since broadcasting does not deal with a "hard" product, increasing profits does not require added investment in raw materials.

2. Stations can be managed by others. Ownership need not be present.

3. Group, decentralized management allows for control.

4. There is a small market for buying and selling. Only a half-dozen companies control all major sales, and the data from all transactions is then made public by the FCC.

5. Financial arrangements offer advantages to investors. An investor may provide up to 75 percent of the value of the station, even if the plant itself is worth less than 10 percent of the station's value.[40]

Point 5 is the most interesting. The FCC does not charge for the use of the spectrum.[41] According to an attorney who frequently deals with broadcast investors, the license represents the lion's share of the value in a communications property.[42] The selling of stations is actually a secondary market for frequency allocation: the equivalent of a "private auction."[43] These limitedly available commodities, combined with the current economy, have attracted much recent activity.[44] It is contended that not charging for spectrum use has actually created the existing scarcity.[45] It is logical to assume that fewer people would actively seek broadcast licenses if the costs of those allocations included a charge for the use of the frequency.

This flurry of activity among buyers and sellers, however, may not result in a broadcast world that is best for either the broadcaster or the listener.[46] Cost-cutting measures have been instituted by all three major television networks in an attempt to streamline operations.[47] In economic terms, the broadcast marketplace does not supply programming to maximize the welfare of the audience.[48]

Despite marketplace rhetoric, a marketplace scheme to valuate the spectrum has never been applied. If the spectrum is to be treated as a market, some determination must be made of the space that exists. However, as has been argued, "deregulatory policy in communications requires that spectrum allocation decisions be made with the explicit goal of encouraging entry, increasing competition, and decreasing the power of currently dominant firms."[49] It has been demonstrated in a variety of contexts that the "lip service" provided by the FCC to the concept of marketplace forces has not, in fact, been a reality. Were it so, the commission would have taken the many opportunities afforded it to expand the number of stations, which it has not, in most cases, elected to do.[50]

Treating the spectrum as a pure marketplace is a gross fallacy. Were this actually done, no government restrictions would exist with respect to what uses might be made of particular frequencies. For example, if broadcasters wanted to transmit television images at 90 MHz (a frequency reserved for FM radio), they should not be precluded from doing so, as is presently the case. The Table of Allocations divides frequencies into more than 450 blocks of communication services.[51] The process of block allocation certainly makes the spectrum familiar to both those who transmit and receive communications, but it also retards innovation and is unresponsive to technological or market changes.[52] There has been some reallocation in "spectrum zoning," allowing certain secondary uses of allocated spectrum, as was done with FM subcarriers.[53]

Not only do restrictions exist between services (such as radio versus television) but additional restrictions exist within designated bands. No commercial broadcaster may use twenty of the one hundred allotted FM

channels (they are reserved for noncommercial use), nor may broadcasters decide it would be in their best interest to have a bandwidth of 0.4
MHz on FM (0.2 MHz is the prescribed bandwidth). In addition, a
broadcaster is proscribed from leasing a portion of his bandwidth to
another party.[54] Finally, and perhaps most important, existing rules limit
the transfer of broadcast rights.[55] Further, a true spectrum marketplace
should have economic incentives to economize use.[56] It is folly to contend
that the government has applied, or intends to apply, free market rules
to the allocation of spectrum space.

Establishing a market for spectrum rights has been discussed for at
least forty years.[57] The numerous criticisms of such an approach can be
summarized as follows:[58]

1. Market allocation would be socially inefficient, due to substan-
    tial existing externalities (primarily between social and private
    value), even when considered on its own terms.[59]

2. The markets in which spectrum users operate are noncompeti-
    tive in nature. Microwave long-distance telephone services may
    compete for spectrum space with other microwave services, such
    as multipoint distribution systems, but they do not compete in
    the marketplace.

3. Major users of the spectrum are government and other public
    agencies. For them to maintain the substantial allocations they
    presently have would require substantial monetary support.
    They would not be able to compete in an equal market.

4. The system would be incapable of achieving broader economic,
    social, and political objectives.

Attempts to apply purely market forces to the broadcast portion of the
spectrum continue to meet with disapproval.[60] In a recent example, the
FCC abandoned a proposal to distribute new radio and television
allocations by lottery, at least in part due to overwhelming opposition
from groups including the National Association of Broadcasters, Federal
Communications Bar Association, Black Media Coalition, and the
Community Broadcasters Association.[61] This despite the fact that the
FCC has had congressional authorization to use lotteries since 1981,[62]
and has conducted more than six hundred lotteries for other services.[63]
Not surprisingly, the finger is often pointed at broadcasters as the force
that most promotes federal regulatory intervention in the broadcasters'
own economic interests.[64]

REGULATORY REALITIES

Broadcasting occupies only a small portion of the available electromagnetic spectrum. Of 17 million authorized transmitting stations in the United States, only 36,000 are for broadcasting and related services.[65] Many more transmitters are authorized for personal (including radio-controlled devices), private land mobile, and industrial services. How much spectrum is dedicated to broadcast uses versus other uses is thus governmental fiat rather than physical law, and is open to periodic review and modification.[66] Frequencies reserved for broadcast use preclude use of that portion of the spectrum for other purposes. Hence, broadcasters lobby against other interests to protect "their" frequencies.[67]

In the developmental days of radio, a decision was made to encourage local broadcasting rather than nationwide broadcast channels. Experiments were authorized with stations using 500 kw of power, ten times the limit eventually established for AM broadcasts.[68] The logic was that by allocating mostly lower powered stations, more stations could be licensed. This was especially true for AM waves, which have a tendency to propagate further at night. Thus the government established its position that more, smaller stations were better for the public interest than fewer, more powerful stations.[69]

A similar situation has recently occurred in television regulatory philosophy. Television was traditionally "full power," with stations allocated according to the Table of Assignments, just as is done with FM radio. In the interest of allowing an increase in available television opportunities, the government established low-power television (LPTV). LPTV is actually nothing new, but simply television operated at lower powers to reach smaller areas.[70] As with AM radio, the lower the power allotment, the greater the number of stations that can be allocated.[71] LPTV stations are "engineered" into the existing scheme of allocations by squeezing stations into areas where they will fit considering existing allocations.[72]

Spectrum management may actually be the cause rather than the solution to any scarcity that exists. Spectrum management policies usually give priority to existing users, requiring new entrants to adjust to the existing environment.[73] The new users may in fact be more efficient users of the spectrum, yet their entry can be prohibited based on the needs of entrenched users. "[T]he relatively deprived users are virtually forced to innovate spectrum-economizing, spectrum-developing technology regardless of its true economic or social merit, whereas those favored with abundant allocations lack any incentive to innovate at all."[74] The

FCC has adopted a policy of awarding licensing preference to "pioneers" who propose innovative communication services or use of technology that improves spectrum efficiency.[75] That telecommunications services that have traditionally been wired communications not requiring any spectrum, are now looking to pioneer preference as a possible alternative to wired circuits is ironic.[76] At the same time, the commission is involved in gradually vacating a portion of the spectrum by encouraging use of nonspectrum media (i.e., wires) for fixed communications.[77]

Trying to shoehorn new technologies into an already-assigned spectrum often results in applying antiquated standards to advanced systems. Digital radio must operate under rules created for analog technology, which fails to take advantage of the technological superiority of the new system.[78] Existing spectrum users resist changes that impinge on them, primarily for economic reasons. Illustrative of the position taken by vested interests in maintaining the status quo is a comment made by AT&T to Congress as it considered "Policy Options for the Spectrum Resource" in 1977.

> The Bell System recognizes that the present process used in the U.S., although imperfect, has not led to chaos, but, in fact, has resulted in the most advanced and extensive use of the radio spectrum. Consequently, changes on purely hypothetical grounds or solely for the sake of change should be avoided. It may be better to merely strengthen the present process where needed than to attempt wholesale changes.[79]

Government discretion alone determines that AM stations occupy 10 kHz of bandwidth each, not some rule of physics. Likewise, no law of physics states that those stations must broadcast only between 500 and 1700 kHz. It is true, however, that some broadcast uses require more bandwidth than others, but the exact proportionality of the difference is disputable. Clearly a TV transmission, which sends video as well as audio, requires more bandwidth than a radio, audio-only signal. The question is whether it requires the equivalent of six hundred AM stations of bandwidth. In other words, the allocation of one TV frequency occupies more than five times the spectrum that is occupied by the *entire* AM band. Situations where the government has attempted to shift spectrum allocation based on predicted usage have been less than prophetic. In the 1980s, bands were shifted to accommodate both direct broadcast satellites (DBS) and cellular telephone. DBS has yet to use its allocated band, while cellular telephone already requires additional allotment.[80] One will never know the demand that would have existed for services whose authorization was denied or delayed by the FCC, such as a new personal radio or air-to-ground telephone service.[81]

While such great disparity between dissimilar services such as audio and video can perhaps be justified, what of the disparity between similar uses? AM and FM broadcasting exist for essentially the same purpose, yet they are not treated similarly. While each has approximately the same number of stations on its band, one FM signal occupies twenty times the bandwidth of one AM signal. The entire AM band actually takes less spectrum space than six FM channels. The assignment of spectrum to its various uses is political. Of all the spectrum assigned for satellite and microwave communication, one-third is reserved for the Department of Defense.[82] This, too, is arbitrary, and obviously unaffected by a marketplace for spectrum.

Interference would seem to be a purely technical question, but this, too, is a regulatory consideration. How much interference can be tolerated is a subjective judgment, subject to increased scrutiny as the spectrum grows more crowded.[83] Some broadcasters fear that as emphasis on the marketplace increases, the government will be willing to tolerate increased interference.[84]

While it is technically possible to transmit a 9 kHz AM signal, regulation and economics have "frozen" the existing system. The bandwidth required for each station and the bandwidth assigned for each purpose are now to a great extent locked in. The furor created by the movement of the FM band, while only a modest investment had been made in transmitters and receivers, attests to the outrage that would occur if bands were suddenly shifted.

An interesting problem, presently before the commission, is high definition television (HDTV). Currently, broadcast television uses a 6 GHz signal to send a conventional audio and video signal. The HDTV systems being proposed cannot be crammed into that "narrow" a frequency.[85] The FCC's advanced television systems committee (chaired by a former FCC chairman) is examining proposals for the new TV system, with a majority of the broadcast interests involved hoping the new system will not cause a realignment of the spectrum.[86] One proposal calls for the HDTV stations to actually use two UHF channels.[87] Other proposals exist, and despite claims that a standard has been established[88] the FCC has set the second quarter of 1993 as its deadline for determining a transmission standard.[89]

New technologies create great difficulty in devising an appropriate regulatory scheme. "As communications technologies have been developed, public policy has lagged far behind."[90] Opening a portion of the spectrum for a new use can take an inordinate amount of time. One prime example is the development of cellular telephone service. The first proceedings were in 1968, yet the first license was not granted until thirteen years later.[91] Similarly, HDTV is experiencing some of the same confusion. While the FCC's advanced television advisory committee worked on details, Congress introduced the Advanced Television Standards Act of 1990. The bill dictated a number of specifics required of the commission and the NTIA.[92] Digital audio broadcasting's (DAB) lagging development is due at least in part to the uncertainty of spectrum assignment. The FCC granted a one-year experimental testing of one DAB system in 1991.[93] At least ten different systems have been outlined requiring from 0.2 to 32 MHz of spectrum.[94] Germany is planning to use VHF Channel 12, Russia proposes using a portion of the FM band, and the United States seems to be leaning toward a higher-frequency S-band, which may not be technically adequate.[95] The matter is far from decided, however, as broadcasters themselves disagree over the suitability of the frequency. As one broadcaster stated, the National Association of Broadcasters' endorsement of L-band has created "a false perception of industry unity."[96] In addition, the U.S. Air Force adamantly opposes reassigning the L-band, claiming it needs the frequencies for flight testing telemetry.[97] Part of the problem may be that technical laymen, such as judges, legislators, and regulatory agencies, fail to see the potential of emerging technologies, and encumber them with regulation based on their own limited vision.[98] As one recent major government study stated:

> Rapid change requires a continuing evaluation of government's proper telecommunications and information role. Yesterday's institutional arrangements have lost and will continue to lose relevance in the face of technical and commercial developments. Domestically, arrangements dating from 1934 and passage of the Communications Act may handicap the introduction of technology, as occurred with cellular mobile telephone and cable television service. Today, a judicial regulatory bottleneck is effecting the wider and more effective distribution of information age benefits.[99]

Traditionally, the Supreme Court has suggested that different media are entitled to different regulatory approaches. The Court frequently attempts to determine what a new technology mostly resembles in order to function from an existing regulatory framework. This is not a novel approach. Telegraph law was modeled on law that had developed in the nineteenth century to regulate railroads.[100] The Court continues to do this. In *Preferred*, the concurrence stated, "the Court must determine whether the characteristics of cable television make it sufficiently analogous to another medium to warrant application of an already existing standard or whether those characteristics require a new standard."[101] Rapid technological changes, however, call into question the premise of applying the First Amendment differently to different media.[102]

If regulatory differences have been based on the difference between print and broadcast, what happens as the new technologies confuse the line dividing them? Pool calls this blurring of lines between media a "convergence of modes."[103] Presently the *Wall Street Journal* and *USA Today* use satellite communications to relay their pages to decentralized printers across the country.[104] Since these papers use electromagnetic frequencies to transmit their information, shouldn't they be subject to similar rules as broadcasters? If it is argued that the spectrum belongs to the public and that its use by private parties obliges them to some public service standard, why aren't all private users of the spectrum, including microwave, mobile telephone, and others, also obligated? The FCC has attempted to distinguish between broadcast and nonbroadcast uses of the spectrum, but it is a difficult and confusing process. For example, multipoint distribution systems (MDS)[105] have been regulated as common carriers, and as such, are not subject to many broadcast regulations. On the other hand, direct broadcast satellites are considered a hybrid of broadcast and nonbroadcast and are subject to some broadcast regulation.[106] The situation is further complicated because both MDS and DBS are microwave systems that can or have been used for pay television. To the receiver, the only difference may be the azimuth of the antenna. This has caused the commission to reexamine its position on what constitutes a broadcast service.[107]

The line between broadcast and nonbroadcast service is not even clear when conventional broadcast signals are involved. Television stations have already begun transmitting newspaper-like data, called teletext, in several markets. Thus a broadcast frequency is being used for what is basically a print service. The information appears on a television screen as words that can be "paged" forward or back, skipped, or stored for later reading.[108] Should teletext be subject to print or broadcast regulation? As new technologies continue to develop, the boundaries dividing media become more and more difficult to define.[109]

SUMMARY

The allotment of spectrum is a valuable commodity. Fortunately, our ability to utilize it more efficiently has constantly increased. Technological advancements improved methods of compressing signals into smaller bandwidths with "cleaner" signals. Receivers capable of separating signals more effectively diminish the need for excessive separations in distance and/or frequency between stations. Techniques such as multiplexing and subcarrier transmissions have put multiple transmissions on frequencies that once carried but one signal.

While transmission and reception technology has improved, demand for spectrum use has increased at least proportionately. Frequencies opened by the Federal Communications Commission for a variety of services are quickly requested, especially in larger markets. In some cases (such as cellular telephone), entire bandwidths have been filled and requests have been filed for increased allocations.

Despite an increasing number of stations on the air, the purchase prices of radio and television stations continue to be above the actual value of the assets. Spectrum users pay nothing to the federal government, yet the value of the frequency allocation is tremendous. As in most other cases, the degree to which the principle applies is proportional to the market size.

Federal regulations attempting to apply market economics to the spectrum have been half-hearted at best. Traditional rationales for distinguishing between communications media are suffering because advancing technologies outdate the regulatory schemes. As lines between various media become increasingly blurred, it will be increasingly difficult to apply differing regulatory analysis based on the type of media.

Chapter 5 examines what opportunities currently exist for individuals desiring a forum for self-expression. With the increase in media channels, is there a concomitant increase in the available opportunities for self-expression? What forums exist, in both the traditional and nontraditional media, that provide access opportunities?

NOTES

1. Comprehensive Policy Review of Use and Management of the Radio Frequency Spectrum, 54 Fed. Reg. 50694, 50703 (1989) (NTIA Request for Comments Dec. 8, 1989) [hereinafter cited as NTIA REVIEW].

2. Originally, FM was given fewer channels, at a lower frequency. To accommodate television, the band was moved higher. To console angry FM

proponents, the bandwidth was doubled. *See* E. KRASNOW & L. LONGLEY, THE POLITICS OF BROADCAST REGULATION 107–117 (1978).

3. NTIA REVIEW, *supra* note 1, at 50698.

4. *Radio Back to Status Quo on 10 kHz*, BROADCASTING, Aug. 10, 1981, at 28–29.

5. I. POOL, TECHNOLOGIES OF FREEDOM 37 (1983).

6. FM stations are allocated according to the Code of Federal Regulations, which contains a table of FM assignments. The channels, occupied or not, are designated to certain markets based on FCC estimations of signal interference from other transmitters.

7. *FCC Releases Revised List for Docket 80–90*, BROADCASTING, July 30, 1984, at 36.

8. "[P]hysical-technical 'saturation' has frequently been alleged in the past, only to be erased by subsequent technical advances." H. LEVIN, THE INVISIBLE RESOURCE 18 (1971).

"Spectrum occupancy" is determined by the NTIA using the radio spectrum measurement system (RSMS), a sophisticated field unit that monitors most of the usable spectrum. Unlike FCC monitoring systems, RSMS is fully automated and capable of more thorough studies. Unfortunately, NTIA has only one such vehicle for the entire United States. NTIA REVIEW, *supra* note 1, at 50704.

9. R. HOROWITZ, THE IRONY OF REGULATORY REFORM 251 (1989).

10. M. KATSH, THE ELECTRONIC MEDIA AND THE TRANSFORMATION OF LAW 114 (1989).

11. NATIONAL TELECOMMUNICATIONS AND INFORMATION ADMINIS-TRATION, TELECOM 2000: CHARTING THE COURSE FOR A NEW CENTURY 15 (1988) [hereinafter cited as TELECOM 2000].

12. Communications businesses today employ more than two million people and generate nearly $300 billion in annual revenues. Symons, *The Communications Policy Process* in 1 NEW DIRECTIONS IN TELECOMMUNICA-TIONS POLICY 275, 276 (P. Newberg ed. 1989). This is quite different from the conditions that existed in the eighteenth century. Chafee asserts freedom of the press was established when the press was an individual medium, not an industry for profit. Z. CHAFEE, GOVERNMENT AND MASS COMMUNICATION 15 (1947).

13. Radio equipment shipments for the United States in 1988 were valued at $54 billion, and is only a portion of spectrum-related industry (the figure includes consumers' purchases of radio and TV receivers as well as equipment used by the stations themselves). Local exchange carriers (telephone companies) added plant valued at $18 billion. NTIA REVIEW, *supra* note 1, at 50694.

14. *Attractiveness of Broadcast Properties Comes at a Price*, TELEVISION/RADIO AGE, July 21, 1986, at 30.

15. This figure represents conventional television stations. It is asserted that low-power television stations can be established for as little as $50,000. Atkin, *The Low Power Elite*, TELECOMMUNICATIONS POLICY 357, 358 (Dec.

1987). A more realistic figure has been stated as $300,000. S. HEAD & C. STERLING, BROADCASTING IN AMERICA 204 (1990).

16. *KTLA to Change Hands in Largest Station Sale Ever*, BROADCAST-ING, April 4, 1983, at 131.

17. *Station Acquisitions Brisk and Prices are High*, TELEVISION/RADIO AGE, July 21, 1986, at 30.

18. Labunski, *May It Rest in Peace: Public Interest and Public Access in the Post-Fairness Doctrine Era*, 11 HASTINGS COMM/ENT L. J. 219, 271 (1989).

19. One estimate is that less than half of a station's value can be attributed to physical assets. Communications Transfer Fee Act of 1987: Hearings on S. 1935 before the Senate Comm. on Commerce, Science and Transportation, 100th Cong., 2d Sess. (April 27, 1988) (statement of Charles H. Kaldec at 59).

20. Emerging Technologies Act of 1989: Hearings on H.R. 2965 before the Subcom. on Telecommunications and Finance of the House Comm. on Energy and Commerce, Nov. 2, 1989 (prepared statement of Alfred Sikes, at 11).

21. *Moms-and-Pops Out of TV Ownership Picture*, ADVERTISING AGE, Feb. 9, 1987, at S8.

22. Estimates are that 65 percent of commercial television stations are owned by someone other than the original licensee. Only 25 percent of commercial radio stations are estimated to be in the original licensee's posses-sion. Spectrum Auctions: FCC Proposals for the Airwaves: Hearings before the Subcomm. on Telecommunications, Consumer Protection and Finance of the House Committee on Energy and Commerce, 99th Cong., 2d Sess. (Oct. 1, 1986) (testimony of Mark Fowler, at 9).

23. L. POWE, AMERICAN BROADCASTING AND THE FIRST AMENDMENT 201 (1987).

24. Note, *The Recognition of Legitimate Renewal Expectations in Broad-cast Licensing*, 58 WASH. U.L.Q. 409 (1980). From 1934 to 1987, only 141 stations lost their licenses. S. HEAD & C. STERLING, *supra* note 15, at 427.

25. *FCC to Applicants: Hurry Up and Wait*, BROADCASTING, Feb. 5, 1990, at 46.

26. Garry, *The First Amendment and Freedom of the Press: A Revised Approach to the Marketplace of Ideas Concept*, 72 MARQ. L. REV. 187, 189, 192–196 (1989).

27. *12-12-12: Fait Accompli*, BROADCASTING, Dec. 31, 1984, at 35–38.

28. *Gauging the Growth in Station Prices*, BROADCASTING April 21, 1986, at 84.

29. *Transfer of TV Properties Went From $750 Million to $6 Billion in Four Years*, TELEVISION/RADIO AGE, June 9, 1986, at 61.

30. *Station and Cable Trading 1986: A Look Back at the Fifth Estate's Record Sales Year*, BROADCASTING, Feb. 9, 1987, 51–91, at 55.

31. Wirth, *Economic Barriers to Entering Media Industries in the United States* in 9 COMMUNICATION YEARBOOK 423–442 (M. McLaughlin ed. 1986).

32. *Id.*, at 441. *See also*, L. POWE, *supra* note 23, at 204–206.

33. J. BUSTERNA, DAILY NEWSPAPER CHAINS AND THE ANTITRUST LAWS 25 (Journalism Monographs 110, 1989).

34. *Brokers See Slow But Steady Cable Sales for 1990*, BROADCASTING, Feb. 5, 1990, at 44; Chan-Olmstead & Littman, *Antitrust and Horizontal Mergers in the Cable Industry*, J. MEDIA ECON. 3 (Fall 1988).

35. The industry norm for determining the sale price of a cable system is now $1,500 per subscriber. *Station and Cable Trading, supra* note 30, at 90.

36. *NCTA Study: Vertical Integration Positive*, BROADCASTING, June 12, 1989, at 33.

37. R. PICARD, MEDIA ECONOMICS 74 (1989).

38. *Id.*, at 77.

39. E. DIAMOND & N. SANDLER, TELECOMMUNICATIONS IN CRISIS 36 (1983).

40. Nicoletti, *Radio Station Returns Get High Ratings from Investors*, BROADCASTING Feb. 23, 1987, at 24. *See also supra* note 19.

41. The government now charges a filing fee, but these amounts are supposedly tied to the costs of administering the license. The charges are not associated with the relative worth of any particular portion of the spectrum.

42. Tillotson, *A Lender's Guide to Broadcasting Stations*, BROADCASTING, April 27, 1987, at 22.

43. NTIA REVIEW, *supra* note 1, at 50702.

44. *Expected Changes in the Economy Set Stage for Aggressive TV Selling*, TELEVISION/RADIO AGE, Feb. 16, 1987, at 14.

45. I. POOL, *supra* note 5, at 141; L. POWE, *supra* note 23.

46. *Current Merger Activity Threatens Financial Stability, Innovation by Broadcasters*, TELEVISION/RADIO AGE, April 14, 1986, at 73.

47. *TV Networks Enter New Cost-Control Era*, BROADCASTING, March 2, 1987, at 70–71.

48. Brennan, *Economic Efficiency and Broadcast Content Regulation*, 35 FED. COM. L. J. 117, 129 (1983).

49. Cornell & Webbink, *The Present Direction of the FCC: An Appraisal*, 73 AM. ECONOMIC REV. 194 (May 1983).

50. *Id.* The authors suggest reduction of channel spacing, new classes of FM stations, VHF drop-ins, low power, MDS, and DBS allocations as examples of the FCC eliminating or impeding new entrants to the spectrum.

51. 47 CFR Sec. 2.106 (1984).

52. NTIA REVIEW, *supra* note 1, at 50697.

53. Webbink, *Radio Licenses and Frequency Spectrum Use Property Rights*, COM. & L. 3, 10 (June 1987).

54. For example, what if a television licensee wished to lease his vertical blanking interval to a local newspaper for its use to provide text services? *See*

Watts, *A Major Issue of the 1980s: New Communication Tools* in THE FIRST AMENDMENT RECONSIDERED 181–193, at 186 (B. Chamberlain & C. Brown eds. 1982).

55. These examples are summarized from Devany, Eckert, Meyers, O'Hara, & Scott, *A Property System Approach to the Electromagnetic Spectrum*, 21 STANFORD L. REV. 1499 (1969).

56. Levin, *Spectrum Allocation Without Market*, 60 AM. ECONOMIC REV. 209 (May 1970); I. POOL, *supra* note 5, at 140; NTIA REVIEW, *supra* note 1, at 50701.

57. The earliest reference uncovered was Herzel, *Public Interest and the Market in Color Television Regulation*, 9 UNIV. CHICAGO L. REV. 802 (1951).

58. Melody, *Radio Spectrum Allocation: Role of the Market*, 70 AM. ECONOMIC REV. 393, 394–395 (May 1980).

59. Coase states that "[i]f we try to imagine the property rights system that would be required and the transactions that would have to be carried out to assure that anyone who propagated an idea or proposal for reform received the value of the good it produced or had to pay compensation for the harm that resulted, it is easy to see that in practice there is likely to be a good deal of 'market failure.'" Coase, *The Market for Goods and the Market for Ideas*, 64 AM. ECONOMICS REV. 384, 389 (May 1974). Coase was speaking not of the spectrum but of the broader ideas market. Still, the principle applies.

60. *But see* TELECOM 2000, *supra* note 11, at 10 ("Our fundamental national economic policy favoring competitive solutions is increasingly relevant.")

61. Carter, *FCC Seeks to Prevent Abuses*, RADIO WORLD, June 13, 1990, at 8.

62. The Omnibus Budget Reconciliation Act of 1981, Pub. L.No. 97–35, 95 Stat. 736–737 (1981).

63. Webbink, *supra* note 53, at 22. Lotteries have been conducted for LPTV, paging systems, and cellular radio.

64. *See e.g.*, H. LEVIN, *supra* note 8; B. OWEN, ECONOMICS AND FREEDOM OF EXPRESSION (1975); R. NOLL, M. PECK, & J. MCGOWAN, ECONOMIC ASPECTS OF TELEVISED REGULATION (1973).

65. S. HEAD & C. STERLING, BROADCASTING IN AMERICA 53 (4th ed. 1982).

66. Spectrum is periodically reallocated to accommodate increased needs by certain users. For examples, radio astronomy was given a channel previously allocated to UHF television, and a number of UHF channels were lost due to increased need for land-mobile communications. S. HEAD & C. STERLING, *supra* note 15, at 67. The House Commerce Committee approved a bill to reallocate 200 MHz of spectrum from government to private use. The FCC supported the bill, the NTIA opposed it. *Spectrum Bill Clears, But Meets Opposition*, RADIO WORLD, July 25, 1990, at 2.

67. *See, e.g., Broadcast Service Loses Out to Land Mobile*, BROADCAST-ING, June 3, 1985, at 34.

68. C. STERLING & J. KITTROSS, STAY TUNED 155 (1978).

69. Of course, 50 kw "clear channels were established, but they were less powerful than the 500 kw tested, and were the exception among stations and frequencies. Of the available frequencies for AM, fewer than one-third were reserved for Class I-A "clears." Using current figures, the Class I-A AMs account for less than 1 percent of all licensed AM stations. *See* BROADCAST-ING YEARBOOK.

70. *LPTV: Still Afloat After a Rough Five Years*, BROADCASTING, Sept. 9, 1985, at 32.

71. LPTV could conceivably be the opportunity for individual access. At least one station in Buffalo, N.Y., has attempted to provide just such an opportunity. Biel, *Empowering the People*, LPTV REPORT Oct. 1989, p. 1. *See infra* chapter five.

72. NTIA REVIEW, *supra* note 1, at 50700.

73. *Id.*, at 50704.

74. H. LEVIN, *supra* note 8, at 3.

75. J. Gross, *Pioneer Preference Approved*, RADIO WORLD, June 26, 1991, at 3.

76. K. Killette, *FCC Helps Wireless "Innovators"*, COMM. WEEK, April 15, 1991, at 29.

77. L. Felker, *FCC Works Spectrum Shift*, RADIO WORLD, May 1991, at 12.

78. Jackson, *Use and Management of the Spectrum Resource* in 1 NEW DIRECTIONS IN TELECOMMUNICATIONS POLICY (P. Newberg ed. 1989).

79. Jackson, *Reactions to the Spectrum Options Paper* in PROCEEDINGS OF THE SIXTH ANNUAL TELECOMMUNICATIONS POLICY RESEARCH CONFER-ENCE 375, 377 (H. Dordick ed. 1979).

80. NTIA REVIEW, *supra* note 1, at 50705–50706.

81. Webbink, *supra* note 53, at 23.

82. J. WICKLEIN, ELECTRONIC NIGHTMARE 9 (1979).

83. *Demand for Spectrum Space Forces FCC to Modify Attitude Toward Interference*, TELEVISION/RADIO AGE, Aug. 15, 1983, at 90.

84. Taylor, *Public Interest vs. Marketplace*, RADIO WORLD, April 26, 1989, at 17.

85. NTIA REVIEW, *supra* note 1, at 50695.

86. Baer, *New Communications Technologies and Services* in 2 NEW DIRECTIONS IN TELECOMMUNICATIONS POLICY 139, 156–161 (P. Newberg ed. 1989).

87. *Broadcasters Ask for HDTV Inquiry*, BROADCASTING, Feb. 23, 1987, at 46–47.

88. *See, e.g., New TV Standards Chosen*, NEW YORK TIMES, March 22, 1990, at D-2.

89. *Where Things Stand*, BROADCASTING, April 2, 1990, at 35, 36.

90. Watts, *supra* note 54, at 184. *See also* Baer, *supra* note 86, at 148. ("Regulation generally is more effective in stable industries than in those where technologies and markets are rapidly changing.")

91. NTIA REVIEW, *supra* note 1, at 50696, n. 12.

92. Felker, *HDTV Landscape May See Change*, TV TECHNOLOGY, July 1990, at 11.

93. F. Beacham, *Westwood To Test L-Band DAB*, RADIO WORLD, June 26, 1991, at 1.

94. *DAB Scoreboard*, RADIO WORLD, July 10, 1991, at 22.

95. J. Gross, *Does the L Stand for Lonely?* RADIO WORLD, Aug. 7, 1991, at 4. Since 1991 the U.S. government now endorses S-Band, rather than L-Band, for DAB.

96. J. Gross, *NAB DAB Stand Fuels Battle*, RADIO WORLD, July 10, 1991, at 14 (quoting Randy Odeneal of Sconnix Broadcasting).

97. S. Crowley, *Air Force Takes Aim at L-Band*, RADIO WORLD, June 26, 1991, at 23.

98. I. POOL, *supra* note 5, at 7.

99. TELECOM 2000, *supra* note 11, at 7.

100. I. POOL, *supra* note 5, at 91–100. *Accord* TELECOM 2000, *supra* note 11, at 9. ("Analogies exist between our modern telecommunications infrastructure and the transportation systems of the industrial age.")

101. Los Angeles v Preferred Communications, 476 U.S. 488, 496 (1986) (Blackmun, J., concurring).

102. Watts, *supra* note 54, at 182.

103. I. POOL, *supra* note 5, at 23, 39–42.

104. J. DOMINICK, THE DYNAMICS OF MASS COMMUNICATION 189 (1987).

105. MDS is a system for transmitting microwave signals to subscribers within about a thirty mile radius. MDS systems typically send subscription services such as HBO or Showtime without the expense associated with connecting cable. L. SINGLETON, TELECOMMUNICATIONS IN THE INFORMATION AGE 71–78 (1986).

106. Hammond, *To Be or Not To Be: FCC Regulation of Video Subscription Technologies*, 35 CATH. U.L. REV. 737 (1986).

107. *Id.*, at 750.

108. For a brief explanation of teletext, *see* L. SINGLETON, *supra* note 105, at 133–141.

109. Compaine, *The Expanding Base of Media Competition*, J. COM. 81 (Summer 1985); Baer, *supra* note 86, at 151.

5   ACCESS ALTERNATIVES

A variety of means exist by which individuals may have an opportunity to practice self-realization through free expression. This chapter analyzes existing means in terms of whether they provide adequate opportunities, how they are utilized now, and how they may be utilized in the future.

CABLE ACCESS

One of the first reported uses of cable access was a system in Dale City, Virginia, begun in 1968.[1] In 1970, a prototypical system established by the New York City Board of Estimates became the first cable access channel required by a governmental agency.[2] Although the New York system does quite well by most standards, the promising start provided in the nation's largest market was not repeated in most other communities.

The movement for cable access was fueled when, in 1972, the Federal Communications Commission (FCC) required that all cable systems in the top one hundred markets provide access channels for their communities.[3] This requirement was pared back significantly when the FCC decided that only those cable systems with 3,500 or more subscribers were required to provide access, and that different access channels no longer had to be provided for government, educational institutions, and the public, but that a single channel could be used to accommodate all.[4] This "taxation by regulation" was in exchange for the government's willingness to let cable grow.[5] Later that same decade, these minimal access requirements were eliminated when the Supreme Court decided that requirement of access channels went beyond the jurisdiction given the FCC by the Communications Act.[6] As a national requirement, cable access existed fewer than eight years. Although the number of cable subscribers, the average number of channels per system, and overall revenues for cable increased, there has been little reference to public access in the popular media.[7]

The extent to which the federal requirement of cable access was enforced while in effect remains in question. According to one source, only 100 of the 750 cable systems in the top one hundred markets had access channels when the requirement was deleted.[8] Communities unaware of the requirement, or choosing not to press for it, saw the conversion of access channels to other uses. Further, a majority of cable systems in the 1970s were not capable of providing more than twelve channels.[9] Thus, cable operators looking for channels to place new services, such as pay cable, local origination,[10] and newly constructed television stations (that fell within the cable company's market, requiring that they be carried) were less enthusiastic about providing public access. FCC figures for 1981 indicate that at least 75 percent of the cable systems in operation at the time provided *no* access channels for government, educational, or public use.[11] A 1984 study put the extent of cable systems offering public access as only 10 percent.[12]

Despite these problems, there are isolated examples of cable access success. As any issue of *Community Television Review* will attest, cable systems in communities large and small have experienced isolated successes in access programming. Some of the more noteworthy examples of cable access success have included:

East Lansing, Michigan: Thirty-five to forty hours per week were programmed on the access channel, with need for a second. In addition, four educational access channels, a municipal channel, and a library channel were all active.[13] Weekly viewership ranges as high as 75 percent of the cable audience.[14]

Encino, California: Coming on line in 1980 (after the elimination of federally mandated access channels), the Encino access program showed great promise. In the first few months of operation, more than two hundred people had been waiting in line to participate in training workshops. More than eight hundred people have completed the *nine hours* of training Valley Cable requires.[15]

Knoxville, Tennessee: Fifty hours per week of access programming.[16]

Bloomington, Indiana: Sixty-eight hours per week of access programming, with little of the repetition customary with access channels.[17]

Twenty to twenty-five of the programs each month were new productions. Surveys conducted in Bloomington show great interest. More than 50 percent of the area's cable subscribers reported they had watched the access channel. More than one-third of the subscribers claimed they watched the City Council meetings on a regular basis, demonstrating an interest in local issues, and a surprising 38 percent cited the access programming as the reason for subscribing to cable.[18]

Austin, Texas: More than nine hundred hours of programming in 1980. Thirteen percent of that programming concerned minority affairs.[19] In 1986, candidates for city council appeared in and/or produced at least twenty public access programs before the election.[20] Austin also provides an excellent example of discussion on controversial issues. "Let the People Speak" host Trella Laughlin has received death threats after airing shows on apartheid, the sanctuary movement, and police brutality of young blacks.[21]

Grand Rapids, Michigan: Approximately four hundred people pay $10 per year for the privilege of participating in public access. In one year, 2,829 hours of programming was aired on the access channel, very little of which was repeated programs (only 310 hours). Of the more than 2,500 hours of original programming produced, only 410 hours were produced by the station's staff. Of the total, 998 hours were programmed public affairs.[22]

Berks County, Pennsylvania: Forty-three different community groups had a monthly program seen by residents in Reading and the surrounding county in 1987. The station averages seventeen hours per week of live programming, all of which affords viewers the opportunity to call in and ask questions of the presenters. In June, 1987, the station received 230 such phone calls (lower than during the winter). Approximately 75 percent of the programming is issue-oriented. One such example is "Inside City Hall," which each week features a different city official speaking and answering questions. The program generates a large percentage of the interactive telephone calls.[23]

New York, New York: One of the best known public access programs is "Paper Tiger." In the first four years, more than sixty original half-hour programs were produced. Originating with media critic Herb Schiller paging through a Sunday *New York Times*, the program has evolved into an irreverent and illuminating look at media. Topics have been diverse: from stereotyping in the media to the breakup of AT&T.[24] Manhattan Cable was carrying 150 hours of public access programming per week in 1987, up from only 20 hours per week in 1971.[25]

Houston, Texas: The public access channel provides the only TV programming in Vietnamese for the city's hundreds of families relocated there.[26]

St. Johnsbury, Vermont: Teenagers out of school and work have produced programs on teen unemployment, vandalism, and alienation, to name only a few subjects. The Gray Panthers are also active participants in public access, and there is frequent interaction via telephone.[27]

Also cited as success stories for cable access have been the channels in Madison and Sun Prairie, Wisconsin; Kettering, Ohio; Rome, Georgia; Columbus, Indiana; Dubuque, Iowa; and Marin County, San Diego and Hayward, California.[28] While these few examples do not demonstrate that cable access channels have been universally successful, they serve to demonstrate that successful access channels have caught on, in small communities and major metropolitan areas, and have dealt with issues of substance.[29] Cable access "has become institutionalized in some markets, while in others it has remained a thorn in the side of cable operators."[30] The belief that cable access has been unsuccessful is an overstatement, based on lack of support from local cable franchisees,[31] inadequate time given to access channels to develop a base of both producers and viewers,[32] expectation of production values similar to those on commercial entertainment programs,[33] and antiquated notions of the number of viewers a program must collect before it is considered a value (a holdover from a broadcasting approach, rather than a narrowcasting approach,[34] that would seem more appropriate to cable communication).[35] A channel watched at least once a week by 18 percent of the community[36] may not be adequate by commercial television standards, but in fact appears to be quite successful for discussion of issues of community interest. A better evaluation results from considering whether the hundreds of people who participate in access programs monthly in each of these communities would have any other viable means of expression available to them. A variety of community groups have continued interest in public access, and would like to see its expansion.[37]

In many communities, cable access has not been given the time necessary for it to be discovered as a viable medium. A survey conducted in Milwaukee showed that a significantly higher percentage of the population was aware of public access in those areas of the city where cable had existed for more than five years than in areas where the system was new (64 percent versus 36 percent).[38] Consistently, viewing was higher where the systems were "mature."[39] It takes "a few years" of public relations work before people become aware of the system and its potential.[40] In 1970, cable access was afforded local political candidates in Waianae, Hawaii. While only 28 percent of those surveyed watched at least one of the ten programs, almost everyone who knew of the programs watched at least one.[41] "While critics point out that viewing levels for such programs are often low, defenders respond with the argument that a program does not have to attract a large audience to be effective. Many elections are relatively close, involving a relatively small number of voters."[42] Although usually cablecast on government rather than public access channels, city council meetings have often served as examples that audiences can be developed over time for issues of public import. A survey in Rockford, Illinois, showed that more than 46 percent of the community watched some of the meetings, and more than 70 percent said they would tune in again.[43] A similar study conducted in Wichita, Kansas, demonstrated not only a 65 percent viewership,[44] but a diverse audience as well. Viewership of the televised meetings had no correlation with any measure of socioeconomic status.[45]

Some argue that the underutilization of existing cable public access channels is proof that no need for public access exists, but that argument is fallacious. First, any new means of communication needs time to be discovered. The invention of radio preceded the first commercial radio station in this country by more than a decade. Second, cable access may not be as unattended as once thought.[46] Third, when viewed as a free speech right, what relevance does the number of users have to its protection? Fourth, the fact that affirmative provisions of free speech via public access are lacking may, in and of itself, retard interest in such opportunities. Free speech attitudes "are influenced by the incentives and obstacles embodied in society's structure and by the values and messages that the structure symbolically proclaims."[47] There is increasing evidence that more "mainstream" communicators are seeing cable access as a viable means of promoting one's message.[48]

Other than concerns that cable access is underutilized, complaints stem from its effectiveness in allowing unpopular viewpoints to be aired. Kansas City has received a certain degree of notoriety for the Ku Klux Klan's use of the cable access channel.[49] The KKK program, "Race and Reason," was seen in 55 cities,[50] and the group is still contacting additional cable systems.[51] Although many cable managers may prefer not to air the programs, they see it as their obligation to do so. Kansas City reinstated its access channel after attempting to prevent KKK programming by deleting the channel.[52] Some cable systems have implemented, or are considering, a requirement that access programming be locally produced, preempting programs produced by national organizations and cablecast at the request of local representatives.[53]

It may in fact be that cable access opportunities are the ultimate free expression vehicle in those communities where it is available and viable. The channel does not consume valuable spectrum and is comparatively inexpensive to operate. Questions of viewership levels, while relevant for discussions of free speech as a means of self-government, are unimportant when free expression is valued for self-realization. Some who oppose cable access channel requirements do so because they mistakenly see the goal of the channels as increasing diversity rather than providing a means for self-fulfillment.[54] Cable access is well suited to this value because "public access is designed less to be seen than experienced."[55] The dynamics of a community may be most relevant in determining the vitality of cable access.[56] One study determined that cable access centers were most likely to be extensively used in communities where the access center was a precondition of the cable system's franchise, and the center had a paid director.[57] The nation's first cable system to serve an entire rural county boasts access channel weekly viewership of 63 percent of cable subscribers.[58] A survey of access viewers showed 60 percent had been involved in, or knew someone involved in, a program, and 70 percent supported the twenty-five cent monthly fee to finance the channel.[59] The cable system's commitment included regularly scheduling the programs, a full-time production manager, and program schedule information in local TV listings.[60] Access channels seem to have been used by communities to the extent individuals have expressed interest, and for the purposes they have deemed appropriate. "Public access has been analogized to an electronic soap box, a modern town square, free-form television, the electronic parallel to the printed leaflet, an apartment building's lobby TV monitor, the anti-channel, spinach and Latin lessons, and Johann Gutenberg's printing press. Public access is all of these."[61] The diverse characterizations of access's utility and function is due, in large part, to the diversity of uses found for access in those communities where cable systems and citizens have allowed channels to exist and prosper. The existence of cable access channels should be seen as a limited public forum, existing for the people within the community to use for noncommercial purposes.[62]

Although cable shows tremendous promise, cable access opportunities cannot be seen as the universal solution to the need for access opportunities as once believed.[63] Public access channels are no longer a federal requirement for franchising.[64] Further, cable access is available only in those areas wired for cable. The most optimistic of estimates predict cable penetration will never exceed two-thirds of American homes.[65]

This still leaves more than 30 percent of the nation without public access. This optimistic estimate also ignores the fact that more than three thousand of the existing cable systems in the United States originate no local programming[66] and that only about one-half of those that do originate programming provide public access channels.[67] This translates to approximately 1,500 cable systems providing public access channels,[68] which is less than 20 percent of the total systems.

COMMUNITY RADIO

A variety of not-for-profit stations exist, or have existed, across the nation, known as community radio stations.[69] These stations are operated to provide an alternative listening choice for local listeners,[70] but they also provide an opportunity for individuals to air their opinions. As one practitioner stated, "[d]ifferences of opinion must find a new medium."[71] Many of these stations were inaugurated on the FM band, because FM has spectrum reserved for not-for-profit stations, but with increased interest in FM, fewer frequencies are available in the noncommercial FM allocation for community stations.[72] With declining interest in AM broadcasting, AM frequencies could become available in a number of communities for just such stations.

Costs for community radio are relatively low, certainly in comparison with television stations. "A community station which goes off the air or loses momentum is viewed as a failure. . . . But unlike television, the stakes in radio are low."[73]

CITIZENS BAND RADIO

A "citizens band" was created by the Federal Communications Commission in 1947.[74] The service was, for the most part, underutilized until the commission made adjustments to the band in 1958. Within two years of the change, 100,000 applications for citizens band licenses had been filed.[75]

Used mostly as a means of locating state police on interstate highways, citizens band (CB) affords individuals the opportunity for low-cost, short-distance two-way communication. CB enjoyed a surge of popularity in the 1970s, due mostly to the oil embargo and the imposition of the 55 mile per hour speed limit.[76] Truckers anxious to cut their travel time used the radios to pass along information about available fuel and speeding traps. Passenger car drivers joined the conversations in increasing numbers. By 1976, almost as many CBs were sold each year as television sets.[77] Applications were arriving at the commission at an incredible rate. In January 1973, 26,682 applications were received. In January 1975, the number was 79,375. By January 1976, 544,742 people were applying for CB licenses.[78] By July of that year, the FCC was processing 200,000 applications per week.[79] By 1978, 30 million CBs were in use in the United States.[80] Even those who did not communicate using CB were quick to adopt the jargon, found in the popular music, books, and movies of the 1970s.[81]

A transceiver complete with microphone and antenna can be obtained for under $100. The low cost was seen as one of CB's endearing characteristics. Class A citizens band lost 80 percent of its allocation to business radio service between 1960 and 1975, primarily because transceivers were more than triple the cost of the more common Class D CB stations.[82] The Class A FM frequencies were actually superior to Class D's AM signals, but mobile units costing up to and above $1,000 lacked mass appeal.[83] The FCC also made it easier for individuals to gain access by dropping the licensing requirement in favor of a permit application.[84] The no-fee application forms were packed with new units for sale, facilitating easier filing.[85]

The band had become overcrowded in some areas of the country, impeding clear reception and discouraging participation.[86] In response to the ever-increasing crowding on the band, the FCC decided to expand the number of channels available from 23 to 40.[87] An expansion had been anticipated for some time, with some predicting as many as 200 available channels.[88] The change, intended to allow the continued growth of CB use, was the cause of its declining popularity, according to CB manufacturers.[89] The higher cost for the sets reduced sales from 11 million in 1976 to less than 2 million in 1980.[90] This occurred despite technological improvements that allowed simultaneous monitoring of several channels.[91] It may simply be that the new medium was no longer new. France, which did not change transceivers as America did, also experienced a drop in popular appeal.[92]

CB has never developed much beyond a medium for highway travelers. After years of sales, the majority of equipment sold is for car or truck use. The majority of CBs are purchased by long-distance truckers who are seeking companionship on their isolated drives.[93] In some cases, CBs have been used by truckers to set up illegal drug transactions.[94] On the other hand, some communities have established CB patrols, similar to neighborhood watch programs, that have effectively curtailed crime.[95] CBs operators have helped during natural disasters.[96]

Citizens band radio never caught on as a medium for the exchange of ideas. "Without doubt, simple, low cost, ubiquitous radio conversation represents the biggest explosion of communications since the invention of the telephone."[97] FCC rules may in fact contribute to CB's lack of acceptance as a public forum for discussion. Commission rules indicate transmission time should be kept short to accommodate many speakers using the same frequency.[98] "The service is not an end in itself (i.e., a hobby or form of recreation), but rather a medium for the brief exchange of definite messages."[99] Ardent CBers refer to people who use the band simply for discussion as "ratchet jaws,"[100] denoting their displeasure with such behavior. Loggers who use the channels to increase safety and efficiency consider simple conversation "garbage."[101] From a free expression perspective, that is unfortunate, because CB "promotes a feeling of neighborliness"[102] and could contribute to public discussion. As with most other communications media, access problems are greatest where the most people desire access.

> In densely populated or traveled areas, the sheer volume of instrumental messages overloads the channel, and places an intersubjective normative inhibition upon "chatter." In open country, drivers who share the prospect of a lonely long-distance journey ease the boredom with lengthy conversations as diverse as those found at a cocktail party.[103]

Despite the belief by some that the medium is primarily to avoid speed traps, one study showed CB enthusiasts seek out social interaction.[104] Several commentators have noted that one of CB's appeals has been the challenge of authority inherent in the content of the transmissions.[105] Research indicates that the argot used expresses a quest for group identity and "a hostility toward the establishment."[106] Although the law requires that each transmission begin with the legal call letters of the speaker, few follow this regulation. Speakers can be as anonymous as they choose to be, often using pseudonyms, or "handles," as an expression of their identity, or perhaps some fantasy.[107] Handles serve as a means for the speakers to characterize themselves to receivers who will never see them.[108] At one point the FCC considered building identifiers into transmitting equipment, but quickly dropped the plan after opposition on civil rights grounds by the American Civil Liberties Union (ACLU) and others.[109]

COMPUTER BULLETIN BOARDS

With an established 3,500 to 4,500 active bulletin boards nation-wide,[110] computerized bulletin boards "provide a significant new channel of communication."[111] New systems continue developing, and most existing boards are growing.[112] Princeton University even uses a system for its weekly alumni newsletter.[113] The boards are already being used by extremist political groups[114] and their low cost (relative to print and broadcast media) makes them quite attractive.[115] A computer bulletin board can be established for as little as $2,500.[116] Their use is increasing, as evidenced by CompuServe. Perhaps best known of the commercially available services, CompuServe boasted more than a quarter of a million members in 1985.[117] In 1990, the figure had grown to 550,000.[118] Computerized "chat services," analogous in many ways to CB transmissions, exist on many of the major services (including CompuServe), and allow individuals to join existing conversations or begin their own group.[119] The world's largest public bulletin board is "Exec PC." The system boasts 150 phone lines and an average three thousand calls per day.[120] There is even a worldwide network for children who want to exchange points of view.[121]

In some ways, perhaps computer bulletin boards have been "too successful" in providing a communications alternative for fringe factions. One bulletin board service available through "Prodigy," was canceled not for financial reasons, but because the owners (IBM and Sears) feared it had become a forum for arguments between Christian fundamentalists and homosexuals.[122] Bulletin boards have been used for such activities as supplying formulas for homemade bombs[123] and establishing sexual contacts.[124] On the other hand, computer bulletin boards are one of the new technologies cited for helping to fuel the student democratic movement in Beijing.[125] CompuServe offers its members a unique forum for communicating with elected officials. When the FCC proposed an increase in telephone rates for computer users, five thousand people sent CONGRESSgrams electronically to senators and representatives.[126]

Bulletin boards are established for a variety of special interests,[127] and sometimes for general interests.[128] If the interest becomes too specific, there is inadequate market to support the service, which may cease to exist. Such was the case with a board operated by the extremist group Aryan Nations.[129] This may provide one example where the economic marketplace and the marketplace of ideas were one and the same. According to one author, "the goal of a free market in the supply of communications has been better achieved with bulletin boards than in the newspaper or broadcasting industry."[130] It may in fact be analogous to the situation that existed for the eighteenth-century pamphleteer.[131] For those who have the money and know-how, computer-linked communities may provide the means for individuals to communicate with others. One participant describes the experience as "a wide-ranging, intellectually stimulating, professionally rewarding, and often intensely emotional exchange with dozens of new friends and hundreds of colleagues."[132] Unlike many other media, computer exchanges do not suffer the limitations of scarcity.[133] Increased demand does not result in inability to access a system, just the need to increase system capacity.

Despite the growth seen in both personal computers and bulletin boards, the "medium" is still in its infancy. A small minority of Americans still access computer bulletin boards.[134] Less than one percent of the American population even has the hardware necessary to access such systems,[135] let alone the technical expertise necessary. Computer interaction requires a certain degree of literacy, both with the printed word and with computer operations. Although line charges may be minimal, they are still higher than those with limited incomes are willing to pay. In addition, at present a large initial investment is necessary in order to get started, putting such a system out of the reach of many. While the opportunity for individual, self-fulfilling expression may be tremendous, it remains to be seen whether this technology will be used by the general public.

DO NOTHING: ADEQUATE ACCESS EXISTS

A plethora of communications media certainly exist, and some contend that adequate means of access already exist to allow a venue to individuals who wish to express themselves. This is *not* the same as the argument from a diversity perspective. Rather than argue that enough different voices exist (emphasizing the listener's right), it can be argued that adequate access means exist for interested speakers through existing media: cable access and community radio stations where they exist, traditional public forums for speeches such as parks and streets, and letters to the editor. While letters to the editor may often be written in an attempt to change minds, they seldom go beyond allowing individuals a forum for their own values and beliefs.[136] They serve Emerson's safety valve function by allowing individuals to "blow off steam."[137]

According to one study, smaller weekly newspapers regard as important letters that reflected positively on the community, while editors of larger daily newspapers consider letters dealing with conflict of greater import.[138] Newspapers thus reflect the communities in which they operate. Letters to the editor can hardly be seen as a means of providing expression opportunities for those denied access in other places. With papers publishing as few as one of ten letters received, and those published representing mainstream viewpoints,[139] it seems that letters to the editor are at best limited access means. Further, the percentage of letters published is lower for major metropolitan dailies,[140] consistent with other forums that are in greater demand in larger cities than in smaller communities (such as broadcast frequencies). One unnamed newspaper with a circulation above 100,000 averages approximately five hundred letters per month, and in the months studied, published 58 percent of the letters received.[141] In the same study, unpublished writers were more likely to submit a cathartic letter.[142] This intimates the limited value letters to the editor serve for self-expression. The situation is no better for magazine letters to the editor. *The Atlantic* publishes only a few of the hundreds of letters it receives each month, and almost all of those published are abbreviated.[143] There is reason to be encouraged, however, as more newspapers commit more space to letters and op-ed pages.[144]

As with letters to the editor, talk radio programs are another forum for those seeking speech opportunities. George Gerbner of the Annenberg School of Communications says the programs "seem to be a safety valve for disaffected and alienated people."[145] The number of stations offering talk radio has increased.[146] Before the growth of FM radio in the late 1960s, the format scarcely existed.[147] Although the programs reflect a great diversity of political viewpoints, the hosts often resent government power and involvement in "telling people what to do."[148]

Talk show hosts are central to the success of the programs, as evidenced by the industry's hiring of famous personalities, such as Jessica Hahn, former Philadelphia mayor Frank Rizzo, and Ronald Reagan.[149] Best known of the radio talk show hosts nationwide is Larry King, heard nightly by an estimated 3.5 million people.[150] In fact, radio talk hosts have seen themselves as instrumental in several grassroots political actions. Protests have been instigated against a congressional pay raise, against Exxon for its reaction to the Valdez oil spill, and against Cat Stevens, the former pop musician who supported the bounty on Salman Rushdie.[151] During the congressional pay raise protest, more than twenty radio hosts encouraged listeners across the country to send more than 75,000 tea bags to Capitol Hill.[152] The campaign elicited criticism not only from Congress[153] but from FCC Commissioner James Quello.[154]

Consumer advocate Ralph Nader calls the hosts' power a "mixed blessing," citing Boston's Jerry Williams' crusade to override the state's mandatory seat belt law.[155] It may in fact be that those benefiting most from the talk radio forum are not the callers, but the hosts.[156]

Traditionally, talk radio has appealed primarily to older audiences.[157] Talk radio is one of the formats found appealing by listeners in the twenty-five-to-fifty-four age group.[158] There is evidence, however, suggesting that the talk radio audience is not only getting younger, but that it is also growing more reflective of the general population.[159] The growing audience diversity is reflected in the trend toward local station specialization. Chicago radio stations have targeted either black or white audiences.[160] While providing a forum to a historically ignored minority, critics claim the black-oriented stations have promoted hatred and division.[161] Touting his upscale audience, Seattle talk radio host Mike Siegel estimates 60 percent of his callers are calling on car phones.[162] It may be simply that the local programs are reflective of the community in which they are located.[163]

As with letters to the editor, talk radio does provide an additional forum for those seeking self-expression, however, the available access is quite limited. Siegal estimates that only 1 percent of his listeners call in. Of those who do, many are screened out because they are repeat callers, they do not fit the station's target demographic, or simply because of lack of time.[164] It is important to note that actually having one's call aired is not necessarily required for the caller to feel satisfied. "Using the telephone to make the call also provides a range of interpersonal gratifications even if the resulting conversation is not broadcast."[165]

SUMMARY

Opportunities for individual expression do exist in a variety of formats, although for a variety of reasons, they have not had universal acceptance. Cable access is no longer federally required, yet is offered by many cable systems as an alternative forum. Whether a cable franchise offers an access channel, and whether that channel is actively used by individuals wanting to speak, often results from a tradition of access commitment by both the cable company and members of the community. Opinions differ as to whether cable access has been "successful." Whether access channels are successful based on their use or level of viewership may be an inappropriate question. Some channels have not existed long enough to be familiar to residents, while some residents may look to the channel in the future to provide their communicative needs.

Citizens band radio could have provided a forum for discussion. Due in part to unrelated circumstances (such as gasoline price increases and reduced highway speed limits), CB evolved instead into a truckers' channel. Government policy further eroded the band's value for public discussion by discouraging its use for "idle chatter."

Computer bulletin boards may be the citizens band of the future, but as yet require expense and expertise to join the conversation. The use of computer bulletin boards has increased in recent years, yet they are, for the most part, still being used by those who might already be considered "communications rich." Penetration of computers into American homes will undoubtedly be related to computer literacy and hardware costs.

Letters to the editor and radio talk shows are existing forums, providing an additional outlet, although access is quite limited. Both venues select participants who discuss topics deemed worthwhile by the editor or host. Letters to the editor are edited for brevity, and talk show hosts have the ability to cut off callers for whatever reason. Nonetheless, they both provide some opportunities for those seeking a forum for expression.

Are there other possibilities for increased expression forums that could be explored? Several proposals before Congress and in scholarly journals argue for alternative systems. Can a system be devised that provides maximum opportunities for those wanting to express themselves, without the constitutional problems associated with requiring media to carry others' messages? Chapter 6 presents one such proposal.

NOTES

1. Note, *Controversial Programming on Cable Television's Public Access Channels: The Limits of Governmental Response*, 38 DE PAUL L. REV. 1051, 1061 (1989). For a review of early cable access, see R. ENGLEMAN, THE ORIGINS OF PUBLIC ACCESS CABLE TELEVISION 1966–1792 (Journalism Monographs 123, 1990).

2. S. Buske, *Status Report on Community Access Programming on Cable* in 3 THE CABLE/BROADBAND COMMUNICATIONS BOOK 102–114 (M. Hollowell ed. 1983).

3. FCC Third Report and Order, 36 FCC 2d. 141, 192 (1972). For a history of cable regulatory development, see Ross & Brick, *The Cable Act of 1984: How Did We Get There and Where Are We Going*, 39 FED. COM. L. J. 27 (May 1987).

4. 47 CFR Sec. 76.201(a) (1974).

5. Wirth & Cobb-Riley, *A First Amendment Critique of the 1984 Cable Act*, 31 J. BROADCASTING & ELECTRONIC MEDIA 391, 393 (1987).

6. FCC v Midwest Video, 440 U.S. 689 (1979).

7. Mitropoulos, *Public Participation, as Access, in Cable TV in the USA*, 302 EKISTICS 385, 386 (1983).

8. G. JABERG & L. WARGO, JR., THE VIDEO PENCIL 23 (1980).

9. Channel capacity is related to the allocation of channels for public-related uses. Moss & Warren, *Public Policy and Community-Oriented Uses of Cable Television*, 20 URBAN AFFAIRS QUARTERLY 233, 237 (1984).

10. Local origination (LO), although often confused with access, is quite different. LO channels are operated by the cable systems themselves for a profit. Their only similarity to access channels is that both are local. The confusion may in part be the design of cable companies attempting to promote "community programming." Alderson, *Everyman TV*, COLUM. JOURNALISM REV. 39, 42 (Jan./Feb. 1981).

11. Moss & Warren, *supra* note 9, at 238.

12. R. GARRAY, CABLE TELEVISION 68 (1988).

13. Buske, *supra* note 2, at 109–110.

14. D. Atkin & R. LaRose, News and Information on Community Access Channels: Market Concerns Amidst the Marketplace of Ideas (paper presented at the Association for Education in Journalism and Mass Communication convention, July 2, 1988, Portland, Ore.) at 3.

15. Buske, *supra* note 2, at 110.

16. *Id.*, at 110–111.

17. Programs have been repeated as often as ten times in one week. Kletter, Hirschhorn, & Hudson, *Access and the Social Environment in the United States of America* in ACCESS: SOME WESTERN MODELS OF COMMUNITY MEDIA 39 (F. Berrigan ed. 1977).

18. Buske, *supra* note 2, at 111–112.

19. *Id.*, at 112.

20. Manley, *Candidates in Austin Enjoy Unrestricted Access*, 9 COMMUNITY TELEVISION REV. 10 (Spring 1986).

21. Wolf, *Cable Access and Social Change: Eight Case Studies*, 9 COMMUNITY TELEVISION REV. 18, 19 (Spring 1986).

22. Telephone interview with Judy Crandall, Programming Coordinator, GRTV (July 13, 1987).

23. Telephone interview with Barbara Cataldi, Program Director, BCTV (July 13, 1987).

24. Hulser, *Paper Tiger Television*, 10 AMERICAN FILM 61 (March 1985).

25. Belkin, *A Look Behind the Scenes at Public Access TV*, NEW YORK TIMES, April 17, 1987, at 19.

26. Kiernan, *To Watch is O.K., But to Air is Divine*, U.S. NEWS & WORLD REPORT 112, 114 (Oct. 16, 1989).

27. T. BALDWIN & D. MCVOY, CABLE COMMUNICATION 96 (1983).

28. *Id.*, at 66.

29. Considerations of what issues are meritorious seem inappropriate. *Id.* Those who take time to prepare their thoughts, appear at the studios, and follow whatever necessary bureaucratic process obviously believe their subject matter adequately important.

30. Kiernan, *supra* note 26.

31. This is not intended to be an indictment of all cable systems. Colony Communications President Robert Turner has added access and local origination to his system. He claims, "We're one more medium in a city, and we have a responsibility to be more than a passive conduit for someone else's program." Bittman, *Colony Pegs Local Access on News*, ADVERTISING AGE 30 (Dec. 6, 1984).

32. A case can be made that, given time, public issue programming will develop. Of twenty-two cable systems in the New York City area surveyed, thirteen (59 percent) reported having a regularly scheduled panel discussion program dealing with public issues. Moss & Warren, *supra* note 9, at 247.

33. Hernandez-Dorow, *Quality of Public Access Television Becomes Subject of Iowa City Debate*, DAILY IOWAN, March 1, 1989, at 3A.

34. Most agree that conventional television "broadcasts" by attempting to achieve a large, heterogeneous audience with its messages. Narrowcasting has come to mean an attempt to reach a substantially smaller, more homogeneous group. One commentator believes that the position that cable channels can narrowcast by reaching only decimal-point percentages of the population is erroneous. Instead, narrowcasting should mean programming that can function at levels 80 percent below those required by broadcasting. W. DONNELLY, THE CONFETTI GENERATION 86–87 (1986).

35. "Community media should not be judged by the same criteria of success as institutionalized media." Kletter, Hirschhorn, & Hudson, *supra* note 17, at 83. One commentator believes access should be compared to pirate radio broadcasts rather than broadcast television. Mitropoulos *supra* note 7, at 387. The committee investigating cable in the early 1970s likened cable not to television but to the printing press. Sloan Commission on Cable Communications, ON THE CABLE: THE TELEVISION OF ABUNDANCE (1971). The Commission cautioned that the analogy could not be pushed too far.

36. Hardenbergh, *Promise vs. Performance: Four Public Access Channels in Connecticut, A Case Study* 13 MASS COMM. REV. 32 (1986). The community is Madison, Connecticut.

37. *See, e.g.*, Katz, *Community Access Television: A Social Service Resource*, 30 SOCIAL WORK 267 (1985) (social workers); Thornton & Greene, *Cable Television and Educational Access: A Reconsideration*, 13 COMMUNITY COLLEGE REV. 47 (1985).

38. Porter & Banks, *Cable Public Access as a Public Forum*, 65 JOURNALISM Q. 39, 41 (Spring 1988).

39. *Id.*

40. T. BALDWIN & D. MCVOY, *supra* note 27, at 98.

41. R. Prisuta, Political/Governmental Utilization of Cable Television (paper submitted to Association for Education in Journalism, April 1, 1976).

42. *Id.*, at 8.

43. *Id.*, at 11.

44. Sharp, *Consequences of Local Government Under the Klieg Lights*, 11 COM. RES. 497, 500 (1984).

45. *Id.*, at 501.

46. *See* Hardenberg, *supra* note 36, at 38. Whether cable access is "adequately utilized" may be one of the more frequently discussed topics. *Local Cable Producers Set Record*, IOWA CITY PRESS-CITIZEN, Feb. 28, 1987, at 3A, col. 4. As early as 1980, three of the four public access channels on Manhattan's cable system were regularly programmed eight hours daily. Many surveys suggest 25 percent of cable subscribers watch access channels. Kiernan, *supra* note 26, at 112. *But see* D. Atkin & R. LaRose, *supra* note 14, at 8 (viewership for community channel 16 percent of audience); Heeter, D'Alessio, Greenberg, & McVoy, *Cableviewing Behaviors: An Electronic Assessment* in CABLEVIEWING 56–57 (C. Heeter & B. Greenberg eds. 1988) (cable access viewing less than 2 percent of total); Advocat, *Cable Offers Access, But Few Watch*, DETROIT FREE PRESS, April 29, 1984, at 1C (less than 1 percent of cable viewing in Columbus, Ohio is of access channel).

47. Baker, *Unreasoned Reasonableness*, 78 N.W.U. L. REV. 937, 1023 (1983).

48. *See* Trufelman, *How To Plug In To Cable TV*, 44 PUB. REL. J. 43 (Sep. 1988) (community access channels as means of reaching client's audience); Gorney, *Laissez-Faire Television*, 41 PUB. REL. J. 12 (March 1985) (public access channels may provide alternative to repealed Fairness Doctrine).

49. S. HEAD & C. STERLING, BROADCASTING IN AMERICA 23 (1990).

50. *Hate TV Pops Up On Cable Channels*, JOPLIN GLOBE, Jan. 1, 1989, at 3E.

51. *Supremacists to Air Show in Springfield*, JOPLIN GLOBE, May 17, 1990, at 2C.

52. S. HEAD & C. STERLING, *supra* note 49.

53. Telephone interview with Jerry Rutherford, TeleCable of Springfield, Mo., Manager, May 18, 1990. *See also* Note, *supra* note 1, at 1104–1105.

54. *See e.g.*, Note, *Access to Cable Television: A Critique of the Affirmative Duty Theory of the First Amendment*, 70 CAL. L. REV. 1393, 1409–1419 (1982).

55. Kiernan, *supra* note 26, at 114.

56. *See e.g.*, Atkin & LaRose, *supra* note 14, at 4–5 (demographics of community influence viewership levels).

57. J. Ledingham, Characteristics of Cable Access Centers in the Top 100 Media Markets (Paper presented at the International Communications Association convention, May 26, 1983, Dallas, Texas).

58. Lang, Blacklock, & Rossing, *Is Anyone Watching?* J. EXTENSION 7, 8 (Summer 1986). The community is Trempeleau, Wisconsin.

59. *Id.*, at 9.

60. *Id.*, at 10.

61. Note, *supra* note 1, at 1060–1061 (citations omitted).

62. *Id.*, at 1105.

63. *See Whitehead on Access: Cable as Common Carrier*, BROADCAST-ING (Sept. 20, 1971), at 43.

64. FCC v Midwest Video, 440 U.S. 689 (1979).

65. Gross, *The State of Cable*, BROADCAST/MANAGEMENT/ENGINEER-ING (May 1985), at 73; Branscomb, *The Cable Fable: Will It Ever Come True*, 25 J. COM. 44 (1975).

66. BROADCASTING YEARBOOK D-3 (1986).

67. Telephone interview with Sue Buske, Executive Director of the National Federation of Local Programmers (Oct. 1, 1986).

68. Note, *supra* note 54.

69. Stations included KRAB Seattle, KBOO Portland, KDNA St. Louis, KCHU Dallas, and KTAO Los Gatos, California. L. MILAM, THE RADIO PAPERS at i (1986).

70. "[W]e see our function at KRAB as one of filling the gaps—of supplementing other stations." *Id.*, at 10.

71. *Id.*, at 4.

72. *Id.*, at 109.

73. Kletter, Hirschhorn, & Hudson, *supra* note 17, at 83.

74. L. BUCKWALTER, KNOW ABOUT CITIZENS BAND RADIO 8 (1966).

75. *Id.*, at 9.

76. OFFICIAL CB DICTIONARY 7 (1976).

77. *Id.*, at 8.

78. *The Bodacious New World of CB*, TIME, May 10, 1976, at 78.

79. Rose, *The Citizens Band Goes Boom*, MOTOR TREND, July 1976, at 67.

80. *CB Radio: Fogbound*, ECONOMIST, July 15, 1978, at 92.

81. Aleong & Chretien, *Can Smokey the Bear Speak French? Adapting CB Lingo in Canadian French*, AM. SPEECH 260 (Winter 1981).

82. Salm, *The Forgotten CB Service*, POPULAR ELECTRONICS, Nov. 1977, at 80.

83. Kahaner, *GMRS Radio—The Uncrowded Citizens Band*, POPULAR SCIENCE, Oct. 1978, at 8.

84. For the commission, the distinction between a license and a permit is substantial. A license requires payment of a fee, and at least a minimal showing of some competence or proficiency. The change parallels that made by the FCC when it stopped requiring third class licenses for radio operators (including a test) in favor of a restricted radiotelephone operator's permit.

85. *CB Today and Where It's Going*, POPULAR ELECTRONICS, April 1978, at 63.

86. *Cashing In On CB*, NEWSWEEK, May 31, 1976, at 64.

87. *CB Rules Changes For 1977*, POPULAR ELECTRONICS, March 1977, at 45.

88. Ethridge, *The CB Fiasco*, MOTOR TREND, April 1977, at 69.

89. *CB Couldn't Keep on Truckin'*, NEWSWEEK, July 21, 1980, at 12.

90. *Id.*

91. Friedman, *Programmed Scanning Brings Back CB Excitement*, POPU-LAR MECHANICS, Aug. 1979, at 78.

92. Prevos, *CB'ers and Cibistes: The Development and Impact of CB Radio in France*, 19 J. POPULAR CULTURE 145, 151 (1986).

93. Bukro, *On The Road, CB Radios Humanize The Long Miles*, CHI-CAGO TRIBUNE, Nov. 16, 1989, at 1–6.

94. Masland, *For a Vocal Minority, Drugs Still a Part of Truckers' Life*, CHICAGO TRIBUNE, March 4, 1990, 7–1; Koziol, *CB Radio Talk Spurs Drug Arrest*, CHICAGO TRIBUNE, Aug. 11, 1989, at 2S–1.

95. Duffy, *A CB Patrol That Works*, POLICE CHIEF, May 1982, at 36.

96. *When a Buddy Meets a Buddy Comin' Through a Crisis*, PSYCHOL-OGY TODAY, May 1979, at 31.

97. *The Bodacious New World of CB*, *supra* note 78.

98. L. BUCKWALTER, *supra* note 74, at 13.

99. *Id.*

100. *CB Couldn't Keep On Truckin'*, *supra* note 89.

101. *Despite Their Limitations, CBs Are, And Will Remain, Popular*, FOREST INDUSTRIES, Nov. 1978, at 51.

102. OFFICIAL CB DICTIONARY, *supra* note 76, at 9.

103. Dannefer & Poushinsky, *The C.B. Phenomenon, A Sociological Ap-praisal*, 12 J. POPULAR CULTURE 611, 614 (1979).

104. Kerbo, Marshall, & Holley, *Reestablishing "Gemeinschaft"?* 7 URBAN LIFE 337, 354 (1978). Their study showed only 10 percent of CB enthusiasts listed avoidance of speed traps as one of their objectives. *Id*, at 343.

105. OFFICIAL CB DICTIONARY, *supra* note 76, at 10; *The Bodacious New World of CB*, *supra* note 78.

106. Ramsey, *The People Versus Smokey Bear: Metaphor, Argot, and CB Radio*, 13 J. POPULAR CULTURE 338, 342 (1979).

107. *See, e.g.*, Dannefer & Kasen, *Anonymous Exchanges: CB and the Emergence of Sex Typing*, 10 URBAN LIFE 265, 271 (1981); Smith, *Gender Marking on Citizens Band Radio: Self-Identity in a Limited-Channel Speech Community*, 7 SEX ROLES 599 (1981).

108. Handley, *What's Your Handle, Good Buddy? Names of Citizens Band Users*, AM. SPEECH 307 (Winter 1979).

109. OFFICIAL CB DICTIONARY, *supra* note 76, at 11.

110. Soma, Smith, & Sprague, *Legal Analysis of Electronic Bulletin Board Activities*, 7 W. NEW ENG. L. REV. 571, 572 (1985).

111. Comment, *An Electronic Soapbox: Computer Bulletin Boards and the First Amendment*, 39 FED. COM. L. J. 217 (1987).

112. Freitag, *As Computer Bulletin Boards Grow, If It's Out There, It's Posted Here*, NEW YORK TIMES, April 2, 1989 at 1–38.

113. Cressy, *The Electronic PAW*, 10 CURRENTS 22 (Oct. 1984).

114. *See* Lowe, *Computerized Networks of Hate*, U.S.A. TODAY, July 1985, at 10; Duggan, *Md. Man Gets Three Years in Bombing*, WASHINGTON POST, Jan. 6, 1990, at A–1 (man involved with bulletin board service that listed formulas for homemade bombs).

115. Petersen, *Going On Line: Whether For Gabbing or Gobbling Facts, Computer Bulletin Board Systems Have Taken Wing*, CHICAGO TRIBUNE, March 16, 1989, at 5–1.

116. Ciarcia, *Turnkey Bulletin-Board System*, BYTE, Dec. 1985, at 93.

117. Uyehara, *Let the Operator Beware*, STUDENT LAW, April 1986, at 28.

118. Telephone interview with Janie Martin, CompuServe, Aug. 9, 1990.

119. *On-Line Chat Services Rekindle CB Spirit, Bring PC Users Together*, PC MAG., June 14, 1988, at 440.

120. Wood and Blankenhorn, *State of the BBS Nation*, 15 BYTE 298 (Jan. 1990).

121. Itzkan, *Citizens of the World*, INCIDER, Oct. 1989, at 104.

122. Coy, *A Computer Bulletin Board Is Unplugged, Silencing Feud*, WASHINGTON POST, Dec. 13, 1989, at G–1.

123. Duggan, *Bomb Data Spread By Computer*, WASHINGTON POST, April 28, 1989, at C–1.

124. *FBI Says Pair Used Sex Message Service In Plot To Nab A Boy, Kill Him On Film*, ATLANTA CONSTITUTION, Aug. 23, 1989, at A–14.

125. McNulty, *Students Run A High-Tech Underground*, CHICAGO TRIBUNE, June 12, 1989, at 1–1; Horvitz, *The Usenet Underground*, WHOLE EARTH REV. 113 (Winter 1989).

126. Koch, *No Sacred Cows*, 14 COMMON CAUSE MAGAZINE, Jan. 1988, at 6.

127. Levitan, *Twelve Special Bulletin Boards*, 9 COMPUTE 51 (May 1987).

128. Hume & Reid, *From Hobbies To Help: It's All On Bulletin Board*, CHICAGO TRIBUNE, Feb. 26, 1989, at 7–2.

129. *Id.*, at 33.

130. Comment, *supra* note 111, at 222.

131. Dembart, *The Law Versus Computers: A Confounding Terminal Case*, L.A. TIMES, Aug. 11, 1985, at 3.

132. Rheingold, *Virtual Communities*. WHOLE EARTH REV. 78 (Winter 1987).

133. Beck, *Control of, and Access to, On-Line Computer Data Bases: Some First Amendment Issues in Videotex and Teletext*. 5 COMM/ENT L. J. 1, 6 (1982).

134. Comment, *supra* note 111, at 222.

135. A personal computer and modem are necessary (in addition to the appropriate software) to access a bulletin board. Kyriakos, *Modem Operandi*, WASHINGTON POST, July 28, 1989, at WW-6. Recent estimates are that fewer than two million Americans have both. *See* Seligman, *Life Will Be Different When We're All On Line*, FORTUNE, Feb. 4, 1985, at 68.

136. L. Ede, Public Discourse and Public Policy: A Case Study (Paper presented at the Annual Meeting of the Oregon Council of Teachers of English, April 6, 1984, Bend, Ore.).

137. Nagel, *Letters to the Editor: A Public Bid for Fame*, COLUMBIA J. REV. 47 (May/June 1974).

138. F. Vasquez & T. Eveslage, Newspapers' Letters to the Editor as Reflections of Social Structure (Paper presented at the Association for Education in Journalism and Mass Communication convention, Aug. 7, 1983, Corvallis, Ore.).

139. K. Starck, Letter Columns: Access For Whom? (Freedom of Information Center Report 237, Feb. 1970) at 5.

140. S. Pasternack, The Open Forum: A Study of Letters to the Editor and the People Who Write Them (Paper presented at the Association for Education in Journalism and Mass Communication convention, July 3, 1988. Portland, Ore.).

141. *Id.*, at 5.

142. *Id.*, at 11.

143. *745 Boylston Street*, ATLANTIC, June 1990, at 6.

144. Powe, *Tornillo*, 1987 SUP. CT. REV. 345, 394–395.

145. *O.K. Caller, You're On the Air*, U.S. NEWS & WORLD REPORT, Feb. 20, 1989, at 12–13.

146. *American Radio Networks Keeps AMs Talking*, BROADCASTING, March 19, 1990, at 55; *More Voices Join Satellite-Delivered Talk Format*, BROADCASTING, Feb. 20, 1989, at 46; *Twenty-four Hours of Talk Available for AMs*, BROADCASTING, Jan. 4, 1988, at 120.

147. Barone & Schrof, *The Changing Voice of Talk Radio*, U.S. NEWS & WORLD REPORT, Jan. 15, 1990, at 51.

148. Klein, *Talk Politics*, NEW YORK, Feb. 27, 1989, 28, at 29.

149. *Names Make News in Radio*, BROADCASTING, March 20, 1989, at 64.

150. Rosellini, *All Alone, Late at Night*, U.S. NEWS & WORLD REPORT, Jan. 15, 1990, at 54.

151. Zoglin, *Bugle Boys of the Airwaves*, TIME, May 15, 1989, at 88.

152. *Hill Steamed Over Radio's Tea Time*, BROADCASTING, Feb. 13, 1989, at 29–30.

153. *Id.*

154. Taylor, *Talk Radio Influence Criticized*, RADIO WORLD, July 26, 1989, at 17.

155. Klein, *supra* note 148, at 29.

156. *See* Palmer, *Don't Blame Talk Radio*, BOSTON GLOBE, July 21, 1989, at 11 (hosts express opinions, which is purpose of free speech).

157. Culter, *Mature Audiences Only*, 11 AM. DEMOGRAPHICS 20 (Oct. 1989).

158. Steinberg, *Radio: Soft Touch a New Age for Medium*, ADVERTISING AGE, Aug. 31, 1987, at S1.

159. Barone & Schrof, *supra* note 147; Armstrong & Rubin, *Talk Radio as Interpersonal Communication*, 39 J. COM. 84, 86 (1989).

160. Schmidt, *Black Talk Radio*, NEW YORK TIMES, March 31, 1989, at A1; Secter & Shryer, *Chicago's Talk Radio Dial Split Along Racial Lines*, LOS ANGELES TIMES, April 2, 1989, at I1.

161. *Chicago Talk Radio Fueling Racism as Mayoral Vote Nears, Group Claims*, ATLANTA JOURNAL, Apr. 1, 1989, at A4.

162. Barone & Schrof, *supra* note 147, at 52.

163. *Id*.

164. Telephone interview with Mike Siegal, Aug. 13, 1990.

165. Armstrong & Rubin, *supra* note 159.

6 A PROPOSAL FOR GOVERNMENT PROVISION OF BROADCAST ACCESS

Ideally, proposals to promote free expression should promote one of the values of free expression while not detracting from either one of the other values or from some other fundamental right. If government can improve the opportunities for individual self-fulfillment while not infringing on the rights of others, either for self-expression or a myriad of other rights (e.g., property), then government should take such action. This chapter proposes that government do precisely that, by providing access channels for public use, thus promoting opportunities for self-fulfillment while not infringing on any other private rights. This apparent conflict is often a target of opponents of the right to media access. As demonstrated in Chapter 1, when First Amendment values conflict with other rights, including other free expression rights, courts are forced to balance between the two. In order to grant access for individual expression, opponents argue, broadcasters or printers must sacrifice their own rights.[1] Access schemes can be devised, however, that do not cause these difficulties.

The most prominent proponent of a right of access to the media has been Jerome Barron,[2] who argued before the Supreme Court on Pat Tornillo's behalf. Barron has argued for a right of access applied not only to broadcasters, but to newspapers as well. His thesis is that, in light of twentieth century conditions, the First Amendment should provide an affirmative right that protects not only speech but also the opportunity to have that speech expressed through viable channels.

Barron takes the position that speech that has no opportunity to be heard is not free speech at all.[3] His ideas of how to provide that opportunity, however, have been greatly criticized,[4] and here is where this proposal differs from Barron's.

Free expression has many values, one of which is self-expression. As asserted in Chapter 1, self-fulfillment is the most inclusive of all the values. If free speech is valued for self-fulfillment, then government is responsible to provide the channels for that opportunity.[5] Regulating access to an entire medium is quite different from mandating access to a particular newspaper.[6] In Justice Rehnquist's comments during oral argument in *Tornillo*, he implied that access requirements were similar to a "right to commandeer someone's printing press."[7] Emerson has argued:

> The state may "own" the airwaves but it cannot withhold the use of such facilities any more than it could withhold the use of the streets or prohibit the manufacture of printing presses. If the electronic media are to fit within the system of freedom of expression, the government must exercise its obligation to make them available to potential participants in the system, both communicators and listeners.[8]

Requiring privately owned media to provide the public access for expression may be a violation of equal protection and due process. It takes private property in the form of the media owner's time or facilities for public good "without just compensation,"[9] especially when doing so to achieve the desired ends is not necessary. The Supreme Court unanimously held that a state could not transform private into public property without just compensation, even for a limited duration.[10] In effect, that is what is done when privately owned media are required by law to provide facilities to others free of charge.[11] This issue, raised in the context of required cable access channels and supported by at least one appeals court, was left unresolved by the Supreme Court.[12] The Court stated that "[t]he Eighth Circuit Court of Appeals intimated, additionally, that the rules might effect an unconstitutional 'taking' of property or . . . might affront the Due Process Clause of the Fifth Amendment. We forgo comment on these issues as well."[13]

Freedom of expression is an anomaly. While the constitution protects speech once it is uttered, laws are indifferent when it comes to providing speech opportunities for citizens.[14] Public forum doctrine, discussed in Chapter 3, is quite particular in mandating fairness in access to the forum, but provides no calculus for determining whether adequate public forums exist. Regardless of the number of communication channels available, the need for government-provided access still exists. Recent proliferation of commercial broadcast media does not address the issue of individual expression, and allusions to the increasing number of stations merely obfuscates the issue.[15] At least one broadcaster asserts that an increase in the attempts at illegal, "pirate" radio broadcasting in America may be due, at least in part, to an inability of individuals to be licensed legally because of regulation and expense.[16] More commercial speech opportunities still do not ensure all individuals the opportunity to express themselves, especially those with the least accepted views, or views counter to the capitalistic goals of privately owned, for-profit media.[17] In this age of intense media competition for advertising revenue, politically controversial speakers may be avoided for fear customers may turn to less "offensive" material.[18] Moreover, some argue that the broadcast licensing process itself, which encourages applicants to provide standardized public interest programming, "minimize(s) ideological diversity among licensees."[19] Almost twenty years ago, the National Commission on the Causes and Prevention of Violence assailed print media for not providing routine access to those with new ideas or grievances.[20]

In fact, the problem of opportunities for dissident viewpoints may be getting worse rather than better.[21] In an age of increased concentration of ownership, media properties bring higher and higher price tags. Emerson has observed that the need for government-provided facilities will increase as economic and technological constraints make it more difficult for the individual to obtain media access.[22] Another commentator argues that preserving maximum use of "public space" (streets and parks in his treatise, but equally applicable to the electromagnetic spectrum) allows for public participation to accommodate both individual liberty and the public agenda as a counterpoint to the "inegalitarian aspects of an influential, elite-dominated press."[23]

More than twenty years ago, the Supreme Court in dicta stressed editorial advertising as "an important outlet for the promulgation of information and ideas by persons who do not themselves have access to publishing facilities."[24] Yet contemporary examples of denial of access to the media by private parties do exist. One case in point is that of the W. R. Grace company and its television commercial "The Deficit Trials," portraying a future America where rampant deficits had destroyed the nation. All three networks initially refused to air the commercial, although the only matter of controversy was the position that the deficit was harmful.[25] The decision not to air "The Deficit Trials" was never challenged legally, perhaps because the Supreme Court in *CBS v DNC* determined that the Fairness Doctrine applied to editorial advertisements (i.e., "advocacy advertising") once they are broadcast, but that broadcasters may decide what ads they choose to accept and which they wish to reject.[26] When a select few individuals have the ability to restrict access, freedom of expression is endangered just as surely as if the restriction had been imposed by the government.[27]

A significant interest in a public forum of some kind does exist. The National Issues Forum, an opportunity to discuss national issues with one's neighbors, existed in only twenty-five communities in 1982. The program has functioned in the form of small group discussions, call-ins for local cable, and even nationwide teleconferences. By 1986, two hundred communities were involved in the project.[28] While two hundred communities is impressive given the lack of any financial support from government or privately owned companies, this, like cable access, falls far short of any nationwide access opportunity.

The concept of government-provided access to communications media is not new, but it has consistently met with disapproval.[29] The criticisms can be characterized as (1) the ineffectiveness of access channels in reaching an adequate audience and (2) the fear that government-operated channels could invite government involvement in content decisions. Typical of the first concern is the statement by Barron:

> Competitive media only constitute alternative means of access in a crude manner. If ideas are criticized in one forum the most adequate response is in the same forum since it is most likely to reach the same audience. . . . The test of a community's opportunities for free expression rests not so much in an abundance of alternative media but rather in an abundance of opportunities to secure expression in media with the largest impact.[30]

Concerns of this sort seem unfounded. Equality of speech is not the issue, nor should it be. Rather, the issue is whether opportunity exists for expression to facilitate self-fulfillment. As our system exists now, it would be foolish to assert that ideas have some equal status, and that the presentation of one issue necessarily results in a balanced presentation of the opposing viewpoint. As a classic example of the inequality of speech, Benno Schmidt cites the 1954 "See It Now" broadcast attacking Senator Joseph McCarthy and his subsequent inept reply.[31] The First Amendment could never have been written to provide equality among speakers, but only equal opportunities. Emerson asserts that "[i]t is not that the system necessarily must provide all participants equal or proportionate facilities for communication. The system does require, however, that there be adequate opportunity for minority viewpoints to be heard—to obtain a foothold from which to grow, if and when accepted."[32] The provision of a "public soapbox" does not require that the audience listen.[33] The belief in equality of speech rather than the opportunity to speak is inconsistent with First Amendment theory and history.

The idea that the government might enter into content decisions is the second general fear concerning access channels. In 1979 the Federal Communications Commission (FCC) issued a ruling on the Fairness Doctrine that affirmed the doctrine as a means for providing open discourse, and committed to its continuance.[34] Unfortunately, government has always been in the business of determining broadcasting content. In reviewing Fairness Doctrine complaints, the FCC subjectively determined whether a station had adequately addressed the concerns of the community. It is obvious that, at least indirectly, the FCC sometimes determined what issues were deserving of attention.[35] The FCC seemed to give great attention to the fact that matters discussed under such an access proposal may not be those of "public importance." There are two responses to this. First, the First Amendment makes no stipulation that only "important" speech is deserving of protection.[36] Second, importance is a relative term. Certainly, those who take time to present their comments cogently, apply in advance for time to speak, and travel to the studios to be recorded must find it significant to do so. If one wishes to protect the First Amendment value of self-fulfillment, it follows that the importance of the expression is self-determined.

Contrary to the FCC's position, government can be a conduit for communication *without* becoming involved in content decisions. Barron has maintained:

> There is an important and fundamental difference . . . between a positive role for the First Amendment which is achieved through a governmentally-sponsored *process* for stimulating the interchange of ideas and a positive role for the First Amendment in which the government contributes substantively to the information process in any way.[37]

If an access opportunity were provided to the general citizenry, mechanisms could be established to prevent content decisions with a minimum of bureaucracy. According to Emerson, "[t]he use of the same facilities by different persons or groups . . . does not ordinarily present very difficult problems of fair accommodation so long as the available facilities are not seriously limited. Usually a first come, first served rule would settle the matter."[38] Whether individuals using such an access channel would be subject to any restrictions (such as on libel or obscenity) was answered by Chief Justice Hughes more than fifty years ago. "Every freeman has an undoubted right to lay what sentiments he pleases before the public; to forbid this, is to destroy the freedom of the press; but if he publishes what is improper, mischievous or illegal, he must take the consequence of his own temerity."[39]

In fact, analogous safeguards already exist for cable access facilities. For example, the Milwaukee Access Telecommunications Authority (MATA) created a first-come, first-served system programming thirty-five hours per week of access television. MATA certified five hundred individuals to use the system, and had seven hundred waiting to train after only two years. MATA is prohibited from pre-screening programs but may penalize rules violations (such as commercial content or obscenity) by imposing a ninety-day or one-year prohibition on use of the channel by the violator. In the first two years of operation, no prohibitions were imposed for program violations.[40]

PRECEDENT FOR COMMUNICATION ACCESS

Precedent exists for government provision of self-expression opportunities. In the sense that government provides exclusive use of the spectrum free of charge to successful applicants, and protects that exclusivity, it is already in the business of providing an expression forum.[41] In addition, second-class mailing privileges and joint operating agreements are examples of the country's commitment to helping media reach the public.[42] Two separate approaches, taken more than a century apart, demonstrate the government's willingness to support measures to expand communication opportunities in other media. What makes these examples even more illuminating is that one involved government provision of the communication medium, while the other involved regulation of existing private enterprise. Further, recent privatization of one, and divestiture of the other, demonstrate the changing regulatory philosophy.

Postal Service

Post roads and establishment of a national postal system were seen as so important that the first Congress incorporated their provision into the Constitution.[43] While many contend the postal system was established for reasons of commerce,[44] it is beyond contention that the system promoted an improved information and communication system.[45] The system could have been privately run, in the same way many other important social needs were satisfied, but instead the Congress passed the act in 1792 giving the postmaster authority over approximately 195 post offices.[46] A private system had been attempted, but was a financial failure.[47] Financial stability of the postal service was also the motivation for federal prohibition of private letter carrier deliveries. The Postal Act of 1845 prohibited competition primarily so that private services could not take over more lucrative routes, leaving the government to provide service in the South and West.[48] Universal service was of concern, and the postal system began establishing rural free delivery in the 1890s to ensure access for all.[49] The government's willingness to subsidize one portion of the mail service by profits from the other demonstrates its willingness to equalize minimum communicative rights for all.[50]

The operation of the postal system remained, for the most part, as it had been structured by Congress in 1792. It was not until 1967, when Postmaster General Lawrence O'Brien recommended that the post office become a nonprofit government corporation, that any substantive changes were adopted.[51] After years of congressional debate, the Postal Reorganization Act was signed in 1970.[52]

Telephone Service

Although not operated by the federal government,[53] policies were also established to promote universal telephone service. Beginning in 1949, telephone service into rural areas was subsidized as a result of federal legislation,[54] much as rural mail delivery was subsidized by more profitable routes. Universal service was advocated in 1908 by AT&T in exchange for its right to operate a regulated monopoly.[55] In AT&T's 1910 Annual Report, company leader Theodore Vail wrote, "[t]he telephone system should be universal . . . affording opportunity for any subscriber of any exchange to communicate with any other subscriber of any other exchange . . . that some sort of connection with the telephone system should be within the reach of all."[56] As with mail service, fear of "cream skimming" (the process of servicing only the more lucrative markets) was used as justification for monopoly.[57] Following World War II, 80 percent of homes in the United States had telephones.[58] Telephone service is now available to virtually every home in America, with 93 percent subscribing.[59] As with postal service, there are other arguments for provision of the service;[60] clearly provision of universal service provides for a nationwide system of communication.

The arguments for deregulating telephone service and eliminating the AT&T monopoly made a great deal of sense after 1960, when universal service was virtually achieved.[61] If AT&T was protected to achieve the national goal of universal service, AT&T's own success suggested such protection was no longer necessary. In fact, however, two subsidy systems were at work in the provision of universal service: subsidizing local rates with long distance income[62] and subsidizing local service for rural markets, or new developments, by income from already built, urban systems. While the consent decree in the divestiture of AT&T lowered long distance rates in exchange for local "access charges,"[63] connection to the phone system remains a constant cost for consumers, regardless of whether the connection is made one block from the electronic switch, or miles from the nearest town. If pricing policy were based on costs, rural areas and small towns would see much higher prices.[64] In addition, line charges for businesses and access charges are well above those for residences receiving the same service.[65]

PROPOSAL SPECIFICS

The provision of a public forum for the discussion of ideas should be the responsibility of a government interested in expanding free expression opportunities. The forum should be provided in a way that expands speech opportunities, while not infringing on speech opportunities currently being used by others. The provision of access channels would provide such a public forum, and at the same time, not infringe on private rights of individual station operators. Public forum cases support the notion that provision of forums may involve costs that the state may assume.[66] There can be costs associated with the administration of the forum, as well as with providing protection for speakers or marches and clean-up afterward.[67] While the state may also impose user fees to cover the costs of administering the forum, as soon as the costs become too high, they preclude some speakers.[68]

Congress should take action to provide opportunities for individual expression by providing the public forum. As early as 1972 there have been questions as to who decides who will speak on access channels, and what subjects are off-limits.[69] It is not the responsibility of government to determine the relative worth of speech, so this forum must be provided without content determinations. The government has in fact operated the Corporation for Public Broadcasting and managed to avoid editorial control.[70] While this may appear only to fill the airwaves with worthless diatribes, it would do far more to guarantee individuals their right of self-expression than the existing system,[71] or any other proposal to date.[72] In *Cohen v California*,[73] the Supreme Court made clear the importance of individual self-expression:

To many, the immediate consequence of this freedom may often appear to be only verbal tumult, discord and even offensive utterance. These are, however, within established limits, in truth necessary side effects of the broader enduring values which the process of open debate permits us to achieve. That the air may at times seem filled with verbal cacophony is, in this sense, not a sign of weakness but of strength.[74]

Individuals interested in expressing themselves on any subject would be able to do so, but would not necessarily be guaranteed listeners. The requisite of the First Amendment is not an audience, but a forum. At present, such a forum is limited.

Since broadcasters currently use the spectrum at no charge, and realize a significant profit from the use of this valuable asset,[75] it would be appropriate to charge a spectrum use fee. A number of other existing proposals support spectrum use fees, often as means to provide general revenue or to support public broadcasting.[76] While spectrum use fees have been considered previously and rejected,[77] such fees would likely pass constitutional muster. Mark Nadel asserts that the First Amendment "permits, and probably even supports, the imposition of economic regulations to facilitate access to all media."[78] The fee could be a flat percentage of gross revenues, similar to cable franchise fees, or a formula based on classification of station, bandwidth of spectrum used, and market size. While the fee based on gross revenue would be logical from the perspective of stations' ability to pay, the latter fee might be more appropriate because it would tax stations based on how much spectrum they occupy and in how much demand that spectrum is. One of the complaints leveled against franchise fees is that their collection as part of general city revenues does not promote the societal goals of the First Amendment, as would be appropriate for a fee on communications activity. [79] Spectrum fees collected to provide a free expression forum would promote just such a value.

It would be most appropriate to locate access channels on the AM band, because those allocations are experiencing the greatest difficulty. [80] AM's inferior reproduction of music when compared with FM is often cited as one of the major AM problems, which is another reason to locate discussion-centered stations on the AM band. [81] In fact, a couple of AM stations in south Florida have attempted to sell blocks of time for $75 to $300 per hour to anyone interested in programming almost anything. [82] Such a station might allow those "screened out" by call-in talk shows (discussed in Chapter 5) to have a forum. It is questionable whether this practice is allowable under FCC regulations for sponsorship identification. The rules currently require program underwriters to be identified, [83] but a change could be easily accomplished. It might be contended that the existence of these stations demonstrates the effectiveness of the marketplace at satisfying existing needs. While the stations are a welcome addition to the existing forums, they are still not as appropriate as government-funded stations would be. Once again, the system favors those with the economic means to speak.

It would also be appropriate to expand access channels to low-power television (LPTV) facilities at some point in the future. Localism has been an important part of the development of LPTV stations. [84] A variety of existing LPTV stations serve the needs of special interests, broadcasting to a specialized audience. For example, Channel 53 in New York programs for Asian-Americans; Channel 58 in Buffalo is targeted to the university community; Channel 45 in Panama City, Florida, is for tourists; Channel 39 in Marshalltown, Iowa, and Channel 11 in Lebanon, Tennessee, serve farmers; Channel 6 in Princeton, Indiana, is run by and for teens; and Channel 65 in Milwaukee programs for blacks. [85] These isolated examples of commercial success, however, do not imply that the marketplace will provide access outlets, because there is no claim that any of these stations will provide access to residents seeking it. What these stations demonstrate is the ability of LPTV stations to do something other than traditional broadcast television and attract an adequate audience.

Since the purpose of the proposed stations is to provide a broadcast expression opportunity to those who otherwise do not have one, it would be most appropriate to locate these stations in markets where no broadcast allocations remain available. The incongruity here is that markets with no available allocations could not make room for access channels without eliminating an existing licensee. Some of the current changes envisioned for the AM band discussed in Chapter 4, such as increased allocation at the upper end, would make a new channel available for access use.

As an alternative to federal provision of access opportunities, states should act to provide the forum. Warren Freedman states that "[t]he state has a legal obligation to ensure a rich matrix of public forums required for the exercise of free speech principles, especially since most state constitution provisions for freedom of speech are directed against private activities, as well as against government actions."[86] State constitutions have been seen as means of supplementing individual rights protected by the federal government.[87] A state constitution was the reason the Supreme Court validated a California right of access to shopping centers in *Pruneyard*,[88] and similar affirmative rights have been established by other states.[89] While states are precluded by federal authority from spectrum allocation, states have successfully argued before the courts for an expanded role in intrastate communication regulation.[90] In addition, nothing prevents states from applying for licenses to operate stations as access channels.

SUMMARY

In the interest of expanding self-expression opportunities for its citizens, the government ought to establish access channels. Access channels, instead of access requirements on existing media, provide expression opportunities for those seeking them, without infringing on the rights of those who own media outlets. This approach recognizes the need to balance between First Amendment values and to avoid conflicts where possible.

These channels would be funded by spectrum fees paid by broadcast licensees and made available to all who wished to use them. The fees would be appropriate because spectrum users currently profit from a government-provided resource, yet pay nothing in return. The use of the fees strictly as a means of improving communication opportunities and advancing First Amendment goals would make their collection more acceptable than earlier fees, proposed merely to provide general revenue. If the fee is truly for use of the spectrum, rather than merely a new tax, it would also be appropriate to base the fee on a formula related to frequency and bandwidth used and the demand on them, rather than a flat percentage of gross revenues or profit.

At first, stations could be established on the AM band, in those communities where no allocations remain available. This would, in fact, mean beginning with the largest markets and developing stations there first. Allocations could be made above 1600 kHz, a portion of band allocated to AM, but as yet unlicensed in this country. It is hoped that low-power television stations would be added to the matrix of available public forums provided by the government at some point in the not-too-distant future, in the similar pattern of spectrum-congested markets first.

NOTES

1. Note, *Access to the Press in Light of the Traditional Concept of Journalistic Freedom*, 8 SUFFOLK U. L. REV. 682, 684 (1974). The Supreme Court embraced this position in CBS v DNC, 412 U.S. 94 (1973). The majority feared mandated access for editorial advertising would be a "further erosion of the journalistic discretion of broadcasters." *Id.*, at 124. This fear was based on assertions made in *Tornillo*, discussed in Chapter 2.

2. Barron's writings on the subject include: *Access To The Press: A New First Amendment Right*, 80 HARV. L. REV. 1641 (1967); *An Emerging First Amendment Right of Access to the Media?* 37 GEO. WASH. L. REV. 487 (1969); *Access—The Only Choice for the Media?* 48 TEX L. REV. 766 (1970); *From Fairness to Access* in A STATE OF SIEGE 133 (M. Barrett ed. 1971); *Public Access to the Media and its Critics* in LIBERATING THE MEDIA 173 (C. Flippen ed. 1973); FREEDOM OF THE PRESS FOR WHOM? 1973; PUBLIC RIGHTS AND THE PRIVATE PRESS, 1981, and; *The Search for Media Accountability* 19 SUFFOLK U. L. REV. 789 (1985).

3. J. BARRON, PUBLIC RIGHTS AND THE PRIVATE PRESS 21 (1981). "Free speech cannot mean much if one has no meaningful forum in which to exercise the right."

4. For criticism of Barron's approach to media access, *see e.g.*, Bagdikian, *Right of Access: A Modest Proposal*, 8 COLUM. JOURNALISM REV. 10 (Spring, 1969) (access right would make news organizations common carriers); Daniel, *Right of Access to the Mass Media—Government Obligation to Enforce the First Amendment?* 48 TEX L. REV. 783 (1970) (impracticality of a right of access); Jaffe, *The Editorial Responsibility of the Broadcaster: Reflections on Fairness and Access*, 85 HARV. L. REV. 768 (1972) (less to fear from private censors than from government); Merril, *Access to the Press: Who Decides?* THE FREEMAN 48 (Jan. 1968) (freedom of the press implies the freedom not to print); address by J. Murray, *The Editor's Right to Decide* (1969) (published by University of Arizona Press) (affirmative dimension of the First Amendment is deceptive reversal of free press); Wulf, *Excess Aging*, 1 CIVIL LIBERTIES REV. 128 (1974) (access confuses circulation of ideas with their adoption).

5. Baker contends that even a marketplace of ideas value of free expression would support an access scheme in order to facilitate equal participation opportunity. Baker, *Scope of the First Amendment Freedom of Speech*, 25 UCLA L. REV. 964, 984 (1978).

6. Nadel, *A Unified Theory of the First Amendment: Divorcing the Medium From the Message*, 11 FORDHAM L. REV. 163, 191 n. 103 (1982).

7. 42 U.S.L.W. 3590 (April 23, 1974) cited in Yodelis, *The Rejection of Florida's Right to Reply Statute: A Setback for a "New Right" of Access to the Press*, 20 N.Y.L.F. 633 (1975).

8. Emerson, *The Affirmative Side Of The First Amendment*, 15 GA. L. REV. 795, 824 (1981) (protection of free expression requires government involvement).

9. "No person shall . . . be deprived of life, liberty or property, without due process of law; nor shall private property be taken for public use, without just compensation." U.S. CONST. amend. V. *See* First English Evangelical Church of Glendale v County of Los Angeles, 482 U.S. 304 (1987) (temporary taking is still a taking); Ruckleshaus v Monsanto Co., 467 U.S. 986 (1984) (trade secrets are similar to property, and are protected by taking clause); Loretto v Manhattan CATV Corp., 458 U.S. 419 (1982) (small volume of space occupied still constitutes illegal taking); Pennsylvania Coal Co. v Mahon, 260 U.S. 393 (1922) ("while property may be regulated . . . , if regulation goes too far it will be recognized as a taking.")

10. Webb's Fabulous Pharmacies, Inc. v Beckwith, 449 U.S. 155 (1980). *See also* Elliot v Sperry Rand Corp., 680 F. 2d 1225, 1228 (8th Cir. 1982); Fountain v Metro Atlanta Rapid Transit Authority, 678 F. 2d 1038, 1042 (5th Cir. 1982) (federal Constitution protects individuals from takings of property for public use without just compensation); Hernandez v City of Lafayette, 643 F. 2d 1188, 1200 (5th Cir. 1981); Rippley v City of Lincoln, 330 N.W. 2d 505, 507 (N.D. 1983) (just compensation clause of Fifth Amendment applicable to states through due process clause of Fourteenth Amendment); Noranda Exploration, Inc. v Ostrom, 335 N.W. 2d 596, 603 (Wis. 1983).

11. *See* Nadel, *supra* note 6, at 197 (private media owners enjoy property rights).

12. FCC v Midwest Video 440 U.S. 689, 709 (1979). However, the Supreme Court decision suggests that if the privately owned forum is indistinguishable from a public forum, it must be treated as public. See the discussion of *Marsh* and the shopping malls cases in Chapter 2.

13. *See also* CBS, Inc. v FCC, 629 F. 2d 1, 23–24 (D.C. Cir. 1980) (access requirement for federal candidates acceptable, distinguishing cable from over-the-air TV); Midland Telecasting Co. v Midessa Television Co., 617 F. 2d 1141, 1146 (5th Cir. 1980) (requirement of signal carriage converts cable to common carrier).

14. Barron, *Access to the Press*, *supra* note 2, at 1641.

15. *Id.*, at 1678. "[C]ompetition within a medium is no assurance that significant opinions will have no difficulty in securing access to newspaper space or broadcast time."

16. *Responsible Piracy*, RADIO WORLD, June 26, 1991, at 5 (letter to the editor by Ed Cole).

17. Note, *Regulation of Commercial Speech: Commercial Access to News-papers*, 35 MD. L. REV. 115 (1975) (state statutes providing limited right of commercial access should be allowed); Comment, *The Right of Access to the Press*, 60 NEB. L. REV. 120 (1970) (denying editorial advertising limits discussion of public affairs).

18. V. KEY, PUBLIC OPINION AND AMERICAN DEMOCRACY 387 (1961) (UAW's difficulty buying time to advocate its position on postwar reconversion); D. LACY, FREEDOM AND COMMUNICATION 69–75 (1965) (advertiser desires audience that is not only large, but that "has not been offended or depressed or startled or shocked or stimulated to resentment or rejection that might unconsciously be attached to the advertised product.") As most stations are owned by corporations needing sufficient revenues to support station purchases (see Chapter 5), the importance of enhancing advertising revenue rather than driving away audience is acute. There have been several instances of boycotts orchestrated by special interests, targeted at media for a variety of content-related reasons, including immorality (Coalition for Better Television) and gun control (National Rifle Association). HEAD & STERLING, BROAD-CASTING IN AMERICA 459 (5th ed. 1987).

19. W. VAN ALSTYNE, INTERPRETATIONS OF THE FIRST AMENDMENT 71 (1984).

20. D. LANGE, R. BAKER, & S. BALL, MASS MEDIA AND VIOLENCE (1969).

21. L. POWE, JR., BROADCASTING AND THE FIRST AMENDMENT (1987).

22. Emerson, *supra* note 8, at 815. The economic and technological constraints alluded to by Emerson are discussed in Chapter 5. Similarly, access to the ballot has often been difficult for those whose beliefs do not coincide with the mainstream. The Supreme Court has been inconsistent in requiring removal of roadblocks. *Compare, e.g.*, Williams v Rhodes, 393 U.S. 23 (1968) (requirements that made it "virtually impossible" for new political parties to be placed on ballot unconstitutional) *with* Jenness v Fortson, 403 U.S. 431 (1971) (some support for party must be shown before its name can appear on ballot). *See* Note, *Early Filing Deadline Unconstitutional: A Trend Toward Strict Scrutiny in Ballot Access Cases*, 18 SUFFOLK U.L. REV. 24 (1984).

23. Baker, *Unreasoned Reasonableness*, 78 N.W.U.L. REV. 937, 978 (1983). Application of public forum analysis to electronic media is discussed in Chapter 3.

24. New York Times Co. v Sullivan, 376 U.S. 254, 266 (1964). *See* New York State Broadcasters Ass'n. v U.S., 414 F. 2d 990, 998 (2nd Cir. 1969) (advertisements on matters of public concern entitled to protection). *Cf.* Lee v Board of Regents, 441 F. 2d 1257 (7th Cir. 1971) (state university newspaper must accept editorial advertisement) *But cf.* Mississippi Gay Alliance v Goudelock, 536 F. 2d 1073, cert. denied 45 LW 3707 (1977) (editor of student newspaper may exclude editorial ads). *Lee* and *Goudelock* both dealt with

another issue (whether the denial was state action). Yet the question of advertising as a means of access for unpopular opinions is still inherent.

25. *The Fairness Doctrine Can Hurt*, BROADCASTING, Mar. 3, 1986, at 67. CBS has a policy not to air commercials that raise controversial issues. F. ROWAN, BROADCAST FAIRNESS 155 (1984). ABC and NBC rejected ad hoc, believing *the content* to be inappropriate and too provocative. CBS finally consented to run the advertisement, provided Grace deleted a line relating to a proposed constitutional amendment. *CBS to Air Grace's Amended Deficit Spot*, NEW YORK TIMES, Aug 21, 1986 at D21. Even after the *CBS* decision, the Grace spot did not air on the network, because the corporation had by then exhausted its annual advertising budget. Behrens, *Going Soft: The Emergence of a Buyers' Market*, CHANNEL FIELD GUIDE '87, Dec. 1986, at 16.

26. CBS v DNC 412 U.S. 94, 125 (1973) (fairness doctrine does not mandate a "system of self-appointed commentators"). *See also* Balsam, *The Media's Right to Refuse Advertising*, 1985 ANN. SURV. AM. L. 699. This "equal access once provided" approach is similar to that adopted by the Court for other, nonbroadcast forums. A city may exclude from car cards on buses a certain class of advertising, such as political ads, as long as it does so uniformly. Lehman v Shaker Heights, 418 U.S. 298 (1974). On a military base, even space open to the public can have nondiscriminatory restrictions on political speeches. Greer v Spock, 424 U.S. 828 (1976). *See* Chapter 2 for a full discussion of these cases.

27. Barron, *Access to the Press*, *supra* note 2, at 1649. While never explicitly enunciated as such, the Court seems to have followed this thinking. *Cf.* U.S. v Storer Broadcasting, 351 U.S. 192 (1956) (ownership limits on broadcast properties constitutional); Associated Press v U.S. 326 U.S. 1 (1945) (restrictive membership policies of AP restraint of trade); NBC v U.S., 319 U.S. 190 (1943) (upholding FCC right to limit network control).

28. Adams, *Access Provides a Forum for Discussions on National Issues*. 9 COMMUNITY TELEVISION REV. 23 (1986).

29. Boylan, *The Ability to Communicate: A First Amendment Right* in THE MASS MEDIA AND MODERN DEMOCRACY 137, 160 (H. Clor ed. 1974).

30. Barron, *Access to the Press*, *supra* note 2, at 1653. It is indeed ironic that in the same journal article, Barron speaks not of equal, but "adequate opportunities for discussion" (at 1656) and of a "minimal right of access" (at 1655). Barron asserts his comment relates to media "responsiveness" rather than equal access. Letter from Jerome A. Barron (Feb. 17, 1987).

31. B. SCHMIDT, FREEDOM OF THE PRESS VERSUS PUBLIC ACCESS 19 (1976).

32. Emerson, *supra* note 8, at 818.

33. Lehman v City of Shaker Heights, 418 U.S. 298, 307 (1974) (Douglas, J., concurring) (while petitioner clearly has right to express views to those who wish to listen, no right to force message on an audience incapable of declining to receive it.) *See also* Consolidated Edison v Public Serv. Comm'n., 447 U.S. 530, 542 (1980) (customers encountering bill insert are not a captive

audience); Erznoznik v City of Jacksonville, 422 U.S. 205, 208–212 (1975) (drive-in theater screen is not so obtrusive as to make passersby a captive audience); Bigelow v Virginia, 421 U.S. 809, 828 (1975) (newspaper advertisement not thrust on a captive audience).

34. In the Matter of the Handling of Public Issues Under the Fairness Doctrine and Public Interest Standard of the Communications Act, 30 FCC 2d 26 (1971). Before the commission had abandoned the doctrine, it rejected alternatives based on content considerations. The Committee for Open Media (COM) submitted a proposal to replace the Fairness Doctrine with access time provided by broadcasters on a first-come basis. According to the FCC, one of the reasons for rejecting the COM proposal was:

> [W]hile the Fairness Doctrine rests on the principle of an informed public, the COM access proposal "is content or issue neutral," focusing instead on "access by speakers to the audience, not on access by the audience to ideas." . . . Neither the COM proposal nor any other "access as substitute" system currently before the Commission, unlike present Fairness compliance, is designed to assure that the public be informed on *controversial issues of public importance*.

Id., at 171–172. Emphasis in original.

35. The FCC has been asked to arbitrate in complaints involving the controversy of an issue's impact, National Football League Players Assn., 39 FCC 2d 248 (1973), whether a program is controversial or merely informational, Central Maine Broadcast System, 23 FCC 2d 45 (1970), and whether a certain issue is a local controversy, Patsy Mink, 59 FCC 2d 984 (1976). In *NFL*, the FCC held a sports commentator's comments regarding football players' pensions was not a controversial issue of public importance. *Central Maine* involved a League of Women Voters program claimed by the station to be merely informational, but determined by the FCC to raise controversial issues. Representative Patsy Mink complained to the FCC when a West Virginia station refused to air anti-strip-mining programming. The FCC ruled in favor of Mink, because to West Virginians, it was a controversy. *See* A. SHAPIRO, MEDIA ACCESS 107–168 (1976).

36. City Council v Taxpayers for Vincent, 104 S. Ct. 2118, 2135 (1984). "Even though political speech is entitled to the fullest possible measure of constitutional protection, there are a host of other communications that command the same respect."

37. Barron, *An Emerging First Amendment Right of Access to the Media?* *supra* note 2, at 507.

38. T. EMERSON, THE SYSTEM OF FREEDOM OF EXPRESSION 364 (1970).

39. Near v Minnesota, 283 U.S. 697 (1931), quoting Blackstone.

40. Telephone interview with Bob Devine, Executive Director of the Milwaukee Access Telecommunications Authority (Aug. 7, 1986). Many

cable systems have some system of training access users. *See* Cable Access in Chapter 5.

41. H. LEVIN, THE INVISIBLE RESOURCE 16 (1971).

42. W. BRASCH & D. ULLOTH, THE PRESS AND THE STATE 621–648 (1986).

43. NATIONAL TELECOMMUNICATIONS AND INFORMATION ADMINISTRATION, NTIA TELECOM 2000: CHARTING THE COURSE FOR A NEW CENTURY 78 (1988) [hereinafter cited as TELECOM 2000].

44. *Id.*

45. *See* R. KIELBOWICZ, NEWS IN THE MAIL 1–56 (1989).

46. W. FULLER, THE AMERICAN MAIL 49 (1972).

47. *Id.*, at 18–21.

48. R. SHERMAN, PERSPECTIVES ON POSTAL SERVICE ISSUES 2 (1980).

49. W. FULLER, *supra* note 45, at 76, 139.

50. Second-class mailing rates, however, do show unequal treatment. The rate is available only to publications requested by one-half or more of recipients, discriminating against unsolicited publications. *See* Gorman, *The First Amendment and the Postal Service's Subscriber Requirement: Constitutional Problems with Denying Equal Access to the Postal System*, 21 UNIV. RICHMOND L. REV. 541 (1987).

51. D. FOWLER, UNMAILABLE 187 (1977).

52. *Id.*, at 192.

53. Congress had at least considered the matter of government ownership of the telephone system. In 1983, the Walker Report stated that government ownership, as was the norm in other countries, might be easier than establishing effective competition. F. HENCK & B. STRASSBURG, A SLIPPERY SLOPE 7 (1988).

54. TELECOM 2000, *supra* note 43, at 79.

55. G. FAULHABER, TELECOMMUNICATIONS IN TURMOIL 6 (1987).

56. W TUNSTALL, DISCONNECTING PARTIES 2–3 (1985).

57. *Id.*, at 24.

58. *Id.*, at 18.

59. *Id.* Removal of the subsidy system, as part of the AT&T divestiture's modified final judgment, may actually have decreased the percentage of the population with basic phone service. The percentage of homes with service in 1984 was higher than 95 percent. Mitchell, *Pricing Subscriber Access to the Telephone Network* in TELECOMMUNICATIONS ACCESS AND PUBLIC POLICY (A. Baughcum & G. Faulhaber eds. 1984), at 70.

60. Often cited as a reason for universal service is the use of the telephone for emergencies.

61. G. FAULHABER, *supra* note 55, at 34, 48.

62. The FCC estimated this subsidy to total $10 billion per year. W. TUNSTALL, *supra* note 56, at 94.

63. G. FAULHABER, *supra* note 55, at 90–92. A telephone access charge is the fee paid to be connected by the local phone company to an interstate system.

64. Noll, *Telecommunications Regulation in the 1990s* in 1 NEW DIRECTIONS IN TELECOMMUNICATIONS POLICY 11, 25 (P. Newberg ed. 1989).

65. Crandall, *Fragmentation of the Telephone Network*, in 1 NEW DIRECTIONS IN TELECOMMUNICATIONS POLICY 49, 64 (P. Newberg ed. 1989).

66. M. YUDOF, WHEN GOVERNMENT SPEAKS 236 (1983).

67. Blasi, *Prior Restraints on Demonstrations*, 68 MICHIGAN L. REV. 1481 (1970).

68. *Id.*, at 1527.

69. Brenner, *TV Access: The New Soapbox*, AMERICA, May 6, 1972, at 477, 479.

70. Canby, *The First Amendment and the State as Editor: Implications for Public Broadcasting*, 52 TEXAS L. REV. 1123 (1974).

71. Often quoted is A. J. Liebling's statement, "[f]reedom of the press is only guaranteed to those who own one." *The Wayward Press*, THE NEW YORKER, May 14, 1960, 105, at 109.

72. In addition to the schemes mentioned above, a system mandating acceptance by commercial media of paid advertising has also been proposed. Sandage, *The Right to Know*, 12 GRASSROOTS EDITOR 4 (1971), and Note, *The Duty of Newspapers to Accept Political Advertising*, 44 IND. L. J. 222 (1969). Of course, this would provide access only to those with economic means. CBS v DNC, 412 U.S. 94, 123 (1973).

73. 403 U.S. 15 (1971). The Supreme Court held a man wearing a jacket bearing the words "fuck the draft" was exercising his constitutionally protected right of free expression.

74. *Id.*, at 24–25.

75. It has been debated whether the spectrum is a public resource. Whether it is or not, it is clearly an asset to commercial broadcasters who could not function without it. The precise value of the spectrum used is discussed in Chapter 4.

76. *See, e.g.*, Geller, *Broadcasting*, in NEW DIRECTIONS IN TELECOMMUNICATIONS POLICY 125, 141 (P. Newberg ed. 1989).

77. *Spectrum Fees Not in Senate Commerce Budget Package*, BROADCASTING, July 31, 1989, at 19.

78. Nadel, *supra* note 6, at 191.

79. Comment, *Cable Television Franchise Fees for General Revenues: The 1984 Cable Act, Wisconsin Law, and the First Amendment*, 5 WISCONSIN L. REV. 1273, 1297 n. 127.

80. *Can AM Radio Be Saved?* BROADCASTING, July 3, 1989, at 20.

81. *AM Radio: The Fidelity Factor*, BROADCASTING, Aug. 21, 1989, at 38.

82. *Selling the Airwaves*, RADIO WORLD, May 24, 1989, at 2.

83. 47 U.S.C. 507.

84. *Localism, HDTV, Hot Topics at NAB Panel*, LPTV REPORT, April 1990, at 1.

85. Biel, *In Our View*, LPTV REPORT, April 1990, at 3.

86. W. FREEDMAN, FREEDOM OF SPEECH ON PRIVATE PROPERTY 78 (1988).

87. Sedler, *The State Constitutions and The Supplemental Protection of Individual Rights*, 16 UNIV. TOLEDO L. REV. 465, 466 (1985).

88. 447 U.S. 74 (1980).

89. *See supra* Chapter 2.

90. *See* Louisiana Public Service Comm'n. v FCC, 476 U.S. 355 (1986) (states allowed to regulate intrastate portion of telephone equipment that can be separated from interstate); People of State of California v FCC, 798 F. 2d 1515 (D.C. Cir. 1986) (federal rule preempting state entry regulation of radio common carriers overruled).

7 CONCLUSION

Freedom of expression has been a central premise of American life for centuries. Despite differences of opinion regarding the precise meaning of the First Amendment, free speech is seen as a positive contribution to our way of life, and steps are constantly being taken to develop that freedom.

Free expression is valued for a variety of reasons including its contribution to the discovery of truth, its relationship to self-governance in a democratic society, its function as a "safety valve" for those dissatisfied with their lot, and as a sort of "fourth branch" of government, acting as a check on government indiscretions. Free expression also has value as a means of self-fulfillment: a part of what it means to be human. A human rights approach to free expression is the most expansive of the values in that it protects not only the right of individuals to speak freely, but also attempts to promote the means by which individuals can be self-actualized. This requires the provision of forums in which individuals can freely express themselves.

Historically, the government has been responsible for maintaining a variety of forums in which individuals could express themselves. The most recognized of these forums is the traditional public forum (such as streets and parks) that the government provides for use by all. Regulation of content or speakers within the forum is limited to logistical considerations, such as the time, place, and manner of the speech. Determination that the government owns a property does not automatically convert it to a public forum, nor does its ownership by private parties indicate its exclusion. Rather, analysis requires an examination of the uses to which the forum historically has been dedicated.

In the area of mass communication media, the government has established a limited right of access to broadcasting facilities while it has emphatically rejected any similar right to print media. Individuals who have been personally attacked have a right of reply, and candidates for federal office have a right to reasonable access during political campaigns. Beyond those two groups, there is no right of access to broadcast media. There was a federal requirement that larger cable systems provide public access channels, but that has been eliminated, and local communities determine whether to require access channels as part of franchise agreements. The only cable access requirement is that of a leased access channel for larger systems. While better than nothing, the forum is available only to those with the economic means to participate.

Differential treatment of print and broadcast media has been questioned in recent years. Proponents of broadcast deregulation cite the vast increase in existing radio and television stations. They further point to the fact that without fail, broadcast outlets outnumber print media available in every market. Those who advocate deregulation from this perspective are confusing the concept of scarcity and the idea of diversity. They ignore the reality that allows entry to print markets while requiring government licensing to broadcast. Especially in major markets, there are still more people wishing authorization to operate stations than there are frequencies available, perhaps due, in part, to the fact that the government authorization to use a limited resource comes free to the user, allowing individuals to profit tremendously from the license. The government then protects this valuable oligopoly by preventing additional broadcast entrants.

While recent federal emphasis has been placed on allowing marketplace forces to regulate in place of government restriction, the broadcast spectrum has never been treated as a marketplace. In addition to the fact that spectrum is given away, its use is tremendously restricted. Those allocated can use their frequency only for its designated purpose, and there is no incentive to use the allocation more efficiently. Individuals cannot elect to "sell off" a portion of their allocation, share it with another, or modify their transmissions in any manner not approved by the federal government.

The management of the spectrum has been a complicated, tedious process, often lagging behind current technological realities. While broadcasting allocations actually occupy a relatively small portion of the spectrum, they are constantly scrutinized because of their value. Broadcasters battle with other spectrum users to increase their allocations, winning some and losing some. The greatest difficulty with the current management of the spectrum is its priority for existing systems. New technologies must find ways of operating within existing technological standards, or eke out a portion of spectrum from an underutilized allocation (or one with a less powerful lobby). Current spectrum users stand as obstacles to new technologies, having no interest in providing space for future competitors nor any economic incentive to do so.

In determining free expression rights, it is often necessary to balance the rights of the speaker with those of the listener. The Supreme Court has reached contrary decisions regarding whose rights are more deserving, often depending on the venue involved. In the area of broadcasting, the listeners' rights seem to have preference over those of the speaker. The Supreme Court seems to have adopted a paternalistic attitude, supported both by Congress and the FCC, that speech able to penetrate the privacy of the home must show deference to the sensibilities and sensitivities of the audience. On the other hand, speech conducted in public places is entitled to greater protection, and may even insult or aggravate the audience.

For the average American, there are a variety of existing forums that allow free expression. In those cities where cable access channels are available, the channels have effectively allowed for individual expression as well as the discussion of important social issues. A number of cable access centers have distinguished themselves as forums for alternative expression. In those few locales where community radio stations exist, they also provide an alternative forum. Citizens band radio could have been the medium to provide individuals the opportunity for self-expression, and still has that potential, but due to regulatory restrictions and historical context, CB has developed into something else for most users. Computer bulletin board services have great potential for allowing individuals to interact with others, but require money and expertise for participation. Computer bulletin boards have the added advantage of virtually unlimited capacity. Unlike broadcast frequencies, increased use does not preclude the entrance of additional speakers. Letters to the editor and call-in talk radio programs also provide a forum for expression, albeit a limited one. The percentage of those actually able to access those forums, and the fact that their remarks are often abridged, limit their value as true forums for public expression.

If the government desires to make forums for expression available, one way is providing broadcast access channels for public use. The channels would be most needed in communities where access is limited, predominantly major cities. The channels could be funded by a spectrum user fee imposed on other users of the broadcast spectrum who are profiting from its use with no monetary benefit being derived by its true owners, the public. Precedent exists for government-supported expression opportunities. Most obviously, the maintenance of streets and parks as traditional public forums implies government willingness to support expression. In addition, however, the government has supported subsidization of both mail and telephone service as a means of affording equal, minimal access to the means of communication. It should be willing to do the same with the broadcast spectrum, the electronic soap box.

The concept of providing access to the media is not a new one, but the proposal contained in this treatise is unique in its recognition of the free speech rights of the owners and operators of currently existing media outlets. There is no assertion that those who own and operate stations should provide free time, or use of their facilities, for the free expression benefit of others. There is, however, the claim that those who gain from use of the spectrum should be expected to pay for its use.

Questions of access have not been resolved. While the FCC continues to contemplate the disposition of political broadcasting rules, and Congress debates fine tuning its earlier cable legislation, the problem of access grows. New technologies increase the demand on spectrum, and access questions, once thought settled in other areas, will undoubtedly become problematic for new media. Research is definitely needed in the area of spectrum management. The task is far too important to be left to politicians or broadcasters, both of whom have vested interests in the outcome, and are likely to support status quo resolutions.

Perhaps the greater contribution of this book is the proposition that free expression for the sake of self-fulfillment is at least as important as for any other reason, including the often argued democratic purpose. As such, this research adopts the position that opportunities for free expression ought to be expanded by the government whenever the prospect presents itself. Free expression as a human right should be not only protected but expanded in ways that benefit individuals and, in turn, society as a whole.

Thomas Emerson provides the four main premises for the value of free expression in a democratic society. While a few may disagree with some of the premises, by and large the problems with the list are usually not with the individual values themselves, but rather with how to resolve conflicts arising whenever the values conflict with one another. Additional research ought to examine ways of resolving the conflict between free expression values in some rational way, especially in areas where the rights of speakers and the rights of listeners conflict.

SELECTED BIBLIOGRAPHY

Abrams, F. 1970. The Press Is Different: Reflections on Justice Stewart and the Autonomous Press. *Hofstra Law Review* 7:563–592.

————. 1987. Review of *Printers and Press Freedom*, by Jeffery Smith. *New York Times Book Review*, 1 Nov., 30.

Adams, B. 1986. Access Provides a Forum for Discussions on National Issues. *Community Television Review* 9, no. 1:23, 38.

Adams, P. 1987. Seeking Audience Feedback. *Phi Kappa Phi Journal* 68, no. 4:18–20.

Adler, M. 1961. *The Idea of Freedom.* 2 vols. New York: Doubleday & Co.

Alderson, J. 1981. Everyman TV. *Columbia Journalism Review*, Jan./Feb.: 39–42.

Aleong, S., and M. Chretien. 1981. Can Smokey the Bear Speak French? Adapting CB Lingo in Canadian French. *American Speech*, Winter:260–268.

Altschull, J. 1984. *Agents of Power.* New York: Longman.

American Radio Network Keeps AM Talking. 1990. *Broadcasting*, 19 March, 55.

AM Radio: The Fidelity Factor. 1989. *Broadcasting*, 21 Aug., 38–40.

Anderson, D. 1983. The Origins of the Press Clause. *UCLA Law Review* 30:455–537.

Armstrong, C. and A. Rubin. 1989. Talk Radio as Interpersonal Communication. *Journal of Communication* 39:84–94.

Atkin, D. 1987. The Low Power Elite. *Telecommunications Policy* Dec.:357–368.

Atkin, D., and R. LaRose. 1988. News and Information on Community Access Channels: Market Concerns Amidst the Marketplace of Ideas. Paper presented at the 71st Annual Convention of the Association for Education in Journalism and Mass Communication, 2–5 July, Portland, Oregon.

Attractiveness of Broadcast Properties Comes at a Price, 1986. *Television/Radio Age*, 21 July, 30.

Baer, W. 1989. New Communications Technologies and Services. In *New Directions in Telecommunications Policy*, vol. 2, ed. P. Newberg. Durham: Duke Univ. Press.

Bagdikian, B. 1969. Right of Access: A Modest Proposal. *Columbia Journalism Review* 8, Spring:10–13.

Baker, C. 1978. Scope of the First Amendment Freedom of Speech. *UCLA Law Review* 25:964–1004.

———. 1981. The Process of Change and the Liberty Theory of the First Amendment. *Southern California Law Review* 55:293–344.

———. 1983. Unreasoned Reasonableness. *Northwestern Univ. Law Review* 78:937–1024.

Baldwin, T., and D. McVoy. 1983. *Cable Communication*. Englewood Cliffs, N.J.: Prentice-Hall.

Balsam, C. 1985. The Media's Right to Refuse Advertising. *Annual Survey of American Law* 1985:699–711.

Barnett, M. 1980. Newspaper Monopoly and the Law. *Journal of Communication* 30:72.

Barnouw, E. 1966. *A History of Broadcasting in the United States*. 3 vols. New York: Oxford Univ. Press.

Barone, M., and J. Schrof. 1990. The Changing Voice of Talk Radio. *U.S. News & World Report*, 15 Jan., 51–53.

Barron, J. 1967. Access to the Press: A New First Amendment Right. *Harvard Law Review* 80:1641–1678.

———. 1969. An Emerging First Amendment Right of Access to the Media? *George Washington Law Review* 37:487–511.

———. 1970. Access—The Only Choice for the Media. *Texas Law Review* 48:766–782.

———. 1971. From Fairness to Access. In *A State of Seige*, ed. M. Barrett. New York: Grossit & Dunlap.

———. 1973a. *Freedom of the Press for Whom?* Bloomington: Indiana Univ. Press.

———. 1973b. Public Access to the Media and Its Critics. In *Liberating the Media*, ed. C. Flippen. Washington, D.C.: Acropolis Books.

———. 1981. *Public Rights and the Private Press*. Toronto: Butterworths.

———. 1985. The Search for Media Accountability. *Suffolk Univ. Law Review* 19:789–814.

———. 1987. Letter to the author. 17 Feb.

Bazelon, D. 1979. The First Amendment and the "New Media." *Federal Communications Law Journal* 31:201–213.

Beacham, F. 1991. Westwood to Test L-Band DAB. *Radio World*, 26 June, 1.

Beck, H. 1982. Control of, and Access to, On-Line Computer Data Bases: Some First Amendment Issues in Videotex and Teletext. *Comm/Ent Law Journal* 5:1–19.

Behrens, S. 1986. Going Soft: The Emergence of a Buyer's Market. *Channels Field Guide '87* Dec., 16.

Benjamin, L. 1985. Radio Regulation in the 1920s: Free Speech in the Development of Radio and the Radio Act of 1927. Ph.D. diss., Univ. of Iowa, Iowa City.

Berger, R. 1977. *Government by Judiciary*. Cambridge: Harvard Univ. Press.

Berman, J. 1989. The Right to Know: Public Access to Electronic Information. In *New Directions in Telecommunications Policy*, vol. 2, ed. P. Newberg. Durham: Duke Univ. Press.

[Bernstein, A]. 1986. Access to Cable: Natural Monopoly and the First Amendment. *Columbia Law Review* 86:1663–1696.

BeVier, L. 1978. The First Amendment and Political Speech: An Inquiry Into the Substance and Limits of Principle. *Stanford Law Review* 30:299–338.

Bezanson, R. 1977. The New Free Press Guarantee. *Virginia Law Review* 63:731–770.

Bickel, A. 1976. *The Morality of Consent*. New Haven: Yale Univ. Press.

Biel, J. 1989. Empowering the People. *LPTV Report*, Oct., 1.

———. 1990. In our view. *LPTV Report*, April, 3.

Bittman, M. 1984. Colony Pegs Local Access on News. *Advertising Age* 6 Dec., 30.

Blasi, V. 1970. Prior Restraints on Demonstrations. *Michigan Law Review* 68:1481–1573.

———. 1977. The checking Value in First Amendment Theory. *American Bar Foundation Research Journal* 2, no. 3:521–649.

[Bloostein, M]. 1987. The "Core" - "Periphery" Dichotomy in First Amendment Free Exercise Clause Doctrine: Goldman v Weinberger, Bowen v Roy and O'Lone v Estate of Shabazz. *Cornell Law Review* 72:827–855.

Bobbitt, P. 1982. *Constitutional Fate*. New York: Oxford Univ. Press.

The Bodacious New World of C.B. 1976. *Time*, 10 May, 78–79.

Bogen, D. 1983. The Origins of Freedom of Speech and Press. *Maryland Law Review* 42:429–465.

Bollinger, L. 1976. Freedom of the Press and Public Access: Toward a Theory of Partial Regulation of the Mass Media. *Michigan Law Review* 75:1–40.

———. 1984. The Press and the Public Interest: An Essay on the Relationship Between Social Behavior and the Language of First Amendment Theory. *Michigan Law Review* 82:1447–1458.

————. 1986. *The Tolerant Society*. New York: Oxford Univ. Press.

Bork, R. 1971. Neutral Principles and Some First Amendment Problems. *Indiana Law Journal* 47:1–35.

Boylan, A. 1974. The Ability to Communicate: A First Amendment Right. In *The Mass Media and Modern Democracy*, ed. H. Clor. Chicago: Rand McNally.

Branscomb, A. 1975. The Cable Fable: Will It Ever Come True? *Journal of Communication* 25:44–56.

Brant, I. 1965. *The Bill of Rights*. New York: Bobbs-Merrill, 1965.

Brasch, W., and D. Ulloth. 1986. *The Press and the State*. Lanham, Md.: Univ. Press of America.

Brennan, T. 1983. Economic Efficiency and Broadcast Content Regulation. *Federal Communication Law Journal* 35:117–138.

Brennan, W. 1979. Press and the Court: Is the Strain Necessary? *Editor & Publisher*, 27 Oct., 10, 33–34.

Brenner, D. 1972. TV Access: The New Soapbox. *America*, 6 May, 477–479.

Brenner, D., and W. Rivers, eds. 1982. *Free But Regulated*. Ames: Iowa State Univ. Press.

Brest, P. 1980. The Misconceived Quest for the Original Understanding. *Boston Univ. Law Review* 60:204–238.

Broadcast Service Loses Out to Land Mobile. 1985. *Broadcasting*, 3 June, 34.

Broadcasters Ask for HDTV Inquiry. 1987. *Broadcasting*, 23 Feb., 46–47.

Broadcasting Publications. 1990. *Broadcasting Yearbook*. Washington, D.C.

Broadcasting's Fairness Doctrine: An Illogical Extension of the Red Lion Concept. 1972. *Richmond Law Review* 6:448–467.

Brokers See Slow But Steady Cable Sales for 1990. 1990. *Broadcasting*, 5 Feb., 44–45.

[Brown, S., and J. Reed]. 1942. Regulation of Radio Broadcasting: Competitive Enterprise or Public Utility. *Cornell Law Review* 27:249–266.

Brunelli, J. 1986. Why Courts Should Not Use Public Forum Doctrine in Considering Cable Operators' Claims Under the First Amendment. *American Business Law Journal* 24:541–570.

Buchanan, G. 1986. Toward a Unified Theory of Governmental Power to Regulate Protected Speech. *Connecticut Law Review* 18:531–579.

Buckwalter, L. 1966. *Know About Citizens Band Radio*. New Augusta, Ind.: Editors and Engineers.

Buske, S. 1983. Status Report on Community Access Programming on Cable. In *The Cable/Broadband Communications Book*, vol. 3, ed. M. Hollowell. Washington, D.C.: Communications Press.

————. 1986. Telephone conversation with author, 1 Oct.

Buss, W. 1989. School Newspapers, Public Forum, and the First Amendment. *Iowa Law Review 74:505–543*.

Busterna, J. 1989. *Daily Newspaper Chains and the Antitrust Laws*. Journalism Monographs, vol. 110. Columbia, S.C.: Association for Education in Journalism & Mass Communication.

[Cahill, S]. 1975. The Public Forum: Minimum Access, Equal Access and the First Amendment. *Stanford Law Review* 28:117–148.

Can AM Radio Be Saved? 1989. *Broadcasting*, 3 July, 20–21.

Canby, W. 1972. The First Amendment Right to Persuade: Access to Radio and Television. *UCLA Law Review* 19:723–758.

————. 1974. The First Amendment and the State as Editor: Implications for Public Broadcasting. *Texas Law Review* 52:1123–1162.

Caristi, D. 1988. The Concept of a Right to Access to the Media: A Workable Alternative. *Suffolk Univ. Law Review* 22:103–130.

Carter, A. 1990. FCC Seeks to Prevent Abuses. *Radio World*, 13 June, 8.

Cashing in on CB. 1976. *Newsweek*, 31 May, 64.

Cass, R. 1979. First Amendment Access to Government Facilities. *Virginia Law Review* 65:1287–1355.

Cataldi, B. 1987. Telephone conversation with author, 13 July.

CB Couldn't Keep On Truckin'. 1980. *Newsweek*, 21 July, 12.

CB Radio: Fogbound. 1978. *The Economist*, 15 July, 92.

CB Rules Changes for 1977. 1977. *Popular Electronics*, March, 45.

CB Today and Where It's Going. 1978. *Popular Electronics*, April, 63–78.

Chafee, Z. 1941. *Free Speech in the United States*. Cambridge: Harvard Univ. Press.

————. 1947. *Government and Mass Communication*. 2 vols. Chicago: Univ. of Chicago Press.

Chamberlain, B. 1979. The FCC and the First Principle of the Fairness Doctrine: A History of Neglect and Distortion. *Federal Communications Law Journal* 31:361–411.

Chan-Olmsted, S., and B. Litman. 1988. Antitrust and Horizontal Mergers in the Cable Industry. *Journal of Media Economics* 1 Fall: 3–28.

[Chase, T]. 1984. Early Filing Deadline Unconstitutional: A Trend Toward Strict Scrutiny in Ballot Access Cases. *Suffolk Univ. Law Review* 18:24–31.

Chevigny, P. 1980. Philosophy of Language and Free Expression, *New York Univ. Law Review* 55:157–194.

Ciarcia, S. 1985. Turnkey Bulletin Board System. *Byte*, Dec., 93–103.

Coase, R. 1974. The Market for Goods and the Market for Ideas. *American Economics Review* 64:384–391.

Cohen, J., and T. Gleason. 1990. *Social Research in Communication and Law*. Newbury Park, Calif.: Sage.

Cohn, M. 1975. Who Really Controls Television? *Univ. of Miami Law Review* 29:482–486.

Compaine, B. 1985. The Expanding Base of Media Competition. *Journal of Communication* Summer:81–96.

[Cook, D]. 1984. Cable Television: The Constitutional Limitations of Local Government Control. *Southwestern Univ. Law Review* 15:181–216.

Cornell, N., and D. Webbink. 1983. The Present Direction of the FCC: An Appraisal. *American Economic Review* 73:194–197.

Crandall, J. 1987. Telephone conversation with author, 13 July.

Crandall, R. 1989. Fragmentation of the Telephone Network. In *New Directions in Telecommunications Policy*, vol. 1, ed. P. Newberg. Durham: Duke Univ. Press.

Creesy, C. 1984. The Electronic PAW. *Currents* 10, no. 9:22–24.

Crowley, S. 1991. Air Force Takes Aim at L-Band. *Radio World*, 26 June, 23.

Culter, B. 1989. Mature Audiences Only. *American Demographics* 11, Oct.:20–29.

Current Merger Activity Threatens Financial Stability, Innovation by Broadcasters. 1986. *Television/Radio Age*, 14 April, 73.

DAB Scorecard. 1991. *Radio World*, 10 July, 22.

Daniel, C. 1970. Right of Access to Mass Media—Government Obligation to Enforce the First Amendment? *Texas Law Review* 48:783–790.

Dannefer, D., and J. Kasen. 1981. Anonymous Exchanges: CB and the Emergence of Sex Typing. *Urban Life* 10:265–287.

Dannefer, W., and N. Poushinsky. 1979. The C.B. Phenomenon, A Sociological Perspective. *Journal of Popular Culture* 12:611–619.

[Deislet, D]. 1982. CBS, Inc. v FCC: Recognition of Candidates' Right of Access to Broadcasting Facilities. *Utah Law Review* 34, no. 3:641–656.

Demand for Spectrum Space Forces FCC to Modify Attitude Toward Interference. 1983. *Television/Radio Age*, 15 Aug., 90.

Despite Their Limitations, CBs Are, and Will Remain, Popular. 1978. *Forest Industries*, Nov., 51.

Devany, A., R. Eckert, C. Meyers, D. O'Hara, and R. Scott. 1969. A Property System Approach to the Electromagnetic Spectrum. *Stanford Law Review* 21:1499–1561.

Devine, B. 1986. Telephone conversation with the author. 7 Aug.

Diamond, E., and N. Sandler. 1983. *Telecommunications in Crisis*. Washington, D.C.: Cato Institute.

Dominick, J. 1987. *The Dynamics of Mass Communication*. New York: Random House.

Donahue, H. 1989. *The Battle to Control Broadcast News*. Cambridge: MIT Press.

Donnelly, W. 1986. *The Confetti Generation*. New York: Holt.

[Douberley, W]. 1969. Resolving the Free Speech—Free Press Dichotomy: Access to the Press Through Advertising. *Univ. of Florida Law Review* 22:293–320.

[Duchek, D]. 1970. The Right of Access to the Press. *Nebraska Law Review* 60:120–136.

Duffy, M. 1982. A CB Patrol that Works. *Police Chief*, May, 36–39.

Dworkin, R. 1978. *Taking Rights Seriously*. Cambridge: Harvard Univ. Press.

———. 1985. *A Matter of Principle*. Cambridge: Harvard Univ. Press.

Ede, L. 1984. Public Disclosure and Public Policy: A Case Study. Paper presented at the Annual Meeting of the Oregon Council of Teachers of English, 6–7 April, Bend, Oregon.

Emerson, T. 1970. *The System of Freedom of Expression*. New York: Random House.

———. 1977. Colonial Intentions and Current Realities of the First Amendment. *Univ. of Pennsylvania Law Review* 125:737–760.

———. 1981. The Affirmative Side of the First Amendment. *Georgia Law Review* 15:795–834.

Engleman, R. 1990. *The Origins of Public Access Cable Television 1966–1972*. Journalism Monographs, vol. 123. Columbia, S.C.: Association for Education in Journalism & Mass Communication.

Ethridge, J. 1977. The CB Fiasco. *Motor Trend*, April, 69–70.

Expected Changes in the Economy Set Stage for Aggressive TV Selling. 1987. *Television/Radio Age*, 16 Feb., 14.

Extended AM Band: Problem or Solution? 1989. *Broadcasting*, 28 Aug., 47.

The Fairness Doctrine Can Hurt. 1986. *Broadcasting*, 3 March, 67.

Fairness Held Unfair. 1987. *Broadcasting*, 10 Aug., 1.

Farber, D., and J. Nowak. 1984. The Misleading Nature of Public Forum Analysis: Content and Context in First Amendment Adjudication. *Virginia Law Review* 70:1219–1258.

Faulhaber, G. 1987. *Telecommunications in Turmoil*. Cambridge, Mass.: Ballinger.

FCC Approves FM Short Spacing. 1988. *Broadcasting*, 19 Dec., 51.

FCC Releases Revised List for Docket 80–90. 1984. *Broadcasting*, 30 July, 36.

FCC to Applicants: Hurry Up and Wait. 1990. *Broadcasting*, 5 Feb., 46–47.

Felker, L. 1990. HDTV Landscape May See Change. *TV Technology*, July, 11.

———. 1991. FCC Works Spectrum Shift. *Radio World*, May, 12.

Fight for Old Glory. 1989. *Newsweek*, 3 July, 18.

Fisher, D. 1982. *The Right to Communicate: A Status Report*. Paris: UNESCO.

Fowler, D. 1977. *Unmailable*. Athens: Univ. of Georgia Press.

Fowler, M., and D. Brenner. 1982. A Marketplace Approach to Broadcast Regulation. *Texas Law Review* 60:206–257.

Francois, W. 1973. Media Access: Romance and Reality. *America*, 22 Sept., 186–188.

Freedman, W. 1988. *Freedom of Speech on Private Property*. New York: Quorum Books.

Friedman, H. 1979. Programmed Scanning Brings Back CB Excitement. *Popular Mechanics*, Aug., 78–80.

Friendly, F. 1975. *The Good Guys, The Bad Guys, and the First Amendment*. New York: Random House.

Fuller, W. 1972. *The American Mail*. Chicago: Univ. of Chicago Press.

[Gaal, B]. 1982. A Unitary Approach to Claims of First Amendment Access to Publicly Owned Property. *Stanford Law Review* 35:121–152.

Garray, R. 1988. *Cable Television*. Westport, Conn.: Greenwood Press.

Garry, P. 1989. The First Amendment and Freedom of the Press: A Revised Approach to the Marketplace of Ideas Concept. *Marquette Law Review* 72:187–234.

Gauging the Growth in Station Prices. 1986. *Broadcasting*, 21 April, 84.

Geller, H. 1975. Does Red Lion Square With Tornillo? *Univ. of Miami Law Review* 29:477–481.

———. 1985. The Role of Future Regulation: Licensing, Spectrum Allocation, Content, Access, Common Carrier and Rates. In *Video Media Competition: Regulation, Economics, and Technology*, ed. E. Noam. New York: Columbia Univ. Press.

———. 1989. Broadcasting. In *New Directions in Telecommunications Policy*, vol. 1, ed. P. Newberg. Durham: Duke Univ. Press.

Geller, H., and J. Yurow. 1982. The Reasonable Access Provision of the Communications Act: Once More Down the Slippery Slope. *Federal Communications Law Journal* 34:389.

[Gold, A]. 1980. The Recognition of Legitimate Renewal Expectations in Broadcast Licensing. *Washington Univ. Law Quarterly* 58:409–438.

Goldberger, D. 1983. Judicial Scrutiny in Public Forum Cases: Misplaced Trust in the Judgment of Public Officials. *Buffalo Law Review* 32:175–220.

Goldstein, P. 1989. Copyright Law and Policy. In *New Directions in Telecommunications Policy*, vol. 2, ed. P. Newberg. Durham: Duke Univ. Press.

Gorman, E. 1987. The First Amendment and the Postal Service's Subscriber Requirement: Constitutional Problems with Denying Equal Access to the Postal System. *Univ. of Richmond Law Review* 21:541–569.

Gorney, C. 1985. Laissez-Faire Television. *Public Relations Journal* 41:12–15.

Gramsci, A. 1977. *Selections from the Prison Notebooks*, ed. Q. Hoare and G. Nowell-Smith. London: Lawrence & Wishart.

Gross, J. 1985. The State of Cable. *Broadcast Management/Engineering* May, 73–86.

———. 1991a. Does the L Stand for Lonely? *Radio World*, 7 Aug., 4.

———. 1991b. NAB DAB Stand Fuels Battle. *Radio World*, 10 July, 14.

———. 1991c. Pioneer Preference Approved. *Radio World*, 26 June, 3.

Grow, J. 1986. Cable Television: Local Governmental Regulation in Perspective. *Pace Law Review* 7:81–126.

Hammond, A. 1979. Meeting Minority Concerns: Structural Versus Regulatory Approaches to Broadcasting. In *Proceedings of the Sixth Annual Telecommunications Policy Research Conference*, ed. H. Dordick. Lexington, Mass.: Lexington Books.

————. 1986. To Be or Not to Be: FCC Regulation of Video Subscription Technologies. *Catholic Univ. Law Review* 35:737–759.

Handley, W. 1979. What's Your Handle, Good Buddy? Names of Citizens Band Users. *American Speech* Winter:307–310.

Hardenbaugh, M. 1986. Promise vs. Performance: Four Public Access Channels in Connecticut. *Mass Comm. Review* 13:32–39.

Head, S., and C. Sterling. 1990. *Broadcasting in America*. 6th ed. Boston: Houghton Mifflin.

Heeter, C., D. D'Alessio, B. Greenberg, and D. McVoy. 1988. Cableviewing Behaviors: An Electronic Assessment. In *Cableviewing*, ed. C. Heeter and B. Greenberg. Norwood, N.J.: Ablex.

Henck, F., and B. Strassburg. 1988. *A Slippery Slope: The Long Road to the Breakup of AT&T*. New York: Greenwood Press.

Herzel, L. 1951. Public Interest and the Market in Color Television Regulation. *Univ. of Chicago Law Review* 9:802–816.

Hill Steamed Over Radio's Tea Time. 1989. *Broadcasting*, 13 Feb., 29–30.

Hocking, W. 1947. *Freedom of the Press*. Chicago: Univ. of Chicago Press.

Hodge, J. 1982. Democracy and Free Speech: A Normative Theory of Society and Government. In *The First Amendment Reconsidered*, ed. B. Chamberlain and C. Brown. New York: Longman.

Hollinrake, J. 1987. Cable Television: Public Access and the First Amendment. *Communication and the Law*, Feb., 3–40.

Horning, R. 1969. The First Amendment Right to a Public Forum. *Duke Law Journal* 19:931–957.

Horvitz, R. 1989. The Usenet Underground. *Whole Earth Review* Winter:113–115.

Horwitz, R. 1989. *The Irony of Regulatory Reform*. New York: Oxford Univ. Press.

Hughes, D. 1987. FCC Eyes HDTV, UHF CPs Frozen. *TV Technology*, Sept., 1.

Hulser, K. 1985. Paper Tiger Television. *American Film* 10:61–63.

Hyde, R. 1987. FCC Action Repealing the Fairness Doctrine: A Revolution in Broadcast Regulation. *Syracuse Law Review* 38:1175–1192.

Immerwahr, J., J. Johnson, and J. Doble. 1980. *The Speaker and The Listener: A Public Perspective on Freedom of Expression*. New York: Public Agenda Foundation.

Itzkan, S. 1989. Citizens of the World. *inCider*, Oct., 104–107.

Jaberg, G. and L. Wargo. 1980. *The Video Pencil*. Washington, D.C.: Univ. Press of America.

Jackson, C. 1979. Reactions to the Spectrum Options Paper. In *Proceedings of the Sixth Annual Telecommunications Policy Research Conference*, ed. H. Dordick. Lexington, Mass.: Lexington Books.

————. 1989. Use and Management of the Spectrum Resource. In *New Directions in Telecommunications Policy*, vol. 1, ed. P. Newberg. Durham: Duke Univ. Press.

Jaffe, L. 1972. The Editorial Responsibility of the Broadcaster: Reflections on Fairness and Access. *Harvard Law Review* 85:768–792.

[Jensen, E]. 1987. An Electronic Soapbox: Computer Bulletin Boards and the First Amendment. *Federal Communications Law Journal* 39:217–258.

Joyce, William. 1988. Review of *Printers and Press Freedom*, by Jeffery Smith. *Journal of American History* 75:924.

Judge Says LA Erred in Refusing Second Cable Franchise. 1990. *Broadcasting*, 15 Jan., 58.

Kahaner, L. 1978. GMRS Radio—The Uncrowded Citizens Band. *Popular Science*, Oct., 8, 10.

Kahn, P. 1988. Media Competition in the Marketplace of Ideas. *Syracuse Law Review* 39:737–794.

Kalven, H. 1965. The Concept of the Public Forum: Cox v Louisiana. *Supreme Court Review* 1965:1–32.

———. 1988. *A Worthy Tradition*. New York: Harper & Row.

Karst, K. 1975. Equality as a Central Principle in the First Amendment. *Univ. of Chicago Law Review* 43:20–59.

Katsh, M. 1989. *The Electronic Media and the Transformation of Law*. New York: Oxford Univ. Press.

Katz, D. 1985. Community Access Television: A Social Service Resource. *Social Work* 30:267–271.

[Keenan, L.] 1972. Broadcasting's Fairness Doctrine: An Illogical Extension of the Red Lion Concept. *University of Richmond Law Review* 6:448–456.

Kerbo, H., K. Marshall, and P. Holley. 1978. Reestablishing "Gemeinschaft"? *Urban Life* 7:337–358.

Key, V. 1961. *Public Opinion and American Democracy*. New York: Alfred A Knopf.

Kielbowicz, R. 1989. *News in the Mail*. New York: Greenwood Press.

Kiernan, M. 1989. To Watch is O.K., but To Air is Divine. *U.S. News & World Report*, 16 Oct., 112–113.

Killette, K. 1991. FCC Helps Wireless "Innovators." *Communications Week*, 15 April, 29.

Klein, J. 1989. Talk Politics. *New York*. 27 Feb., 28, 30.

Kletter, R., L. Hirschhorn, and H. Hudson. 1977. Access and the Social Environment in the United States of America. In *Access: Some Western Models of Community Media*, ed. F. Berrigan. Paris: UNESCO.

Koch, T. 1988. No Sacred Cows. *Common Cause Magazine* 14, no. 1:6–7.

Koppel, R. 1983. The Applicability of the Equal Time Doctrine and the Reasonable Access Rule to Elections in the New Media Era. *Harvard Journal on Legislation* 20:499–539.

Krasnow, E., and L. Longley. 1978. *The Politics of Broadcast Regulation*. New York: St. Martin's Press.

Krattenmaker, T., and L. Powe. 1985. The Fairness Doctrine Today: A Constitutional Curiosity and An Impossible Dream. *Duke Law Journal* 1985, 151–176.

[Krug, P]. 1985. Cable Television Franchise Fees for General Revenue: The 1984 Cable Act, Wisconsin Law, and the First Amendment. *Wisconsin Law Review* 5:1273–1303.

KTLA to Change Hands in Largest Station Ever. 1983. *Broadcasting*, 4 April, 131.

Labunski, R. 1989. May It Rest in Peace: Public Interest and Public Access in the Post-Fairness Doctrine Era. *Hastings Comm/Ent Law Journal* 11:219–290.

Lacy, D. 1965. *Freedom and Communications*. Carbondale: Univ. of Illinois Press.

Ladenson, R. 1983. *A Philosophy of Free Expression and Its Constitutional Applications*. Totowa, N.J.: Rowman & Littlefield.

Lang, M., K. Blacklock, and B. Rossing. 1986. Is Anyone Watching? *Journal of Extension* Summer:7–10.

Lange, D., R. Baker, and S. Ball. 1969. *Mass Media and Violence*. Washington, D.C.: Government Printing Office.

[Langway, R]. 1984. The Public Forum and the First Amendment: The Puzzle of the Podium. *New England Law Review* 19:619–645.

LaPierre, D. 1973. Cable Television and the Promise of Program Diversity. *Fordham Law Review* 42:25–124.

Lazarus, R. Changing Conceptions of Property and Sovereignty in Natural Resources: Questioning the Public Trust Doctrine. *Iowa Law Review* 71:631–716.

Ledingham, J. 1983. Characteristics of Cable Access Centers in the Top 100 Media Markets. Paper presented at the Annual Meeting of the International Communication Association, 26–30 May, Dallas, Texas.

Levin, H. 1970. Spectrum Allocation Without Market. *American Economic Review* 60:209–218.

———. 1971. *The Invisible Resource*. Baltimore: Johns Hopkins Press.

Levitan, A. 1987. Twelve Special Bulletin Boards. *Compute* 9:51.

Levy, L. 1985. *Emergence of a Free Press*. New York: Oxford Univ. Press.

Lewis, A. 1979. A Preferred Position for Journalists? *Hofstra Law Review* 7:595–627.

Liebling, A. 1960. The Wayward Press. *The New Yorker*, 14 May, 105–112.

Lippmann, W. 1922. *Public Opinion*. New York: The Free Press.

[Lipsky, A]. 1976. Reconciling Red Lion and Tornillo. *Stanford Law Review* 28:563–588.

Lively, D. 1988. Fairness Regulation: An Idea Whose Time Has Gone. *Washington & Lee Law Review* 45:1379–1390.

Localism, HDTV, Hot Topics at NAB Panel. 1990. *LPTV Report*, April, 1, 18.

Locke, J. 1966. *The Second Treatise of Government*, ed. J. Gough. New York: Barnes & Noble.

LPTV: Still Afloat After a Rough Five Years. 1985. *Broadcasting*, 9 Sept., 32.

MacFarlane, L. 1985. *The Theory and Practice of Human Rights*. New York: St. Martin's Press.

[Magnus, R., C. Perry, L. Richards, and M. Wickliffe]. 1982. Access Rights to the Media After CBS v DNC. *Howard Law Journal* 25:825–853.

Manley, P. 1986. Candidates in Austin Enjoy Unlimited Access. *Community Television Review* 9, no. 1:10–11.

Martin, H. 1990. FCC Adheres to Fairness "Corollaries." *Broadcast Engineering*, July, 8.

Martin, J. 1990. Telephone interview, Aug. 9.

McGill, I. The Market for Corporate Control in the Broadcasting Industry. *Federal Communications Law Journal* 40:39–87.

Meiklejohn, A. 1948. *Free Speech and Its Relation to Self Government*. New York: Harper & Brothers.

———. 1951. The First Amendment and the Evils that Congress Has A Right to Prevent. *Indiana Law Journal* 26:10–25.

———. 1961. Is the First Amendment an Absolute? *Supreme Court Review* 1961:245–261.

———. 1965. *Political Freedom*. New York: Oxford Univ. Press.

[Melnick, A]. 1982. Access to Cable Television: A Critique of the Affirmative Duty Theory of the First Amendment. *California Law Review* 70:1393–1420.

Melody, W. 1980. Radio Spectrum Allocation: Role of the Market. *American Economic Review* 70:393–397.

Merrill, J. 1968. Access to the Press: Who Decides? *The Freeman*, Jan., 48–53.

Middleton, K., and B. Chamberlain. 1988. *The Law of Public Communication*. New York: Longman.

Milam, L. 1986. *The Radio Papers*. San Diego: MHO & MHO Works.

Mill, J. [1859] 1975. *On Liberty*, ed. David Spitz. New York: W. W. Norton & Company.

Milton, J. 1975. *The Complete Prose Works of John Milton*, ed. D. Wolf. 7 vols. New Haven: Yale Univ. Press.

Milton, J. 1927. *Areopagitica and Other Prose Writings*, ed. W. Haller. New York: Macmillan.

Mitchell, B. 1984. Pricing Subscriber Access to the Telephone Network. In *Telecommunications Access and Public Policy*, ed. A. Baughcum and G. Faulhaber. Norwood, N.J.: Ablex.

Mitropoulos, M. 1983. Public Participation, as Access, in Cable TV in the USA. *Ekistics* 302:385–392.

Moms-and-Pops Out of TV Ownership Picture. 1987. *Advertising Age*, 9 Feb., S8.

More Voices Join Satellite-Delivered Talk Format. 1989. *Broadcasting*. 20 Feb., 46–47.

Moss, M. and R. Warren. 1984. Public Policy and Community-Oriented Uses of Cable Television. *Urban Affairs Quarterly* 20:223–254.

[Mueller, W]. 1989. Controversial Programming on Cable Television's Public Access Channels: The Limits of Governmental Response. *DePaul Law Review* 38:1051–1120.

Murray, J. 1969. *The Editor's Right to Decide*. Tucson: Univ. of Arizona Press.

NAB Opposes Academic Panel's Proposal for "Free" Political Airtime. 1990. *TV Today*, 12 Mar., 1.

Nadel, M. 1982. A Unified Theory of the First Amendment: Divorcing the Medium From the Message. *Fordham Law Review* 11:163–224.

Nagel, G. 1974. Letters to the Editor: A Public Bid for Fame. *Columbia Journalism Review*, May/June, 47–48.

Names Make News in Radio. 1989. *Broadcasting*, 20 March, 64–65.

NCTA Study: Vertical Integration Positive. 1989. *Broadcasting*, 12 June, 33.

Neisser, E. 1985. Charging for Free Speech: User Fees and Insurance in the Marketplace of Ideas. *Georgetown Law Journal* 74:257–362.

Nemming, C. 1969. Negative and Positive Press Freedom. *IPI Report*, Sept.

Neville, R. 1974. *The Cosmology of Freedom*. New Haven: Yale Univ. Press.

Nicoletti, R. 1987. Radio Station Returns Get High Ratings from Investors. *Broadcasting*, 23 Feb., 24.

Noll, R. 1989. Telecommunications Regulation in the 1990s. In *New Directions in Telecommunications Policy*, vol. 1, ed. P. Newberg. Durham: Duke Univ. Press.

Noll, R., M. Peck, and J. McGowan. 1973. *Economic Aspects of Television Regulation*. Washington, D.C.: Brookings Institution.

Official CB Dictionary. 1976. New York: Book Craft-Guild.

O.K., Caller, You're On the Air. 1989. *U.S. News & World Report*, 20 Feb., 12–13.

On-Line Chat Services Rekindle CB Spirit, Bring PC Users Together. 1988. *PC Magazine*, 14 June, 440.

Owen, B. 1975. *Economics and Freedom of Expression*. Cambridge, Mass.: Ballinger.

[Pappas, N]. 1987. In Defense of Monopoly Cable Television Franchising: Defining the First Amendment Rights of the Public and the Cable Operator Under the Public Forum Doctrine and Natural Monopoly Theory. *Rutgers Computer & Technology Law Journal* 13:137–235.

Parsons, P. 1987. *Cable Television and the First Amendment*. Lexington, Mass.: D. C. Heath & Co.

Pasternack, S. 1988. The Open Forum: A Study of Letters to the Editor and the People who Write Them. Paper presented at the 71st Annual Convention of the Association for Education in Journalism and Mass Communication, 2–5 July, Portland, Oregon.

Picard, R. 1985. *The Press and the Decline of Democracy*. Westport, Conn.:
    Greenwood Press.
————. 1989. *Media Economics*. Beverly Hills, Calif.: Sage.
Pool, I. 1983. *Technologies of Freedom*. Cambridge: Harvard Univ. Press.
Porter, G., and Banks, M. 1988. Cable Public Access as a Public Forum.
    Journalism Quarterly 65:39–45.
Powe, L. 1987a. *American Broadcasting and the First Amendment*. Berkeley:
    Univ. of California Press.
————. 1987b. Tornillo. *Supreme Court Review* 1987, no. 8:345–396.
Prevos, A. 1986. CB'ers and Cibistes: The Development and Impact of CB
    Radio in France. *Journal of Popular Culture* 19:145–154.
Prisuta, R. 1976. Political/Governmental Utilization of Cable Television.
    Paper submitted to the Association for Education in Journalism, 1
    April.
Radio Back to Status Quo on 10 KHz. *Broadcasting*, 10 Aug., 28–29.
Ragan, F. 1971. Justice Oliver Wendell Holmes Jr., Zechariah Chafee Jr., and
    the Clear and Present Danger Test for Free Speech. *Journal of
    American History* 58:23–45.
Ramsey, R. 1979. The People Versus Smokey Bear: Metaphor, Argot, and
    CB Radio. *Journal of Popular Culture* 13:338–344.
Rawls, J. 1982. The Basic Liberties and Their Priorities. In *The Tanner
    Lectures on Human Values*, vol. 3, ed. S. McMurrin. Provo: Univ. of
    Utah Press.
Redish, M. 1982. The Value of Free Speech. *Univ. of Pennsylvania Law
    Review* 130:591–645.
————. 1984. *Freedom of Expression: A Critical Analysis*. Charlottesville,
    Va.: The Michie Co.
Regulation of Commercial Speech: Commercial Access to Newspapers. 1975.
    Maryland Law Review 35:115–133.
Reich, C. 1988. Affirmative Action for Ideas. *Case Western Reserve Law
    Review* 38:632–640.
Reid, T. 1988. An Affirmative First Amendment Access Right. *Communica-
    tions and the Law*, June, 39–58.
[Resneck, W]. 1969. The Duty of Newspapers to Accept Political Advertising.
    Indiana Law Journal 44:222–241.
Responsible Piracy. 1991. *Radio World*, 26 June, 5.
Rheingold, H. 1987. Virtual Communities. *Whole Earth Review* Winter:78–
    80.
Rose, P. 1976. The Citizens Band Goes Boom. *Motor Trend*, July, 66–68.
Rosellini, L. 1990. All Alone, Late at Night. *U.S. News & World Report*, 15
    Jan., 54–55.
Ross, S., and Brick, B. 1987. The Cable Act of 1984: How Did We Get There
    and Where are We Going. *Federal Communications Law Journal*
    39:27–52.

Rosse, J. 1980. The Decline of Direct Newspaper Competition. *Journal of Communication* 30:65.

Roth, R. 1962. *John Dewey and Self Realization*. New York: Greenwood Press.

Rousseau, J. 1950. *The Social Contract*. Translated by G. Cole. New York: Dutton.

Rowan, F. 1984. *Broadcast Fairness*. New York: Longman.

Rudman, R. 1989. The Marketplace Model: Fixing Something That's Broken. *Broadcast Management/Engineering*, Jan., 82.

Rutherford, J. 1990. Telephone conversation with author, 18 May.

Salm, W. 1977. The Forgotten CB Service. *Popular Electronics*, Nov., 90–91.

Sandage, C. 1971. The Right to Know. *Grassroots Editor* 12:4–7.

Scanlon, T. 1972. A Theory of Freedom of Expression. *Philosophy and Public Affairs* 1:204–224.

Schauer, F. 1982. *Free Speech: A Philosophical Inquiry*. New York: Cambridge Univ. Press.

———. 1986. The Role of the People in First Amendment Theory. *California Law Review* 74:761–788.

Schmidt, B. 1976. *Freedom of the Press Versus Public Access*. New York: Praeger.

———. 1978. Pluralistic Programming and Regulation of Mass Communications Media. In *Communications for Tomorrow*, ed. G. Robinson. New York: Praeger.

Schmueli, E. 1980. The Right to Self-Realization and its Predicaments. In *The Philosophy of Human Rights*, ed. A. Rosenbaum. Westport, Conn.: Greenwood Press.

Sedler, R. 1985. The State Constitutions and the Supplemental Protection of Individual Rights. *Univ. of Toledo Law Review* 16:465–505.

Seligman, D. 1985. Life Will Be Different When We're All On Line. *Fortune* 4 Feb., 68–72.

Selling the Airwaves. 1989. *Radio World*, 24 May, 2.

745 Boylston Street. 1990. *The Atlantic*, June, 6.

Shapiro, A. 1976. *Media Access*. Boston: Little, Brown & Co.

Sharp, E. 1984. Consequences of Local Government Under the Klieg Lights. *Communication Research* 11:497–517.

[Shelledy, D]. 1982. Access to the Press: A Teleological Analysis of a Constitutional Double Standard. *George Washington Law Review* 50:430–464.

Shepard's United States Citations. 1990. 12 vols., 6th ed. Colorado Springs: McGraw-Hill.

Sherman, R. 1980. *Perspectives on Postal Service Issues*. Washington, D.C.: American Enterprise Institute for Public Policy Research.

Siegal, M. 1990. Telephone conversation with the author, 13 Aug.

Singleton, L. 1986. *Telecommunications in the Information Age.* Cambridge, Mass.: Ballinger.

Sloan Commission on Cable Communications. 1971. *On the Cable: The Television of Abundance.* Washington, D.C.

Smith, A. 1989. The Public Interest and Telecommunications. In *New Directions in Telecommunications Policy,* vol. 1, ed. P. Newberg. Durham: Duke Univ. Press.

Smith, C. 1989. *Freedom of Expression and Partisan Politics.* Charlotte: Univ. of South Carolina Press.

Smith, J. A. 1988. *Printers and Press Freedom.* New York: Oxford Univ. Press.

Smith, J. J. 1981. Gender Marking on Citizens Band Radio: Self-Identity in a Limited-Channel Speech Community. *Sex Roles* 7:599–606.

[Smith, T]. 1986. Reexamining the Reasonable Access and Equal Time Provisions of the Federal Communications Act: Can These Provisions Stand if the Fairness Doctrine Falls? *Georgetown Law Journal* 74:1491–1520.

Soma, J., P. Smith, and R. Sprague. 1985. Legal Analysis of Electronic Bulletin Board Activities. *West New England Law Review* 7:571–611.

Spectrum Bill Clears, But Meets Opposition. 1990. *Radio World*, 25 July, 2.

Spectrum Fees Not in Senate Commerce Budget Package. 1989. *Broadcasting*, 31 July, 19.

Spitzer, M. 1989. Broadcasting and the First Amendment. In *New Directions in Telecommunications Policy,* vol. 1, ed. P. Newberg. Durham: Duke University Press.

Starck, K. 1970. *Letter Columns: Access For Whom?* Freedom of Information Center Report 237. Columbia, Mo.

Station Acquisitions Brisk and Prices Are High. 1986. *Television/Radio Age*, 21 July, 30.

Station and Cable Trading 1986: A Look Back at the Fifth Estate's Record Sales Year. 1987. *Broadcasting*, 9 Feb., 51–91.

Steinberg, J. 1987. Radio: Soft Touch a New Age for Medium. *Advertising Age*, 31 Aug., S1–2, 6.

Sterling, C., and J. Kittross. 1978. *Stay Tuned.* Belmont, Calif.: Wadsworth.

Stern, J., E. Krasnow, and R. Sendowski. 1983. The New Video Marketplace and the Search for a Coherent Regulatory Philosophy. *Catholic Univ. Law Review* 32:529–602.

Stewart, P. 1975. Or of the Press. *Hastings Law Journal.* 26:631–637.

Stone, G. 1974. Fora Americana: Speech in Public Places. *Supreme Court Review* 1974:233–280.

Summary of Broadcasting and Cable. 1990. *Broadcasting*, 11 June, 86.

Sweeney, B. 1984. The Marketplace of Ideas: An Economic Analogy for Freedom of Speech. Paper presented at Annual Convention of the Association for Education in Journalism and Mass Communication, Gainesville, Fl., 6 Aug.

Symons, H. 1989. The Communications Policy Process. In *New Directions in Telecommunications Policy*, vol. 1, ed. P. Newberg. Durham: Duke Univ. Press.

Taylor, C. 1979. What's Wrong With Negative Liberty. In *The Idea of Freedom*, ed. A. Ryan. New York: Oxford Univ. Press.

————. 1989a. Public Interest vs. Marketplace. *Radio World*, 26 April, 17.

————. 1989b. Talk Radio Influence Criticized. *Radio World*, 26 July, 17.

Television Information Office/Roper. 1987. *America's Watching: Public Attitudes Toward Television*. New York.

[Thomas, G]. 1970. The Listener's Right to Hear in Broadcasting. *Stanford Law Review* 22:863–902.

Thornton, L., and J. Greene. 1986. Cable Television and Educational Access: A Reconsideration. *Community College Review* 13:47–53.

Tillotson, D. 1987. A Lender's Guide to Broadcasting Stations. *Broadcasting*, 27 April, 22.

[Toomey, K]. 1974. Access to the Press in Light of the Traditional Concept of Journalistic Freedom. *Suffolk Univ. Law Review* 8:682.

Transfer of TV Properties Went From $750 Million to $6 Billion in Four Years. 1986. *Television/Radio Age*, 9 June, 61.

Tribe, L. 1978. Toward a Metatheory of Free Speech. *Southwestern Univ. Law Review* 10:237–245.

Trufelman, L. 1988. How to Plug In to Cable TV. *Public Relations Journal* 44:43–44.

Tucker, D. 1985. *Law, Liberalism and Free Speech*. Totowa, N.J.: Rowman & Allanheld.

Tunstall, W. 1985. *Disconnecting Parties*. New York: McGraw-Hill.

TV Networks Enter New Cost-Control Era. 1987. *Broadcasting*, 2 March, 70–71.

12-12-12: Fait Accompli. 1984. *Broadcasting*, 31 Dec., 35–38.

Twenty-four Hours of Talk Available for AMs. 1988. *Broadcasting*, 4 Jan., 120–121.

Uyehara, K. 1986. Let the Operator Beware. *Student Law*, April, 28–33.

Van Alstyne, W. 1984. *Interpretations of the First Amendment*. Durham: Duke Univ. Press.

Vasquez, F., and T. Eveslage. 1983. Newspapers' Letters to the Editor as Reflections of Social Structure. Paper presented at 66th Annual Convention of the Association for Education in Journalism and Mass Communication, 6–9 August, Corvallis, Oregon.

Volner, I. 1974. Broadcast Regulation: Is There Too Much "Public" in the Public Interest? *Univ. of Cincinnati Law Review* 43:267–289.

Watts, D. 1982. A Major Issue of the 1980s: New Communication Tools. In *The First Amendment Reconsidered*, ed. B. Chamberlain and C. Brown. New York: Longman.

Webbink, D. 1987. Radio Licenses and Frequency Spectrum Use Property Rights. *Communications and the Law*, June, 3–29.

When a Buddy Meets a Buddy Comin' Through a Crisis. 1979. _Psychology Today_, May, 31–32.
Where Things Stand. 1990. _Broadcasting_, 2 April, 35–36.
Whitehead on Access: Cable as Common Carrier. 1971. _Broadcasting_, 20 Sept., 43.
Wicklein, J. 1979. _Electronic Nightmare_. Boston: Beacon Press.
Wilson, L. 1988. Minority and Gender Enhancements: A Necessary and Valid Means to Achieve Diversity in the Broadcast Marketplace. _Federal Communications Law Journal_ 40:89–114.
Wirth, M. 1986. Economic Barriers to Entering Media Industries in the United States. In _Communications Yearbook_, vol. 9, ed. M. McLaughlin. Beverly Hills, Calif.: Sage.
Wirth, M., and Cobb-Reiley. 1987. A First Amendment Critique of the 1984 Cable Act. _Journal of Broadcasting & Electronic Media_ 31:391–407.
Wolf, B. 1986. Cable Access and Social Change: Eight Case Studies. _Community Television Review_ 9, no. 1:18–21.
Wood, L., and D. Blankenhorn. 1990. State of the BBS Nation. _Byte_ 15; Jan.:298–304.
Wright, R. 1985. A Rationale from J. S. Mill for the Free Speech Clause. _Supreme Court Review_ 1985, no. 4:149–178.
Wulf, M. 1974. Excess Access. _Civil Liberties Review_ 1:128–130.
Yodelis, M. 1975. The Rejection of Florida's Right to Reply Statute: A Setback for a "New Right" of Access to the Press. _New York Law Forum_ 20:633–642.
Yudof, M. 1983. _When Government Speaks_. Berkeley: Univ. of California Press.
Zoglin, R. 1989. Bugle Boys of the Airwaves. _Time_, 15 May, 88–89.

CASES

Abrams v U.S., 250 U.S. 616 (1919).
Adderly v Florida, 385. U.S. 39 (1966).
Alderwood Associates v Washington Environmental Council, 635 P.2d 102 (1981).
Amalgamated Food Employees Union v Logan Valley Plaza, Inc., 391 U.S. 308 (1968).
American Radio Association v Mobile S.S. Association, 419 U.S. 215 (1974).
Associated Press v U.S., 326 U.S. 1 (1945).
Batchelder v Allied Stores International, 445 N.E. 2d 590 (1983).
Berkshire Cablevision v Burke, 571 F. Supp. 976 (D.R.I. 1983).
Bigelow v Virginia, 421 U.S. 809 (1975).
Board of Airport Commissioners v Jews for Jesus, 55 U.S.L.W. 4855 (1987).
Bolger v Young Drug Products Corp., 463 U.S. 60 (1983).
Bond v Floyd, 385 U.S. 116 (1966).

Boos v Barry, 56 U.S.L.W. 4254 (1988).
Breard v Louisiana, 341 U.S. 622 (1951).
Brown v Louisiana, 383 U.S. 131 (1966).
Buckley v Valeo, 424 U.S. 1 (1976).
Cantwell v Connecticut, 310 U.S. 296 (1939).
Carey v Brown, 447 U.S. 455 (1980).
CBS v DNC, 412 U.S. 94 (1973).
CBS v FCC, 453 U.S. 367 (1981); 629 F.2d. 1(D.C. Cir. 1980).
Central Hardware Co. v NLRB, 439 F.2d. 1331, *vacated* 407 U.S. 539
        (1972).
Chaplinski v New Hampshire, 315 U.S. 568 (1942).
City Council v Taxpayers for Vincent, 466 U.S. 789 (1984).
Clark v Community for Creative Non-Violence, 468 U.S. 268 (1984).
Cohen v California, 403 U.S. 15 (1971).
Cologne v Westfarm Associates, 469 A2d 1201 (Conn. 1984).
Connecticut Southern Federation of Teachers v Board of Education Members,
        538 F.2d. 471 (2d Cir. 1976).
Connick v Myers, 461 U.S. 138 (1983).
Consolidated Edison v Public Service Commission, 447 U.S. 530 (1980).
Cornelius v NAACP Legal Defense & Education Fund, 473 U.S. 788 (1985).
Cox v Louisiana, 379 U.S. 536 (1965).
Cox v New Hampshire, 312 U.S. 569 (1941).
Curtis Publishing Co. v Butts, 388 U.S. 130 (1967).
Davis v Massachusetts, 167 U.S. 43 (1897).
Denis v U.S., 341 U.S. 494 (1951).
Dunn & Bradstreet v Greenmoss Builders, 472 U.S. 749 (1985).
Edwards v South Carolina, 372 U.S. 229 (1962).
Elliot v Sperry Rand Corp., 680 F. 2d 1125 (8th Cir. 1982).
Erznoznik v City of Jacksonville, 422 U.S. 205 (1975).
FCC v League of Women Voters, 468 U.S. 364 (1984).
FCC v Midwest Video Corp., 440 U.S. 649 (1979).
FCC v National Citizens Committee for Broadcasting, 436 U.S. 775 (1978).
FCC v Pacifica Foundation, 438 U.S. 726 (1978).
FCC v Pottsville Broadcasting, 309 U.S. 134 (1940).
Federal Elections Commission v Massachusetts Citizens for Life, 107 S. Ct.
        616 (1986).
Federal Trade Commission v raladam Co., 283 U.S. 643 (1931).
Feiner v New York, 340 U.S. 315 (1951).
First English Evangelical Lutheran Church of Glendale v County of Los
        Angeles, 482 U.S. 304 (1987).
First National Bank of Boston v Bellotti, 435 U.S. 765 (1978).
Fountain v Metro Atlanta Rapid Transit Authority, 678 F. 2d 1038 (5th Circ.
        1982).
Fowler v Rhode Island, 345 U.S. 67 (1952).
Frisby v Schultz, 56 U.S.L.W. 4785 (1988).

Garrison v Louisiana, 379 U.S. 64 (1964).
Gertz v Welch, 418 U.S. 323 (1974).
Grayned v City of Rockford, 408 U.S. 104 (1972).
Greer v Spock, 424 U.S. 828 (1976).
Gregory v Chicago, 394 U.S. 111 (1969).
Griffin v California, 380 U.S. 609 (1965).
Hague v CIO, 307 U.S. 496 (1939).
Harper & Row Publishers v Nation Enterprises, Inc., 471 U.S. 539 (1985).
Hazelwood School District v Kuhlmeyer, 108 S. Ct. 562 (1988).
Hefron v International Society for Krishna Consciousness, 452 U.S. 640
    (1981).
Herbert v Lando, 441 U.S. 153 (1979).
Hernandez v City of Lafayette, 643 F. 2d 1188 (5th Cir. 1981).
Houchins v KQED, 438 U.S. 1 (1978).
Hudgens v NLRB, 424 U.S. 507 (1976).
Hynes v Mayor of Oradell, 425 U.S. 610 (1976).
Illinois Migrant Council v Campbell Soup Co., 519 F.2d. 391 (7th Cir. 1975).
International Association of Machinists v Street, 367 U.S. 740 (1961).
Jamison v Texas, 318 U.S. 413 (1943).
Jennes v Fortson, 403 U.S. 431 (1971).
Jones v North Carolina Prisoners Union, 433 U.S. 119 (1977).
Kleindienst v Mandel, 408 U.S. 753 (1972).
Kovacs v Cooper, 336 U.S. 77 (1949).
Kunz v New York, 340 U.S. 290 (1951).
League of Women Voters v FCC, 468 U.S. 364 (1984).
Lee v Board of Regents, 441 F.2d. 1257 (7th Cir. 1971).
Lehman v City of Shaker Heights, 418 U.S. 298 (1974).
Linmark Associates v Willingboro, 431 U.S. 85 (1977).
Lloyd Corp. v Tanner, 407 U.S. 551 (1972).
Lorain Journal Co. v U.S., 342 U.S. 143 (1951).
Loretto v Manhattan CATV Corp., 458 U.S. 419 (1982).
Los Angeles v Preferred Communications, 476 U.S. 488 (1986).
Louisiana Public Service Commission v FCC, 476 U.S. 355 (1986).
Lovell v City of Griffin, 303 U.S. 444 (1938).
Madison Joint School District v Wisconsin Employees Relation Commission,
    429 U.S. 167 (1976).
Marsh v Alabama, 326 U.S. 501 (1946).
Martin v City of Struthers, 319 U.S. 141 (1943).
Metromedia v City of San Diego, 453 U.S. 490 (1981).
Miami Herald Publishing v Tornillo, 418 U.S. 241 (1975).
Midland Telecasting Co. v Midessa Television Co. 617 F. 2d 1141 (5th Cir.
    1980).
Mills v Alabama, 384 U.S. 214 (1966).
Mine Workers v Illinois Bar Association, 389 U.S. 217 (1967).

Minneapolis Star & Tribune v Minnesota Commissioner of Revenue, 460 U.S. 575 (1983).
Minnesota State Board for Community Colleges v Knight, 465 U.S. 271 (1984).
Mississippi Gay Alliance v Goudelock, 536 F. 2d. 1073 (5th Cir. 1976), cert. denied, 430 U.S. 982 (1977).
Monitor Patriot Co. v Roy, 401 U.S. 265 (1971).
Muir v Alabama Educational Television Commission, 688 F.2d. 1033 (5th Cir. 1982).
Myers v U.S., 272 U.S. 52 (1926).
NAACP v Claiborne Hardware Co., 458 U.S. 886 (1982).
NBC v US., 319 U.S. 190 (1943).
Near v Minnesota, 283 U.S. 697 (1931).
New York State Broadcasters Association v U.S., 414 F. 2d. 990 (2nd Cir. 1969).
New York Times v Sullivan, 376 U.S. 254 (1964).
New York Times v U.S., 403 U.S. 713 (1971).
Niemotko v Maryland, 340 U.S. 268 (1951).
Noranda Exploration, Inc. v Ostrom, 335 N.W. 2d 596 (Wis. 1983).
Pacific Gas & Electric v Public Utilities Commission, 475 U.S. 1 (1986).
Paris Adult Theatre v Slaton, 413 U.S. 49 (1972).
Pennsylvania Coal Co. v Mahon, 260 U.S. 393 (1922).
People of State of California v FCC, 798 F. 2d 1515 (D.C. Cir. 1986).
Perry Educational Association v Perry Local Educators Association, 460 U.S. 37 (1983).
Pickering v Board of Education, 391 U.S. 563 (1968).
Pittsburgh Press Co. v Human Relations Commission, 413 U.S. 376 (1973).
Police Dept. of the City of Chicago v Mosley, 408 U.S. 92 (1972).
Pruneyard Shopping Center v Robins, 447 U.S. 74 (1980).
Public Utilities Commission v Pollak, 343 U.S. 451 (1952).
Red Lion Broadcasting v FCC, 395 U.S. 367 (1969).
Rippley v City of Lincoln, 330 N.W. 2d 505 (N.D. 1983).
Robins v Pruneyard Shopping Center, 447 U.S. 74 (1980).
Rosenblatt v. Baer, 383 U.S. 75 (1966).
Roth v U.S., 354 U.S. 476 (1957).
Rowan v U.S. Post Office Department, 397 U.S. 728 (1970).
Ruckleshaus v Monsanto Co., 467 U.S. 986 (1984).
Saia v New York, 334 U.S. 558 (1948).
Schad Alliance v Smith Haven Mall, 488 NE2d 1211 (N.Y. 1985).
Schneider v State, 308 U.S. 147 (1939).
Southeastern Promotions, Ltd. v Conrad, 420 U.S. 546 (1975).
Spence v Washington, 418 U.S. 405 (1974).
Telecommunications Research and Action Center v FCC, 806 F.2d. 1115 (1986).
Terminiello v Chicago, 337 U.S. 1 (1949).

Texas v Johnson, 57 USLW 4770 (1989).
Thomas v Collins, 323 U.S. 516 (1945).
Time v Firestone, 424 U.S. 448 (1975).
Tinker v Des Moines School District, 393 U.S. 503 (1969).
Twentieth Century Music Corp. v Aiken, 422 U.S. 151 (1975).
U.S. Postal Service v Greenburgh Civic Association, 453 U.S. 114 (1981).
U.S. v Grace, 461 U.S. 171 (1983).
U.S. v Midwest Video, 406 U.S. 649 (1972).
U.S. v Southwestern Cable, 392 U.S. 157 (1968).
U.S. v Storer Broadcasting, 351 U.S. 192 (1956).
U.S. v Zenith Radio Corp., 12 F.2d. 614 (N.D. Ill. 1926).
Village of Schaumburg v Citizens for Better Environment, 444 U.S. 620
       (1980).
Village of Skokie v National Socialist Party, 373 N.E. 2d 21 (1978).
Virginia Board of Pharmacy v Virginia Consumers Council, 425 U.S. 748
       (1976).
Webb's Fabulous Pharmacies, Inc. v Beckwith, 449 U.S. 155 (1980).
Whitney v California, 274 U.S. 357 (1926).
Widmar v Vincent, 454 U.S. 263 (1981).
Williams v Rhodes, 393 U.S. 23 (1968).
Winters v New York, 333 U.S. 507 (1948).
Wolston v Reader's Digest, 443 U.S. 157 (1978).
Woodland v Michigan Citizens Lobby, 378 NW2d 337 (Mich. 1985).
Young v American Mini Theatres, 427 U.S. 50 (1976).

GOVERNMENT DOCUMENTS

Broadcast Regulation Reform 1983: Hearings Before the Subcommittee on
       Telecommunications, Consumer Protection & Finance of the House
       Committee on Energy & Commerce, 98th Congress, 1st Session
       (1983).
Cable Communications Policy Act, 47 USC (1985) Sec. 541(c).
Cable Television Report and Order, 36 FCC 2d. 143 (1979).
Carter-Mondale, 74 FCC 2d. 623 (1979).
CATV & TV Repeater Services, 26 FCC 403 (1959).
Central Maine Broadcast System, 23 FCC 2d 45 (1970).
Code of Federal Regulations, Volume 47.
Commerce Department Study. Print and Electronic Media: The Case for First
       Amendment Parity. S. Print. 98–50, 98th Congress, 3 May, 1983.
Communications Transfer Fee Act of 1987: Hearings on Senate Bill 1935
       before the Senate Committee on Commerce and Transportation, 100th
       Congress, 2nd Session, 27 April, 1988.
Comprehensive Policy Review of Use and Management of the Radio Fre-
       quency Spectrum. 54 Fed. Reg. 50694 (1989).

Department of Commerce, Bureau of the Census. 1990. *Statistical Abstract of the United States*.

Emerging Technologies Act of 1989: Hearings on H.R. 2965 before the Subcommittee on Telecommunications and Finance of the House Committee on Energy and Commerce, 2 Nov., 1989.

Fairness Doctrine Inquiry, 102 FCC 2d. 145 (1985).

First Report and Order, 38 FCC 683 (1965).

First Report and Order, 20 FCC 2d. 201 (1969).

In re Commission Policy Enforcing Sec. 312(a)(7), 68 FCC 2d. 1079 (1978).

In re Complaint of Syracuse Peace Council, 4 FCC Rcd. 5045 (1987).

In re Infinity Broadcasting Corp., 3 FCC Rcd. 930 (1987).

In the Matter of the Handling of Public Issues Under the Fairness Doctrine and Public Interest Standard of the Communications Act, 30 FCC 2d 26 (1971).

Memorandum Opinion & Order in Docket 16574, 8 FCC 2d. 721 (1967).

National Football League Players Association, 39 FCC 2d 248 (1973).

National Telecommunications and Information Administration. 1988 *Telecom 2000: Charting the Course for a New Century*.

Nine kHz Channel Spacing for AM Broadcasting, 88 FCC 2d. 290 (1981).

Omnibus Budget Reconciliation Act of 1981. Pub. L. No. 97–35, 95 Stat. 736–737 (1981).

Second Report and Order, 23 FCC 2d. 816 (1970).

Spectrum Auctions: FCC Proposals for the Airwaves. Hearings before the Subcommittee on Telecommunications, Consumer Protection and Finance of the House Committee on Energy and Commerce, 99th Congress, 2d session. 1 Oct., 1986.

Statistical Abstract of the United States, 110th ed. U.S. Bureau of Census, 1990.

Syracuse Peace Council, Memorandum Opinion & Order, 2 FCC Rcd. 5043 (1987).

Third Report and Order, 36 FCC 2d. 141 (1972).

1 Stat. 124 (1790).

United States Code, Volumes 15, 47.

INDEX

About the Author

DOM CARISTI is Assistant Professor of Communications at Missouri Southern State College. In addition to teaching, he manages K57DR, the college's low-power television station, and he is Chair of the Law and Policy Division of the Broadcast Education Association. His articles have appeared in several journals, including *Suffolk University Law Review*.